# EQUITY AND TRUSTS

The University of Law

# EQUITY AND TRUSTS
## THIRD EDITION

Rebecca Northrop

Published by
The University of Law
2 Bunhill Row
London EC1Y 8HQ



British Library Cataloguing in Publication Data

A catalogue record for this book is available from the British Library

ISBN 978 1 80502 217 6

# Preface

This book is part of the 'Foundations of Law' series of textbooks, designed to support postgraduates in their study of the core subjects of English law.

It is anticipated that the reader can then move on to studies for their professional examinations (eg the SQE and BSB assessments) comfortable that they have an understanding of foundational legal principles.

Each textbook aims to provide the reader with a solid knowledge and understanding of fundamental legal principles and rules. The series aims to give the reader the opportunity to identify and explore areas of critical interest whilst also identifying practice-based context.

For those readers who are students at The University of Law, the textbooks are used alongside other learning resources to best prepare students to meet outcomes of the Postgraduate Diploma in Law and related programmes.

We wish you every success as you learn about English Law and in your future career.

The legal principles and rules contained within this textbook are stated as at 1 May 2025.

# Contents

# Table of Cases

# Table of Legislation

# 1 Principles of Equity and Trusts

**LEARNING OUTCOMES**

By the end of this chapter, you should be able to:

- discuss equitable concepts using appropriate terminology;
- explain the concept of a trust and understand its basic structure;
- identify different beneficiaries' interests and their distinguishing features;
- appreciate the different contexts in which trusts arise; and
- understand equitable remedies devised as alternatives to common law damages.

## 1.1 Introduction

Ask a non-lawyer to define 'criminal law' and you will no doubt elicit an intelligent response. Ask them to define 'equity' and you will probably be met with a blank look. Go further and ask someone to explain a 'trust' and you will most probably be met with a discussion of 'the super-rich', 'hidden money', 'tax avoidance and money laundering'.

However, equity is a body of law in its own right whose impact is seen everywhere. Originally administered solely by the Court of Chancery rather than the common law courts, it can now be deployed in the decisions of all courts. Despite its negative press, equity and its most notable invention, the trust, affects divorce and family lawyers, private client advisers who draft wills and assist with tax planning, conveyancers and property specialists, as well as commercial, corporate and banking lawyers.

There are references to trust funds in newspapers and online – for instance, the 'Jai Ho' trust created by the makers of the 2008 film *Slumdog Millionaire* for the movie's child stars, Sir Elton John's charitable foundation and the like. Yet, trusts affect us all, not just those people with access to wealth and expensive financial advisors. When making a will giving substantial amounts to infant children, a trust is likely to be created. An individual may, sooner or later, contribute to a pension scheme to plan for their future; this is another example of a trust. Trusts also play an important part in the ownership of land, and equitable principles have historically shaped some of the duties owed by directors to their companies and partners in a business.

Trusts, however, are not the only invention of equity. For example, litigants who are not content with the common law remedy of damages will be thankful that equity introduced a range of other remedies including an 'injunction', which is a court order to stop the defendant from doing something, eg, being violent to a partner or divulging trade secrets, or compelling the defendant to do something, eg, delivering or surrendering documents.

## 1.2 Historical background of equity

By studying the historical development of equity it is possible to appreciate its pervasive nature, the way in which it interacts with common law, and how the law of conscience underlies many equitable claims.

In the late 12th and 13th centuries, numerous lords of the realm joined the military forces about to embark on the Crusades. The expectation was that they would be away for months, if not years. While abroad, the lords were concerned about the protection of their land and the collection of feudal rents and taxes. The law at the time did not allow a wife to own property in her own right and any children may be too young or inexperienced. A solution would be to ask a third party to act as a protector and caretaker. Accordingly, land was transferred to the third party on the understanding that they would manage the estate for the benefit of the departing lord's wife and children. However, in some instances, as soon as the lord departed, duplicitous third parties claimed the land for themselves, forcing the wife and children from the feudal castle.

The 'common law' at the time would not protect the wife and children. A judge would simply say that the third party was the legal owner of the land; the wife and her offspring had no rights whatsoever. So, the disappointed would-be litigant, such as the crusader lord and his family, not receiving justice in the common law courts, were forced to petition the King for redress. The King might declare that the third party had acted against good conscience and order them to carry out the lord's original wishes. At that time, it was said that the third party held the land 'to the use' of the wife and her children. Today, we would say that the third party, as a trustee, held the land on trust for them.

In due course, the King delegated dealing with these kinds of petitions to his Lord Chancellor. Eventually, the petitions went directly to the Chancellor. 'Conscience' played a key role in the development of equity largely due to the input of these successive Chancellors who were ecclesiastics. By the late 1400s, there was a Court of Chancery and a body of decisions called equity.

As mentioned earlier, equity does not only include trusts. It also covers equitable remedies such as injunctions, dealings with land and mortgages, the administration of estates of deceased persons, partnerships, the setting aside of written instruments and many other apparently unrelated topics. The reason the topics are so disparate is that equity was never originally intended to be a separate system of law. It grew alongside the common law, which it supplemented as and when particular facts required it. The need to supplement the common law lay in its rigidity. If a legal problem fitted precisely into a previously recognised cause of action, then a claim could be made in the common law courts. There were, however, only a limited number of recognised causes of action, and if the problem was not covered by one of them, there was no remedy; and the common law was not inclined to extend their number.

However, by the 19th century, equity became just as inflexible as the common law. Dickens commented most forcibly upon the slowness of the process in *Bleak House*. There were very few judges who would hear Chancery cases. It was difficult to know to which court you should present your case. If you picked the wrong one, you had to start again. Any case requiring both common law and equitable remedies meant starting two actions.

The Judicature Acts 1873 and 1875 created one Supreme Court, albeit with different divisions: Chancery for equity cases and the Queen's Bench for common law cases. Each division may, however, determine a point of equity in any case.

## 1.3 Equitable maxims

As equity progressed, the courts developed a series of short general statements of principle which underpinned the running of equity. Referred to as 'equitable maxims', these basic tenets act as guidance to the court on how to approach matters before them. There are numerous examples of judicial decisions being made with reference to one or more of these maxims.

Some of the more widely used maxims (which are referenced throughout this textbook) follow.

### 1.3.1 'Equity will not suffer a wrong to be without a remedy'

Arguably this maxim is the foundation of equity as it developed to address the inflexibility of the common law and its failure to recognise the rights of some claimants where something more than monetary compensation was the effective remedy. Equity seeks to provide a remedy to ensure a fair result in the circumstances. You will see examples of this discussion in **Chapter 6** under implied trusts.

### 1.3.2 'Whoever comes to equity must come with clean hands'

While it has been said that 'equity does not demand that its suitors shall have led blameless lives', equity does demand fairness from the claimant as well as the defendant. A remedy in equity will not be available to the claimant who has not behaved in good conscience (legally rather than morally) themselves in the matter in dispute. The Duke of Argyll sought to prevent his wife's injunction claim against him on the grounds that her known adultery meant she did not have clean hands. He failed as the adultery was an irrelevant consideration in the case (*Argyll (Duchess) v Argyll (Duke)* [1967] Ch 302).

### 1.3.3 'Equity will not assist a volunteer'/'Equity will not perfect an imperfect gift'

Equity will not uphold the claim of a volunteer – somebody who has not provided consideration for a particular transaction. The main application of the maxim is where a donor purports to make a gift to the donee, but the gift is not effective, and the donor retains the legal title. Equity will not perfect such an imperfect gift. A similar application can apply to beneficiaries under a trust, also volunteers. Equity will enforce the rights of the beneficiaries where the formalities for the creation of a valid trust are complied with. However, where an issue arises with the constitution of the trust, the starting point is that equity will not enforce the trust. This will be discussed further in **Chapter 3** when considering the constitution of trusts.

### 1.3.4 'Delay defeats equity'

It is accepted in common law and in equity that undue delay in bringing a claim will cause a claimant to lose their legal rights. Claims under common law are subject to limitation, and equitable claims may be subject not only to limitation but also to laches, a guard against unreasonable delay. Given the discretionary nature of equity, the court decides what is an unreasonable delay in the circumstances. This will be covered in **Chapter 7** and **8** when looking at fiduciary duties and remedies against trustees.

### 1.3.5 'Equity is equality'

As far as possible, equity will work on the basis that parties are treated on an equal basis so far as their rights and responsibilities are concerned.

### 1.3.6 'Equity looks to intent rather than form'

In other words, equity is more concerned with the substance of the transaction than with the form it takes. Equity looks to the spirit of the agreement and its desired outcome rather than to the enforcement of the technical rules surrounding it.

## 1.4 What is a trust?

A trust describes a relationship where a binding obligation is placed on a person – a 'trustee' – to look after property for the benefit of another – a 'beneficiary' – or for a purpose permitted by law. Notice that there is an obligation placed on the trustee. This obligation can be enforced by the beneficiary. This is a direct descendant of the 'use', discussed earlier.

A trust allows for the separation of the control of property from its enjoyment and use. The trustee has management and control of the property subject to the trust (the 'trust property'), but the beneficiary is the 'real' owner in the sense that they enjoy the benefit of the property.

> ***Example***
>
> *A grandfather, Gerald, wishes to make a gift of £100,000 for the benefit of his granddaughter, Sally, aged 2. Sally is to receive the capital (the £100,000) at 18. In the meantime, Gerald wants someone to invest the £100,000 and pay out anything needed to give Sally a good education. It clearly would not be sensible for Gerald to give such a large sum to a 2-year-old. Gerald could manage the money himself on Sally's behalf, but he is not in the best of health, and he would rather someone else act as trustee for Sally. Tara has agreed to do the job. So Gerald creates the trust and is called 'the settlor' (the person creating a trust in their lifetime); Tara is the trustee; and Sally is the beneficiary.*

Gerald's trust is an example of an 'express trust' – a trust which is set up intentionally. Gerald could seek to give the same amount to Sally but by way of a trust only to be effective when he dies. In this circumstance, Gerald would be identified as 'the testator' but the same principles would apply.

In order to create his trust, Gerald would take three steps:

(a) He would select his trustee or trustees (which he has done in the example).

(b) He would arrange for the transfer of the £100,000 (it is common to refer to the trust property as 'the Trust Fund' or 'the Trust Capital') to Tara as trustee.

(c) He would lay out the terms of the trust, usually in a written document.

Trusts are clever devices which can be used to achieve much more sophisticated dispositions of property than outright gifts. An outright gift transfers complete ownership to the recipient or recipients. However, when settlors or testators create trusts, they can give the beneficiaries a specific benefit without giving them outright ownership. They are also able to define the benefit the beneficiaries are to receive from the property or carve up benefits between different beneficiaries.

### 1.4.1 Features of a trust

When the trust is created, trustees are given the management or control of the trust property, and equity recognises that the trustees hold the legal title or interest in the trust property. The beneficiaries have the benefit of the property; it is equity that recognises this interest in the property and so the beneficiary has an equitable interest in the trust property sitting alongside the trustee's legal interest.

**Figure 1.1** The legal and equitable interests in Gerald's trust

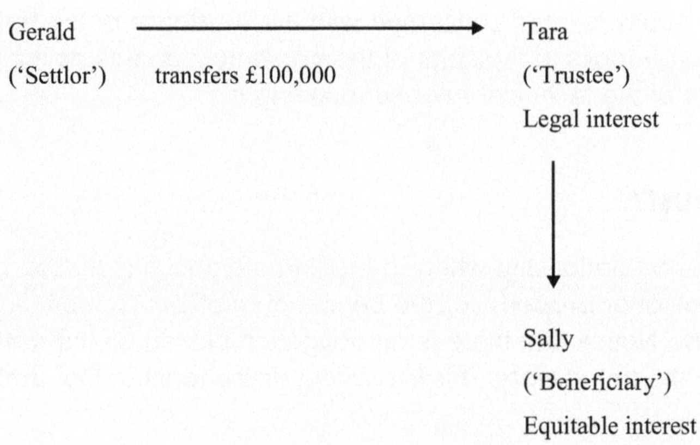

Equitable interests are also known as 'beneficial interests', which describes more clearly the nature of the beneficiary's interest.

There are practical consequences to this separation of the legal and equitable interests (or 'titles' as they are sometimes called).

### 1.4.2 Legal interest held by the trustee

The fact that trustees hold the legal title enables them to manage the trust property. As far as the outside world is concerned, the holder of the legal title, the trustee, is the owner of the trust property. In Gerald's example, Tara may pay the £100,000 into a bank or building society account, and the account will be in her name. The bank or building society will send statements to Tara and account to her for interest. The same would apply to any other property purchased with the £100,000. For example, if Tara were to buy company shares with the money, the company would register Tara as the owner and would send her the dividends.

If the trust contains land, as legal owner, the trustee will be registered as proprietor at the Land Registry and will collect the rents earned from it. As the legal owner, it would be the trustee who would be able sell the land. The beneficiary cannot give away the land (the legal title) because they do not hold the legal title (but as can be seen in **1.4.4**, they can give away their equitable interest in that land).

In contrast to an outright owner, however, trustees are obliged to hold the property for the benefit of those possessing the equitable title. This obligation to hold the property is the trust. To create a trust, some kind of property must be involved; under an employment contract, an employee may owe a duty of loyalty to the employer, but this does not make the employee a trustee. The employee is not holding property for the benefit of the employer.

The beneficiaries get the benefits from the trust property. However, they do not get the benefits direct from the bank, building society or company; rather, they get the benefits indirectly by enforcing the trust obligation against the trustee.

To guard against the trustees misusing the trust property, the law imposes very rigorous duties on them. The duties derive from statute and case law (and can be varied by settlors or testators when they create the trust). The duties underpin the requirement that trustees deal with the trust property in accordance with the terms of the trust (*Guardian Trust & Executors Company of New Zealand v Public Trustee of NZ* [1942] AC 115, PC). This ensures that the beneficiaries get the benefit intended for them. Further, trustees must do their best for the trust. They owe a duty to invest the trust property so that it brings in a reasonable return and, unlike outright owners not subject to any trust, must avoid speculative investments. If trustees breach a duty, the beneficiaries can sue them to make good any loss from the trustees' own money.

### 1.4.3 Equitable interest held by the beneficiary

From the beneficiary's perspective, their equitable interest gives them two rights: personal and proprietary.

Beneficiaries have a *personal* right to enforce the trustees' duties and to seek an account of or compensation for any breaches. It is called a 'personal' right because it is enforceable against the trustees personally.

However, beneficiaries also have a *proprietary* right - an ownership interest in the trust property itself. The significance of this proprietary right is twofold:

(a) First, it can be enforced not only against the trustee, but also against successors in title (ie people who subsequently get the legal title to the trust property). Two examples will help to illustrate this principle:

> ***Example 1***
>
> *A sole trustee dies. All of their property (including the legal title to the trust property) will pass by operation of law to their 'personal representatives' (the people who will wind up the deceased's estate and share it out according to the deceased's will or under the intestacy rules determined by statute and/or statutory instrument). However, the trust property will not pass as part of the trustee's estate; it will still be held on trust for the original beneficiaries. The beneficiaries' proprietary interest binds not only the original trustee but also, when they die, the trustee's personal representatives who acquire legal title to the trust property.*

> ***Example 2***
>
> *A sole trustee goes bankrupt. All their property (and the legal title to the trust property) will pass to their 'trustee in bankruptcy', whose job it is to satisfy the claims of the creditors. However, the trustee in bankruptcy cannot use the trust property for this purpose; the beneficiaries' proprietary interest means that the trust property is preserved for the beneficiaries and will not be available for creditors. The trustee in bankruptcy will hold the trust property for the original trust beneficiary.*

(b) Secondly, the proprietary nature of a beneficiary's interest means that it is itself an item of property (just like shares in a company or money in a bank) which, in certain circumstances, can be sold or given away.

There is one type of third party who will not be bound by the trust, and that is a bona fide purchaser for value who has no notice of the beneficiaries' rights (known as 'equity's darling'). Where a purchaser acts in good faith, gives full valuable consideration and has no knowledge of the trust's existence (either actual knowledge or knowledge which a reasonable purchaser would have acquired if enquiries were made - 'constructive notice' - or knowledge which could be 'imputed' from the knowledge held by the purchaser's agent), the purchaser takes the purchased property free from the beneficiaries' interests. The beneficiaries cannot assert their rights against the property in the bona fide purchaser's hands (but they can sue the trustees for any loss in a claim for breach of trust).

Given that a trust involves separate ownership of the legal and equitable interests, a sole trustee cannot hold on trust for themselves alone. In that situation, there is no trust - the 'trustee' is the outright owner, with no obligation to hold it for another. Here, as there is no trust, the legal owner is said to also be the 'beneficial owner'.

## 1.5 Creation of trusts

### 1.5.1 Creation of an express trust in settlor's lifetime

A settlor may create an express trust in their lifetime in one of two ways:

(a) *Settlor declares themselves as the trustee.* The simplest way to create a trust is for the owner of an asset to declare that they hold the asset for the benefit of someone else. They might say, 'From now on, I am going to hold the money in my account at National Westminster Bank, Park Street, Chester on trust for Hetty.' Such a 'declaration of trust' will make the original owner a trustee for Hetty.

(b) *Settlor transfers property to trustees on trust.* Here, the settlor does not retain legal title to the asset but transfers it to trustees to hold on trust for a designated beneficiary. The trustees may number one or more; settlors commonly choose two trustees, so that one can keep an eye on the other and so that there is someone to carry on if one trustee should die. The trustees may be professionals, relatives or friends. The settlor may even choose a beneficiary (but a sole trustee cannot be the only beneficiary - there would be no trust).

The settlor may make themselves a beneficiary. However, as stated above, the settlor cannot make themselves a sole trustee holding on trust for the settlor alone.

Once trusts have been created properly, settlors cannot change their minds and recover the property for themselves beneficially (unless they reserved a power of revocation when the trust was created, which is possible but comes with potential tax consequences to the settlor so is rare). It is the beneficiaries who enforce the trustees' duties, not the settlor. Thus, unless settlors make themselves trustees or beneficiaries, they have no say in how the trust is run once it is validly created.

### 1.5.2 Creation of express trusts by will

A person (historically called a 'testator' if male, or a 'testatrix' if female) can create trusts in their wills. As in lifetime, this is an alternative to making a gift directly to the beneficiary. Property can be given to trustees to hold on the beneficiary's behalf. However, such trusts do not take effect until the testator dies. Thus, until the testator dies, a named beneficiary has merely the *hope* of receiving their gift or interest under a trust (sometimes called a mere 'expectancy').

Normally, the executors (the estate's personal representatives named by the deceased in their will to carry out the administration of the estate) are also appointed as the initial trustees of any trust arising under the will. However, it is also possible for specific trustees who are not the estate's executors to be appointed.

There are two ways in which a trust may appear in a will:

(a) *A specific gift to be held on trust* - here a monetary amount or an asset or group of assets are distinguished in the will from all other assets, and trustees are instructed to hold the specific fund or property for the beneficiaries.

(b) *Residuary gift on trust* - the gift of residue is a gift of what remains in the estate after the payment of the deceased's debts, the settlement of any tax due on the estate, and the distribution of any specific gifts (ie monetary legacies, specific assets) to the relevant beneficiaries. Effectively, this is the remainder of the property in which the deceased had an interest when they died.

***Example of a residuary gift on trust***

*I GIVE all the rest of my estate whatsoever and wheresoever not otherwise disposed of by this my will to my Executors and Trustees on trust for such of my children Anna and Paul who attain twenty-five and if more than one in equal shares.*

### 1.5.3 Implied trusts

Not all trusts are created expressly. There are two types of implied trusts: 'resulting' trusts and 'constructive' trusts:

(a) *Resulting trusts.* Resulting trusts are implied in certain defined situations. An example is where a person has monetarily contributed to the purchase of an asset which is registered in the name of some other party. The legal owner is presumed to be holding the purchased asset on a resulting trust for the person who provided the money.

(b) *Constructive trusts.* Constructive trusts arise in certain circumstances when it would be unconscionable for the legal owner of property to deny the claimant an equitable interest. For example, say that Gary buys a house in his sole name, but his partner, Hannah, pays part of the purchase price on the understanding that she would get an interest in the property. In these circumstances, the court is likely to say that Gary holds the legal title on a constructive trust for himself and Hannah in equity.

**Chapter 6** will consider resulting and constructive trusts in more detail.

## 1.6 Different types of express trust

A settlor or testator can create different types of express trust either in their lifetime or by will. Which type of trust to use is very much a reflection of the specific circumstances - both as to whether a trust is the appropriate vehicle for giving away property and, if yes, what type of trust would be suitable in those circumstances.

### 1.6.1 Fixed trusts

These trusts are called 'fixed trusts' because the terms of the trust define the *share* of the trust property which the beneficiary will receive. There are a number of examples of fixed trusts:

#### (a) 'On trust for X for life remainder to Y'

This type of trust creates 'successive interests'; this means that it creates beneficial interests which take effect one after the other. X (who is called the 'life tenant') has a 'life interest'; Y (who is called 'the remainderman') has an 'interest in remainder'. However, it does not mean that X enjoys all the trust property first and then Y gets what is left. The trustees pay only the trust *income* to X during their lifetime. Trust income will consist of recurring receipts from the invested trust property, such as interest from banks and building societies, dividends on company shares and rent from land. When X dies, the trustees will transfer the trust property itself (the money, shares and land) to Y, whereupon the trust will come to an end. The trust property is called 'trust *capital*'.

This type of trust can also be referred to as an 'interest in possession' (IIP) trust as a beneficiary has immediate possession of a right of enjoyment of trust property (ie a right of residence) or a right to the income from the property (*Pearson v IRC* [1980] STC 318 (HL)).

#### (b) 'On trust for A if A attains 21, but if A dies before then, for B'

Here, A's interest is conditional (or 'contingent') on A attaining 21. In the meantime, the trustees will look after the trust property for the benefit of A. If A dies before attaining the age of 21, A's interest fails, and B becomes entitled. The example trust in **1.5.2** is another example of a contingent trust.

#### (c) 'On trust for Z' where Z is an infant or cannot manage their affairs for some other reason

In these circumstances, it would not be appropriate to transfer large sums of money to Z by way of outright gift. A trust is used here not so much to carve up the beneficial interests, but to ensure that the property is managed by trustees for the benefit of Z.

#### (d) 'On trust for C' where C is an adult with full mental capacity

This is called a 'bare trust' because the trustees hold on trust for a sole adult beneficiary possessing full mental capacity absolutely (with no limitations or conditions attached). This is an unusual type of trust because the trustees must handle the trust property as the beneficiary dictates. Indeed, the beneficiary can end the trust at any time, by demanding that the trustees transfer legal title to them so that they become the outright owner (*Saunders v Vautier* (1841) 4 Beav 115).

Bare trusts may be created expressly and are quite common in the investment world. For example, owners of a large portfolio of company shares might transfer legal title of the shares to a 'discretionary portfolio manager' (stockbroker or financial adviser) who will manage them on their behalf. The manager needs the legal title to be able to sell shareholdings at short notice and reinvest the money. However, they will hold the legal title on a bare trust for the original owner. The manager is sometimes called a 'nominee'. The original owner, of course, can end the arrangement at any time and get the legal title to the shares transferred back to them.

Bare trusts also arise when a beneficiary under one of the other types of trust considered earlier becomes solely and absolutely entitled to the trust property. For example, in the trust 'for X for life remainder to Y', when X dies, if Y is an adult with full mental capacity, Y is solely entitled to the trust property absolutely. At this point, the trust converts into a bare trust. In due course, the trustees will transfer legal title to the trust property to Y, whereupon the trust will end (see also **1.7.4**)

### 1.6.2 Discretionary trusts

A discretionary trust gives the trustees a discretion as to the amounts any beneficiary may receive and/or whether particular beneficiaries receive anything at all. An example would be if the settlor gives property to the trustees 'to hold on trust for such of my children and in such shares as my trustees think fit'.

Why would a settlor not want to specify what each child should receive? When a settlor sets up a trust, they may be providing for a distribution to beneficiaries many years hence, and unless they are clairvoyant they will not know what the beneficiaries' circumstances will be at that time. Some of the children may be wealthy with no need for additional trust funds; some may be more needy or deserving than others. A discretionary trust allows the trustees to respond to changes in circumstances when the time comes for distribution of the trust property.

No individual has an equitable interest under a discretionary trust until the trustees exercise their discretion in that individual's favour. In the meantime, each individual just has a hope that the trustees will choose them. Therefore, until such persons are allocated an interest by the trustees, they are called 'objects' rather than beneficiaries.

## 1.7 Understanding beneficial interests

The nature of a beneficial interest under a trust varies depending on the terms of the trust. It is important to understand the nature of any beneficial interest in order to be able to identify:

(a) whether the beneficiary's interest is unconditional or conditional and liable to fail if the condition is not satisfied;

(b) when the beneficiary will get their interest; and

(c) what the beneficiary is entitled to receive.

There are several elements to consider, and they have specific terminology. A beneficial interest may be described in any or all of the ways identified in **Table 1.1**.

**Table 1.1** Nature of beneficial interests

| Identify | Description of interest | | |
|---|---|---|---|
| Conditional or unconditional? | Vested | or | Contingent |
| When does interest arise? | In Possession | or | In Remainder |
| What does interest include? | Absolute | or | Limited |

### 1.7.1 Vested and contingent interests

A beneficiary has a *vested interest* if that beneficiary exists and does not have to satisfy any conditions imposed by the terms of the trust before becoming entitled as of right to trust property.

**_Example_**

*Vikram gives £50,000 to trustees to hold 'on trust for my daughter, Chanda'.*

*Chanda does not have to satisfy any conditions before she is entitled to the £50,000, so her interest is vested. If Chanda is aged at least 18, she can require the trustees to pay the £50,000 to her as she can give the trustees a 'good receipt' for the trust property.*

*If Chanda is aged under 18, she cannot give a good receipt. The trustees will hold the £50,000 until Chanda reaches 18. Despite being under 18, Chanda's interest is still vested. This is best illustrated by considering what would happen to the £50,000 if Chanda died under the age of 18. As Chanda was entitled to the money, it forms part of her personal estate and will pass to whoever inherits from Chanda on her death.*

A beneficiary has a *contingent interest* if their right to that interest is conditional upon the happening of some future event that *may not* happen, or if the beneficiary is not yet in existence (eg a trust 'for my grandchildren' and the settlor does not yet have any grandchildren). A common contingency relates to beneficiaries attaining a certain age, perhaps reflecting a settlor or testator's lack of confidence in their financial acumen or lifestyle when at a young age. However, it should be noted that a settlor or testator's ability to impose a contingency age that is too far in the future is not looked on favourably by the courts - beneficiaries are felt to have certain rights to their own financial independence and autonomy as young adults (*Wright v Gater* [2011] 2881 (Ch)).

When the condition is satisfied, the beneficiary's interest then becomes vested. If the condition is not satisfied, the beneficiary never becomes entitled to the trust property and their interest fails. The settlor usually provides for what should happen in this event by making a substitutional gift. If the settlor does not so provide, they have failed to dispose of the whole beneficial interest in the property. In another example of a resulting trust, the trust property will have to be returned to the settlor. Once the interest fails, the trustees will hold the trust property on a resulting trust for the settlor (or their estate, if the settlor has died by this point). This will be discussed further in **Chapter 6**.

**_Example_**

*Vikram gives £50,000 to trustees to hold 'on trust for my daughter, Chanda, provided she reaches the age of 25, and if she does not then for my brother, Sashi'.*

*Whilst Chanda is alive and under 25, her interest is contingent. If she reaches 25, her interest becomes vested, and she can require the trustees to pay her the £50,000. If she dies under the age of 25, Sashi would be entitled to the £50,000, not Chanda's estate.*

*If Vikram had not stated what was to happen if Chanda did not reach 25, the £50,000 would instead be held on resulting trust for Vikram (or his estate if he had died by this time).*

### 1.7.2 Interests in possession and interests in remainder

A beneficiary has an *interest in possession* if they can enjoy that interest immediately. A beneficiary has an *interest in remainder* if they cannot enjoy it immediately but instead have to wait until some other beneficiary's right of use and enjoyment expires. The interest is said to be 'postponed'.

**Example**

*Sarah gives £500,000 to trustees to hold on trust 'for my husband, Hugh, for life and on his death for my son, Peter'.*

*Hugh has an interest in possession because he is entitled to immediate enjoyment of the property held in the trust. The effect of the phrase 'for life' means that Hugh will only be entitled to receive the income generated from investing the £500,000 (see* ***1.6.1*** *above). He will receive this for the rest of his life.*

*While Hugh is alive, Peter must wait to enjoy the trust property, and so Peter has an interest in remainder. When Hugh dies, his interest does not pass under his will. Instead, Peter's interest 'falls into possession' and he is then entitled to enjoy the trust property. However, Peter is not limited to enjoying just the income in the same way as Hugh. Peter will be entitled to the capital held by the trustees.*

The fact that enjoyment of the interest is postponed to the future does not necessarily make it contingent or limited. Although Peter's interest in the example cannot be enjoyed whilst Hugh is alive, he does not have to satisfy any conditions (Hugh's death is a future event that will happen) and so his interest is vested as well as being in remainder. This means that if Peter were to die before Hugh, the vested interest in remainder would form part of Peter's personal estate and would pass to whomever inherited it from him. When Hugh dies, Peter's heirs would be entitled to the capital held by the trustees.

### 1.7.3 Absolute and limited interests

A beneficiary may have an interest which is *limited* to only the income generated by investing the capital held in the trust, or an *absolute* interest in the capital of the trust, or in both income and capital.

The word 'income' describes the receipt of money which is regular or recurring as opposed to a one-off payment. For example, a person's salary is income. The profit made on the sale of a house is more in the nature of a one-off payment and is capital (unless that person is a builder and sells houses all the time).

Using the example in **1.7.2** above, Hugh has a limited interest as he has an interest in the trust income only. He will never have the right to enjoy the capital. His interest in the income can also be described as vested and in possession. An interest in income only will normally be limited in duration, eg for the duration of that beneficiary's life.

Peter has an absolute interest as his interest is in the capital. He will be entitled to this once Hugh dies. His interest in the capital can be described as vested and in remainder.

### 1.7.4 The changing nature of beneficial interests

The nature of a beneficial interest may change according to the circumstances. For example, an interest may begin as contingent and/or in remainder but eventually become vested and/or in possession. If a beneficiary's interest is *vested and in possession and not limited in enjoyment,* the beneficiary is described as 'absolutely entitled'.

**Example**

*'£10,000, on trust for my daughter Hetty provided she reaches the age of 21'.*

*Hetty has just reached 21 and the trustees have not yet transferred the money to Hetty. While she was under the age of 21, Hetty had a contingent interest in the £10,000. However, once she reached 21, she attained a vested interest in possession of the whole of the trust property (not limited to just enjoying income). There is no one else with a right to the £10,000, and Hetty will be able to give a good receipt to the trustees for the money as she is over 18.*

Where trustees hold trust property for a beneficiary who is an adult and who has a vested interest in possession not limited in any way, this is described as a bare trust (see **1.6.1**). At this point, according to *Saunders v Vautier* (1841) 4 Beav 115, this sole adult beneficiary of sound mind with a vested interest in the trust property can bring the trust to an end by asking the trustees to hand the whole trust fund over to them personally or to other trustees (for instance, setting up a new trust with new trustees).

This rule has been extended to include trusts which have more than one beneficiary. A group of beneficiaries can end the trust by calling for a transfer of trust property to themselves or to other trustees if *all* the beneficiaries under the trust *who could possibly become entitled*:

(a) are in existence and ascertained;

(b) are 18 or older and of sound mind; and

(c) agree to the proposed course of action.

'All the beneficiaries under the trust who could possibly become entitled' means that, between them, they must be absolutely entitled (ie there is no other person with a potential interest in the fund).

### 1.7.5 The nature of the beneficial interest under a discretionary trust

What is the nature of the beneficial interests under a trust 'for such of my children at such times and in such shares as my trustees shall in their absolute discretion decide'? As discussed in **1.6.2**, a discretionary trust gives the trustees a discretion as to the amounts any beneficiary may receive and/or whether particular beneficiaries receive anything at all. Here, the objects do not (as individuals) have any equitable interest until such time as the trustees exercise their discretion in the objects' favour. The objects do have the right to require the proper administration of the trust but have no proprietary interest.

Notwithstanding this, it is arguable that objects under a discretionary trust could bring the trust to an end under an application of *Saunders v Vautier*, provided all the objects are ascertainable, legally competent and in agreement (*Re Smith* [1928] Ch 915).

**Figure 1.2** Summary – requirements for use of *Saunders v Vautier*

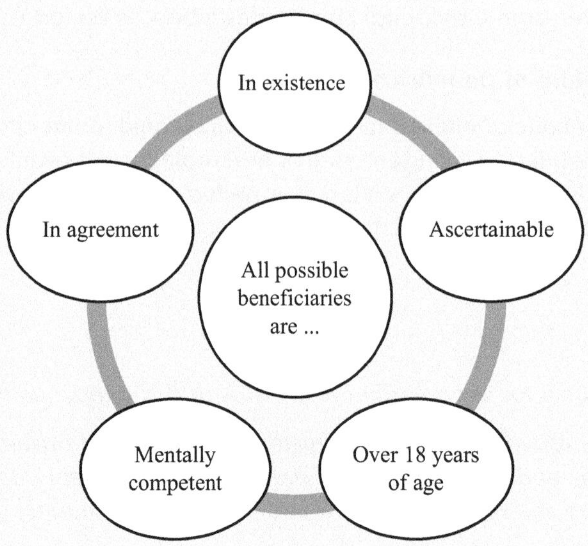

## 1.8 Trusts in context

Equity and the trust relationship do not just have a use in the family context of providing gifts and succession planning. Equity and trusts also have significant roles to play in other areas.

### 1.8.1 Buying a home

Trusts are used widely in land law and conveyancing when individuals jointly purchase a property. It is possible for such co-owners to use a trust to clearly define their interests (equally or differing) in the property they have purchased. Implied trusts can also be employed where co-owners have not expressly defined their interests for themselves (**see Chapter 6**).

### 1.8.2 Charities

Many charities exist as trusts. These are public trusts given that they are recognised as a way in which the public can support causes of interest to them (considered in more detail in **Chapter 4**).

### 1.8.3 Private clubs and associations

Many private clubs and associations (such as sports clubs) operate in a way comparable to trusts. Members pay their subscriptions to participate in the club's activities and use its facilities. The body of the membership will fluctuate as members join and then leave the club, but in paying their subscriptions members agree to be bound by the club's constitution. The constitution will set out the club's rules - how the club's assets are to be held, how meetings are run, who calls the AGM, how many are needed for a quorum, who can sign cheques on the club's bank account etc. The rules may also say that if the club is wound up, the remaining assets (surplus subscriptions etc) will be divided between the members. A few members will volunteer, or be persuaded, to be on the club's committee - treasurer, secretary etc - and the property of the club is often held by such committee members (as trustees) on trust for the members. A discussion about trusts in this context appears in **Chapter 4**.

### 1.8.4 Pensions

Many people pay a significant proportion of their income into a pension fund over the course of their working life. If it is an occupational pension scheme, the employer will also contribute. The pension fund will be held by trustees on trust for the members (ie the present and future pensioners). The trust device allows the management of the fund to be vested in a few (the trustees) but gives equitable interests in the fund to hundreds (or even thousands) of members. The pension's trustees are subject to the rigorous duties imposed on trustees by trusts law, and the members maintain their equitable interests in the pension fund despite the insolvency of the company or the pension trustees.

While the trust concept lies at the heart of such pension schemes, it has been overlain by statutory provisions. In the 1990s, the Maxwell scandal involved fraudulent breaches of trustee duties, and the misappropriation of the pension fund caused many employees of the *Daily Mirror* to lose their pensions. This led to statutory intervention in the form of the Pensions Act 1995.

### 1.8.5 Collective investment schemes

In a similar vein to pensions, unit trusts, investment clubs and time share schemes involve people contributing to a common investment venture. In a unit trust, an investment manager raises money from members of the public; the idea is that the contributions are pooled, invested and the profits shared between the contributors. Again, equitable means of preventing abuse by trustees and policing trusts, while stringent, were not considered adequate and were supplemented by a statutory regulatory system (Financial Services and Markets Act 2000, as amended).

### 1.8.6 Trusts and insolvency

When an individual is made bankrupt or a company goes into liquidation, their property is divided among their creditors according to a strict order of priority. Ordinary unsecured creditors (those who did not take a charge over the debtor's property) appear at the bottom of that order, and, in many cases, there will be insufficient property left to give them more than a small percentage of what they are owed.

Suppose that you supply a machine to a company. You allow the company two months' credit to pay for the machine. Before it makes the first payment, the company goes into liquidation. If you had to rely on your contractual rights to payment, you would rank as an unsecured creditor and would not recover much. If you had had the foresight to stipulate that the company held the machine on trust for you until payment, you would be in a much stronger position; you would have an equitable interest in the machine and, according to what was said earlier, that would make you the 'real' owner of the machine. This would mean that you could immediately recover your property (the machine) and need not take your place in the queue of creditors. The use of trusts in these circumstances will be discussed in more detail in **Chapter 5**.

### 1.8.7 Fiduciary duties

Equity imposes trustee-like duties (which are called 'fiduciary duties') on certain people who occupy positions of trust (in addition to trustees, this would also apply to company directors and partners in a business). Thus, equity has been used to impose standards of honesty and good faith in certain business relationships, not just the relationship between the trustees and the beneficiaries. These duties will be discussed in **Chapter 8**.

### 1.8.8 Trusts in business

In *Westdeutsche Landesbank Girozentrale v Islington London Borough Council* [1996] AC 669, Lord Browne-Wilkinson laid down the framework in which he saw trusts arising:

> Equity operates upon the conscience of the owner of the legal interest. In the case of a trust, the conscience of the legal owner requires him to carry out the purposes for which the property was vested in him (express or implied trust) or which the law imposes on him by reason of his unconscionable conduct (constructive trust).

It can be seen from this quote that Lord Browne-Wilkinson thought that the conscience of the legal owner formed the basis of all trusts. In particular, such a (constructive) trust can be *imposed* by the law where the legal owner is guilty of unconscionable conduct. The possible imposition of constructive trusts makes commercial lawyers nervous: lawyers define the terms of business relationships in carefully drafted contracts; the subsequent imposition of a constructive trust will change what the parties have agreed. This can potentially lead to uncertainty.

While the trust has 'become a valuable device in commercial and financial dealings' (Lord Browne-Wilkinson in *Target Holdings v Redferns* [1995] 3 All ER 785), there remains an ongoing uneasiness about the courts applying equitable principles, which evolved in the context of family trusts, to large-scale commercial situations traditionally governed by the law of contract. Even Lord Browne-Wilkinson suggested that only fundamental principles of trust law should apply in commercial situations; the specialist rules developed in relation to traditional trusts should be applicable only to those traditional trusts and not to trusts of a different kind.

## 1.9 Equitable remedies

The only remedy available under the common law is compensatory damages. In addition to recognising the trust relationship, equity also recognises that in certain circumstances a remedy of damages or compensation is insufficient. In the face of the perceived inflexibility of the common law and given that equity does not like for a wrong to be without a remedy (see **1.3.1**), the court's equitable jurisdiction has given rise to a number of alternative remedies which can be sought by claimants.

### 1.9.1 Injunctions

An injunction is a court order which either compels a party to do a particular act (a *mandatory* injunction) or restrains a party from doing a particular act (a *prohibitory* injunction). Examples of behaviour which can be prevented through a prohibitory injunction include trespass and release of confidential information. A mandatory injunction might be deployed to force the demolition of a house built without planning permission.

Any judge who has jurisdiction to conduct the trial of a claim has the power to grant an injunction. However, they are generally granted only when the claimant has established a serious issue to be tried and damages will not be an adequate remedy.

Injunctions are granted at the discretion of the court on either an interim or final basis. An interim (or interlocutory) injunction is awarded either prior to or during the proceedings dealing with the dispute and is intended to maintain the status quo while the matter is being decided. A search order is a form of mandatory interim injunction used to compel entry into premises to preserve incriminating evidence which might otherwise be destroyed or concealed. Similarly, a freezing order is an interim order which seeks to prevent the dissipation or removal of disputed assets from the jurisdiction while proceedings are ongoing.

A final or perpetual injunction is awarded as a remedy after a final determination of a claimant's rights. Such an injunction means that it is not necessary to bring further actions in respect of every infringement of the rights so determined.

Failure to comply with an injunctive court order is a contempt of court. Severe penalties (including imprisonment) can be imposed.

### 1.9.2 Specific performance

Specific performance is a court order compelling a defendant to comply with the terms of a contract. There must a valid and enforceable contract and, as with injunctions, the order will only be made where damages do not provide an adequate remedy. Specific performance is often ordered in cases dealing with land, given that there is an assumption that each piece of land is distinctive. Similarly an order might be given for assets other than land where the item is unique and not easily replaced.

The court will only order specific performance in circumstances where it will be able to supervise the performance to ensure compliance with the order.

The court will generally not order specific performance of contracts for personal services so requiring a person to work for the claimant (although it might be possible to obtain an order preventing the defendant from working for someone else, by way of an injunction as in *Lumley v Wagner* (1851) 1 De G M & G 604).

### 1.9.3 Rectification

Under rectification, the court will agree to order the correction of an executed written document which does not accurately reflect what the parties intended. An order can be sought to correct mistakes in most cases; however, the correction has to be to the document itself (ie missing words etc) not to the nature of or an error in the transaction itself.

The mistake can be common to both parties to the contract or can be unilateral where only one party has made a mistake with the knowledge of the other.

The claimant seeking rectification has to evidence both the parties' actual intention and that the executed document does not accurately reflect that.

### 1.9.4 Recission

An order for recission brings a contract to an end, returning the parties to their pre-contractual position. It is possible to obtain recission at common law. For instance, a contract will be void at law if the subject matter of the contract no longer exists. However, the circumstances giving rise to recission in equity are wider:

- where there is a mistake as to the 'legal character or nature of a transaction or as to some matter of facts or law which is basic to the transaction' (Lord Walker, *Pitt v Holt* [2013] UKSC 26);
- where one party exerted undue influence over the other in negotiations and there has been a lack of free will. The undue influence can be presumed in certain close relationships; in other cases the influence must be proved;
- where there has been a misrepresentation, whether fraudulent or innocent;
- where there has been unconscionable conduct by one party in the negotiation process (ie taking advantage of the weak position of the other and the agreement is oppressive and exploitative).

A claimant to these equitable remedies does not have to be in a trust relationship to have recourse to them. All courts are able to award all these equitable remedies on a discretionary basis. The only limit to a claimant's ability to seek such remedies will be the equitable bars such as an excessive delay in bringing proceedings or the unclean hands of the claimant (linked to the equitable maxims discussed earlier in **1.3**).

As enforcers of the trust, equity provides beneficiaries with their own remedies in the context of their trust relationship. These remedies are available regardless of whether the beneficiaries and the trust have incurred loss. These remedies will be discussed specifically in later chapters of the book.

## 1.10 Example of a discretionary trust

An example of a discretionary trust has been provided in the **Appendix**. It highlights the structure and contains some of the provisions which could be encountered in a document produced by the Private Client department of a solicitor's firm. The precise wording would be amended in light of a settlor's specific instructions and circumstances. There is a commentary on some of the clauses at the end, as well as an indication of where some matters arising from the content of the example will be discussed elsewhere in this textbook.

**ACTIVITY Review your understanding – beneficial interests**

During their lifetime, a settlor gives £500,000 to trustees upon trust.

(1) Identify the nature of Xavier's beneficial interests in each of the following examples:

  (a) 'For my children, Xavier and Nadine, now living in equal shares.'
  (b) 'For my children, Xavier and Nadine, who attain 21 years and if more than one in equal shares.' (Xavier is 14 and Nadine 16)
  (c) 'For my son Xavier for life thereafter for his children, Anna and Clare, in equal shares.'
  (d) 'For my wife, Nina for life, thereafter for my son Xavier.'

(2) Can Xavier bring these trusts to an end using the rule in *Saunders v Vautier*?

  (a) 'On trust for Xavier and Nina in equal shares.' Xavier is 18 and Nina 21; neither suffer from any mental incapacity.

(b) 'On trust for Xavier for life, then for Nina for life and then to Nina's children living at Nina's death.' Xavier is 50, Nina is 38 and has two infant children.
(c) 'On trust for my children, Xavier, Nina, and Lucy, as reach the age of 21 and if more than one in equal shares.' Xavier is 23, Nina is 20, and Lucy 19.
(d) 'On trust for my children, Xavier, Nina, and Lucy, as reach the age of 25 and if more than one in equal shares.' Xavier is 23, Nina is 20, and Lucy 19.
(e) 'On trust for my children, Xavier, Nina and Lucy in such shares as my trustees think fit.'

**COMMENT**

(1) Xavier's interests in the examples are:

(a) 'For my children, Xavier and Nadine, now living in equal shares.'
- vested (no conditions attached to the gift);
- in possession (no other person entitled to an interest before him; Nadine has the same interest as him);
- absolute (he is entitled to share the capital).

(b) 'For my children, Xavier and Nadine, who attain 21 years and if more than one in equal shares.' (Xavier is 14 and Nadine 16)
- contingent (his entitlement is conditional on attaining 21);
- in possession (as above);
- absolute (as above, subject to reaching 21).

(c) 'For my son Xavier for life thereafter for his children, Anna and Clare, in equal shares.'
- vested (no condition imposed);
- in possession (no other person entitled to an interest before him);
- limited (he is only entitled to income).

(d) 'For my wife, Nina for life, thereafter for my son Xavier.'
- vested (no condition imposed; he has to wait for Nina to die before getting actual enjoyment, but that is regarded as a postponement, not a condition);
- in remainder (there is someone with an interest in priority to him - Nina);
- absolute, because he will be entitled to capital when Nina dies.

(2) Can Xavier end the example trusts under *Saunders v Vautier*?

(a) Yes, as Xavier and Nina are all legally competent (*sui juris*) they can end the trust (provided they both agree) by compelling the trustees to transfer the trust property to them or to other trustees.
(b) No, while *Saunders v Vautier* does apply to trusts containing successive interests, here Nina's children are infants, and some may be unborn (at 38, Nina could have more children). Therefore, *Saunders v Vautier* cannot apply here as some beneficiaries are not *sui juris* and some are not yet ascertained.
(c) Yes, as here the three children are 'between them absolutely entitled to the trust fund'. This is because Xavier has satisfied the condition ('to reach the age of 21') and so, even if Nina and Lucy both died under 21, according to the wording of the trust Xavier would be entitled to everything. Assuming they can agree, Xavier, Nina and Lucy can end the trust now (they are legally competent). (Whether Xavier would agree to this is a different question. After all, although no doubt loving them dearly, if either of his sisters were to die before reaching 21, his share would be increased.)

(d) No, as here the three children are not 'all the beneficiaries under the trust who could possibly become entitled'. All three could die before reaching the age of 25, in which case someone else would become the beneficiary. Accordingly, the fact that Xavier, Nina and Lucy are not between them absolutely entitled would prevent *Saunders v Vautier* applying.

(e) Yes, providing Xavier, Nina and Lucy agree. As objects they are ascertainable and *sui juris*; according to *Re Smith* [1928] Ch 915, *Saunders v Vautier* does apply to such a discretionary trust.

**SUMMARY**

- It is important to appreciate the pervasive quality of equity and, in particular, the trust.
- People create trusts for any number of reasons and these reasons will determine the form of trust to be used – fixed interest, successive interest, contingent, discretionary – and how they are created. The type of the trust will also determine how it will work once created.
- A trust is an example of a situation where different people can own different interests in the same item of property at the same time; in most trusts, the trustee owns the legal interest, whereas the beneficiary has the equitable interest in the trust property. It is this divided relationship that is recognised by equity.
- A beneficiary's equitable interest can be classified in different ways – vested/contingent, in possession/in remainder, absolute/limited. This classification will tell a great deal about a particular beneficiary's entitlement.
- Equity and trusts can operate in situations beyond the private family scenario, for instance, in a commercial context when considering pensions or insolvency, in a social context when considering membership of a sports organisation, or in the creation and administration of charities. However, there is a commonality to the underlying concepts and principles regardless of the circumstance.
- Equity also recognises a series of remedies which offer an alternative to damages in situations where monetary compensation is not sufficient or appropriate – needing to restrain behaviour, bring about compliance with the terms of a contract, correct a written document which does not reflect intention, or end a contract which has been negotiated in circumstances of mistake, undue influence or unconscionable behaviour.

# 2 Creating Express Trusts - The Declaration of Trust

**LEARNING OUTCOMES**

By the end of this chapter, you should be able to:

- understand the ways by which a person may seek to benefit another person;
- recognise the differences between an outright absolute gift and a trust and the differences between a fixed trust and a discretionary trust;
- discuss the elements required in a valid declaration of trust;
- explain the relevant rules and tests used to determine whether the different elements of the declaration are valid; and
- analyse the contents of declarations of trust to identify whether they are valid or not.

## 2.1 Introduction

There are numerous motivations for people to give away their property, by way of gift or trust, in their lifetime or on their death by will. Generous sentiments for family and friends obviously have their part to play, but succession and tax planning may also be considerations.

The obvious way in which a person (the 'donor') can give property to another is to make an outright gift. The recipient of the gift ('the donee') would become the absolute owner of the property in question, with complete control over it, able to deal with it as they wish. This is regardless of whether the gift is made during the donor's lifetime or is made by will on their death.

**Figure 2.1** Outright gift to X

**DONOR** ⟶ **DONEE (X)**
transfers property to — management and enjoyment of the property

While this may be the obvious course of action, any donor must ensure that they comply with the various technical rules which govern the making of even something as straightforward as a gift. A donor must do 'all that is necessary' (*Milroy v Lord* (1862) 4 De GF & J 264) to render the gift binding on them. These rules relate to the capacity and intention of the donor to make the gift as well as ensuring sufficient certainty in the definition of the property to be given away and the identification of the donee.

However, the donor may consider that it would be inappropriate for the donee to receive an outright gift - the donee might be too young, have a perceived reckless lifestyle, or have a disability which renders outright ownership impractical. As discussed in **Chapter 1**, this is when a donor might look to create a trust. This is a more structured way of bestowing a benefit as the donee's enjoyment of the property being given away would be dictated by the terms of the trust. As with gifts, creating a trust also requires compliance with a series of rules so that a valid trust is created.

## 2.2 Ways of creating a trust

In *Milroy v Lord*, Turner LJ detailed what is considered to be a classic statement of how gifts and trusts are made. In addition to making an on outright gift to the donee, he said that a person could also consider:

(a) a transfer to trustees to hold on trust for the person to be benefited; or

(b) during their lifetime, a declaration of self as trustee for the person to be benefitted.

### 2.2.1 By transfer to trustees

This involves the transfer of the trust property to the chosen trustee or trustees and a declaration which directs those trustees to hold the money on trust for the beneficiary. In that declaration, the person creating the trust is generally free to define the obligations imposed on the trustees and the nature of the beneficiary's entitlement. The trustees consequently hold the legal title and manage the money for the benefit of the beneficiary, eg by investing it. The beneficiary has the equitable interest.

**Figure 2.2** Transfer to trustees to hold on trust for X

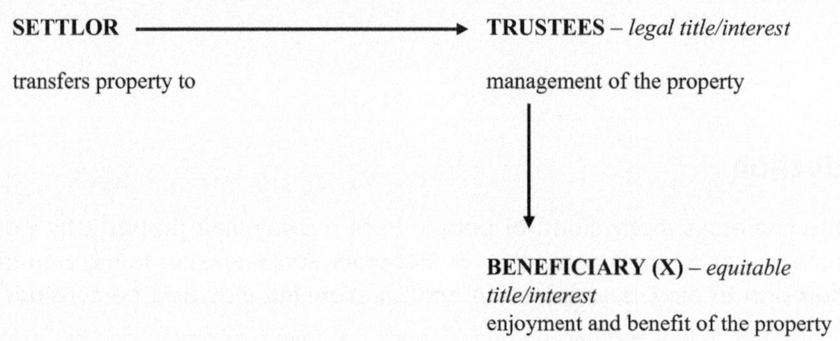


Such a trust can be created *inter vivos* (in lifetime) and may also appear in a will only to have effect on a testator's death.

### 2.2.2 Self as trustee

Alternatively, in their lifetime, a settlor can declare themselves to be the chosen trustee, directing themselves to hold the money on trust for the beneficiary on whatever terms they deem appropriate. The settlor retains the legal title but is now managing the money for the benefit of the beneficiary who again has the equitable interest.

**Figure 2.3** Declaration of self as trustee to hold on trust for X

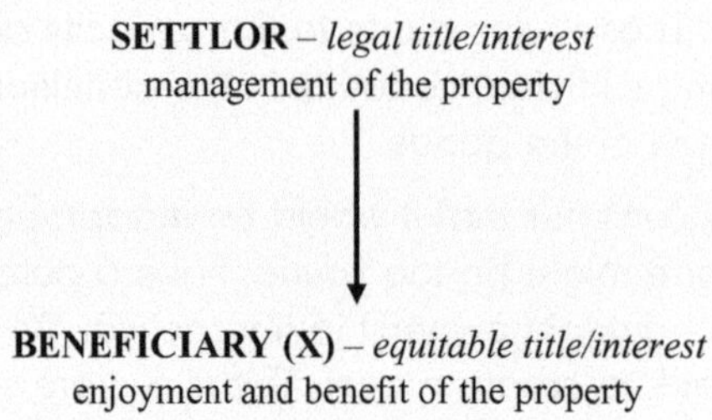

In both circumstances, it is necessary for the relevant rules to be complied with when declaring the trust. This chapter will consider these rules.

Additionally, where necessary (ie where there is/are third party trustee(s)), the subject-matter of the trust must be transferred in the correct manner for the proposed transaction to be valid. This is known as 'constituting' a trust. The 'correct manner' in which to constitute a trust is discussed in **Chapter 3**.

## 2.3 A valid declaration of trust

What differentiates an outright gift from a trust is a valid declaration of trust which imposes an obligation on the trustee (whether a third party or the settlor themselves) to hold the property for the benefit of another (the beneficiary or beneficiaries).

What amounts to a valid declaration of trust? **Figure 2.4** outlines the elements comprised in a declaration of trust.

**Figure 2.4** The components of a declaration of trust

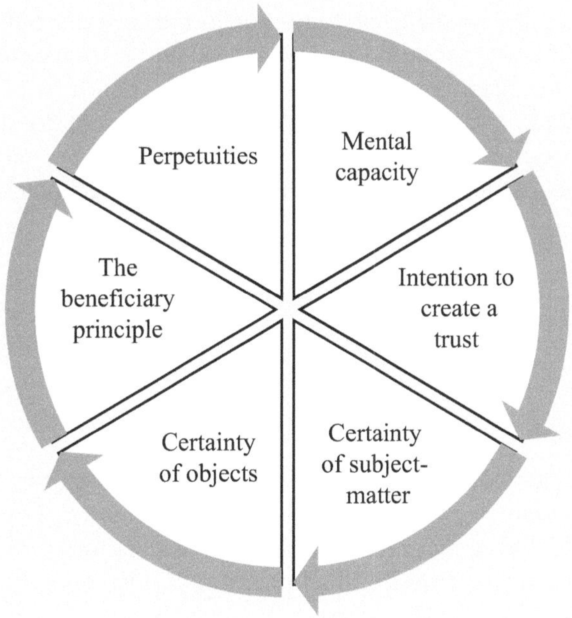


To be valid, a declaration (whether *inter vivos* or in a will) must comply with *all* its component parts, namely:

(a) mental capacity;

(b) evidence of a certain intention to create a trust;

(c) a clear definition of the subject-matter of the trust and the respective beneficiaries' interests in that trust property;

(d) the description of the intended objects (the beneficiaries) being objectively clear;

(e) compliance with the beneficiary principle; and

(f) the relevant rules against perpetuity being satisfied.

There is also the additional issue of whether any written formalities must be completed (see **2.4**).

Together, elements (b), (c) and (d) are often referred to as 'the three certainties' (as originally stated by Lord Langdale in *Knight v Knight* (1840) 3 Beav 148).

Where there is a perceived issue with any of these required elements, it will sometimes fall to the courts to resolve the matter. Trustees may occasionally require interpretive guidance, and again courts could be asked to make an 'order for directions' (CPR 1998, Part 64) to clarify the meaning of the words used.

### 2.3.1 Capacity

Capacity relates to being able to understand the nature of a transaction and its consequences. Under s 1 of the Mental Capacity Act 2005, a person is 'assumed to have mental capacity unless it is established that they lack capacity'. The degree of required understanding varies according to the nature and value of the asset being given away. An asset or amount of small value relative to the rest of a settlor's assets will require a low degree of understanding. However, sometimes a higher degree of understanding is necessary.

***Re Beaney* [1978] 1 WLR 770**

A mother who was suffering from senile dementia made a gift of her house, her only substantial asset, to one daughter. This had the effect of disinheriting her other two children. In these circumstances, the required degree of understanding was high and included being able to understand the claims of all potential donees. The mother was found not to have been capable of understanding this, and the gift was accordingly held void. It was the effect of the gift of her main asset which was crucial.

Any person under the age of 18, as a minor, lacks capacity for legal purposes. A trust of any property created by a minor is voidable if repudiated within a reasonable time of the minor attaining 18 years of age (Family Reform Act 1969, s 1).

### 2.3.2 Certainty of intention

There must be the intention on the part of the settlor or testator to create a trust. Owners of property may deal with property in a variety of different ways. For example, the owner of money may transfer it to another person pursuant to a contract, or by way of gift, or in order to make the other person a trustee. This last event, a trust, only comes into existence if this is the owner's intention.

In *Milroy v Lord*, Turner LJ stressed the importance of intention – 'if the [benefit] is intended to be effectuated by one of the modes [a gift or a trust] ... the court will not give effect to it by applying another of those modes'. Thus if a donor fails to make a valid gift in favour of the donee, the court would not 'save' the gift by pretending that what the donor had really intended to do was to create a trust in the donee's favour.

The intention to create a trust involves the intention of the owner to impose a legally binding obligation on the recipient of the property to deal with the property in a certain way. It is necessary, therefore, to examine the words used by the owner. The words they use need to be sufficiently certain to fix the conscience of the recipient to deal with the property in the specified way.

Where called upon to examine the words used by the settlor or testator, the court will 'give effect to the intention ... wherever it can be ascertained' (Lord Langdale MR in *Knight v Knight* (1840) 3 Beav 148). However, it is not necessary for settlors or testators to use a particular form of words to create a trust. In accordance with the equitable maxim, 'Equity looks to intent rather than form' (see **1.3.6**), any wording, or even conduct, which manifests an intention to impose the trust obligation on the trustee will be sufficient. The use of the word 'trust' somewhere would obviously help.

***Paul v Constance*** **[1977] 1 WLR 527**

Mr Constance lived with, but was not married to, Mrs Paul. He received £950 compensation for an industrial injury. They went to the bank, intending to open a joint account for the money, but on the advice of the bank manager opened an account in Mr Constance's sole name. The parties treated the account as their joint money, paying in their joint bingo winnings. Mr Constance stated frequently that 'the money is as much yours as mine'. The court accepted that these words, together with the course of conduct in relation to the bank account, amounted to an express declaration of trust on Mr Constance's part. There is no need to pinpoint one particular instance. When he died intestate, the bank account did not, therefore, pass under intestacy to his wife (whom he had not seen for many years) but was held on trust for Mrs Paul.

It is insufficient, however, to use 'precatory' words. Examples of such words would be a transfer of £1,000 to John 'in full confidence that' or 'hoping that' or 'believing that' or 'expecting that' he will benefit Betty. Up until the second half of the 19th century, the courts were willing to find an intention to create a trust where the settlor used such precatory words. Judicial attitudes then changed. *Re Adams and Kensington Vestry* (1884) 27 ChD 394 held that no trust was created where the settlor used such precatory words. In this case, the words used were 'in full confidence that she will do what is right'; failing to provide directions as to what the testator intended this to mean resulted in a widow not being subject to any binding obligation.

Certainty of intention to create a lifetime trust goes to a settlor's intention to give up ownership of the asset of the trust property in favour of third party trustees for the benefit of the beneficiaries. A settlor who retains extensive powers for themselves over the fund and its management may find the attempted creation of the trust held to be 'a sham' if the true effect of the trust and its administration means that the settlor has actually retained ownership and control (*Rahman v Chase Bank (CI) Trust Co Ltd* [1991] JLR 103; *JSC Mezhdunarodniy Promyshlenniy Bank v Pugachev* [2017] EWHC 2426 (Ch); *Webb v Webb* [2020] UKPC 22).

### 2.3.3 Certainty of subject-matter

There are two aspects to certainty of subject-matter - there needs to be a clear description of both the trust property and the respective interests of the beneficiaries in that property. Without certain subject-matter, the trustees' job would be impossible. If they do not know what the trust property is, how can they perform their duties to manage and invest it? How can they administer the trust for the benefit of the beneficiaries and distribute the trust fund properly if they do not know what the beneficiaries' respective interests are?

#### 2.3.3.1 Description of trust property

When creating the trust, the settlor (or testator) must identify the trust property clearly. For example, it is no use the settlor (or testator) trying to create a trust over 'some of my finest silver' or 'my best land'. It would be impossible for the trustees to identify which silver or land was intended. Similarly, trusts of shares or paintings cannot be valid unless the settlor makes it clear which shares or paintings are to be held on trust.

In a will, a trust for the 'bulk of my estate' which provides no indication of what constitutes 'the bulk' is uncertain (*Palmer v Simmonds* (1854) 2 Drew 221). However, a trust of the 'residue of my estate' will be certain. While at the time of the will, the extent of the residue would have been unknown, the residue will become ascertainable when the will has effect on the testator's death. At this time, the extent of the debts and tax to be paid as well as all other valid gifts and/or trusts will be known. The fact that it is not a definite amount until death is immaterial because the will has no effect until the testator dies.

Issues can arise if a settlor owns a collection of a particular item, quantifies the part to be held on trust but does not segregate that part from the rest.

For example, a settlor owns 500 ICI shares. The settlor declares: 'From now on I am holding 100 of my ICI shares on trust for Imran.' Here the settlor does not state which particular shares they mean and does not segregate them from the rest of the shareholding. Would the subject-matter of this example trust be certain?

***Re London Wine Company (Shippers) Ltd*** **[1986] PCC 121**

When a wine company went into liquidation, buyers of wine sought to establish that the wine they had paid for, and which remained stored in the company warehouse, was held on trust for them. As the wine was not segregated from the general stock of wine, they could not establish a trust as the subject-matter of any trust was uncertain. The settlor (here the wine company) would have had to identify which chattels (out of their larger collection of chattels) they intended to form the subject-matter of the trust.

On the basis of the decision in *Re London Wine*, it would seem that the example trust would be invalid due to a lack of certainty of subject-matter. However, consider the case of *Hunter v Moss.*

***Hunter v Moss*** **[1994] 1 WLR 452**

Moss was the owner of 950 shares in a private company. He wanted the finance director (Hunter) to own the same number of shares as the managing director, and the court found that Moss had tried to declare himself a trustee of 50 of his shares for Hunter. Moss later sold the 950 shares and Hunter claimed part of the sale proceeds. Moss had never done anything to differentiate which block of 50 shares from the holding of 950 shares was to be the subject-matter of the trust. It was held that there was a valid trust of 50 shares for Hunter. The first instance judge distinguished *Re London Wine* because chattels, such as bottles of wine, are not identical, and so it is essential for the settlor to specify exactly which ones are intended to be subject to the trust. Shares of the same class in the same company, on the other hand, are indistinguishable from each other. Therefore, the settlor does not need to stipulate exactly which 50 is meant.

In *Hunter v Moss*, the Court of Appeal went further. It stated that the *Re London Wine Co (Shippers) Ltd* decision related to tangible assets whereas *Hunter v Moss* concerned intangible assets, namely company shares. Accordingly, it is possible to create a valid trust of an unascertained part of a bulk of intangible assets. It should be noted that this decision has been criticised.

When dealing with trusts of money, it does appear necessary to separate the trust money from other money held by the trustee. Consider these two examples from commercial cases where the claimants sought to exercise their proprietary rights under a trust and obtain protection in the circumstance of the trustee's insolvency.

***Re Lewis's of Leicester Ltd*** **[1995] 1 BCLC 428**

*Background*

Lewis's owned a department store and had granted licences of parts of its floor space to traders on a 'shop within a shop' basis. The traders paid their takings into Lewis's tills and some of these takings were paid into a separate bank account in Lewis's name. Lewis's went into liquidation. The traders argued that the money in the bank account was held on trust for them and should not be available to Lewis's creditors on the insolvency.

*Decision*

Robert Walker J held that the traders were able to recover the money held in the bank account because there was a valid trust for them. The subject-matter was certain because, by placing the money in a separate account, it had been segregated from Lewis's other money.

***Mac-Jordan Construction Ltd v Brookmount Erostin Ltd*** **[1992] BCLC 350**

*Background*

Mac-Jordan agreed to conduct some building work for Brookmount. Brookmount paid for the work in instalments, but, as is usual in a building contract, the contract allowed Brookmount to retain 3% of each instalment for a period to cover costs should the work turn out to be defective. The contract provided that the retained monies were to be held on trust for Mac-Jordan. Brookmount went on to retain over £100,000 but did not pay this money into a separate bank account. Brookmount went into liquidation. Mac-Jordan claimed an interest under the trust.

*Decision*

Mac-Jordan was not successful in its arguments. While there had been an intention to set up a trust of the retained money, this had not been accomplished because there was uncertainty of subject-matter. The retention monies had not been segregated from Brookmount's other funds. The key fact was that they had not been placed in a separate bank account.

The subject-matter of a trust is certain if the settlor gives a workable formula for calculating the amount. In *Re Golay* [1965] 2 All ER 660, where a beneficiary was to be given a 'reasonable income', the court decided that this term was sufficiently objective to provide an 'effective determinant' to enable the court to decide how much income to give the beneficiary. The court would be guided by the level of the beneficiary's previous income. However, it is very unlikely that a gift of capital, eg 'a reasonable legacy', would be valid.

#### 2.3.3.2 Beneficial interest must be certain

The nature of the beneficiary's interest must be clear. Does the beneficiary have a life interest or an absolute interest? Is the beneficiary's interest contingent on attaining a certain age?

It must also be clear what shares the beneficiaries will respectively enjoy. For example, does a beneficiary have a third or a quarter share?

***Boyce v Boyce* (1849) 16 Sim 476**

A will left the following provision: 'My two houses to my daughters, Maria whichever she might choose and the other to Charlotte.'

Maria died before choosing her house and as a consequence the disposition failed due to lack of certainty of subject-matter. It was not possible for Charlotte to select for herself. Both houses reverted back to the deceased's estate under a resulting trust.

However, in a couple of circumstances, it is not necessary to specify the exact share of a beneficiary:

(a) Under a discretionary trust where settlors do not want to specify the shares of the beneficiaries, preferring to leave this decision to their trustees. It is possible to create a discretionary trust without offending this aspect of the certainty of subject-matter rule. The beneficiaries' shares are regarded as certain if they are to be determined by the trustees. If the trustees do not undertake this task, then the court will.

(b) Where a trust (or gift) is made for a group of beneficiaries, but the settlor does not specify the shares each member of the group is to receive; they are assumed to be equal. For example, 'to my trustees on trust to divide it between my children living at my death' is silent as to the share of each child but the shares are certain because they are assumed to be equal (see **1.3.5**).

### 2.3.4 Certainty of objects

The certainty of objects rule requires the settlor or testator to define the beneficiaries with sufficient clarity when declaring the trust. In the same way that you cannot create a trust of 'my best silver', you cannot create a trust for 'my greatest fans' because it is not possible to identify these beneficiaries. Without this certainty, the declaration would be invalid.

There are a number of reasons why trusts with uncertain objects are impracticable and should fail:

(a) The trustees could not perform their duty to distribute the trust fund to the right beneficiaries unless they are able to identify who the beneficiaries are.

(b) If trustees do not perform their duties at all, or perform them incompetently, the beneficiaries can complain to the court. The court should ensure that the trustees' duties are carried out correctly. The court can fulfil this function only if it is able to ascertain who the beneficiaries are (and so who has the right to complain).

(c) Beneficiaries enforce trustees' duties. They would want to complain to the court if, say, trustees distribute to people who are not beneficiaries. How can they do this if the definition of the beneficiaries is so hopelessly unclear that nobody knows who is and is not a beneficiary?

Usually there is no problem if the settlor (or testator) names the beneficiaries. For example, if a will gives '£10,000 on trust for Vijay Patel', the beneficiary is certain unless the testator knew two Vijay Patels. In *Re Jackson* [1933] Ch 237, a testatrix left a gift 'to my nephew, Arthur Murphy'. Unfortunately, she had three nephews called Arthur Murphy. Evidence was accepted to identify which of them she intended to benefit. In the absence of such evidence, there would be uncertainty of object.

There will also be no trust for Vijay if he dies before the testator. In this situation, the intended trust will *lapse* (the subject matter of a lapsed specific trust falls into the residuary estate; a lapsed residuary trust passes under the intestacy rules to the testator's statutory next of kin).

Certainty of objects is more likely to cause a problem in a trust for a 'class' of objects (ie where the testator or settlor gives a general description of the beneficiaries but does not name them individually). Examples of class gifts include 'on trust for my friends' or 'for my relatives'. In all cases one has to decide whether the description of beneficiaries is clear enough to enable the trustees to administer the trust and distribute the trust property. If it is not, the trust fails to have effect.

The courts have developed different tests for assessing whether beneficiaries are certain depending on the type of trust. The correct way to approach the problem is to apply the appropriate legal test, depending on whether the disposition is a fixed or discretionary trust. Given that there are different tests, it is necessary to decide whether the declaration is for a fixed or discretionary trust. Only then can the relevant certainty of objects test be identified and then applied to the trust in question, so determining whether the trust is valid or not.

#### 2.3.4.1 Certainty of objects - fixed trusts

Fixed trusts were discussed in **Chapter 1**. Under a fixed trust, the trustees have no discretion as to how the trust property is to be allocated between the beneficiaries. The settlor (or testator) has stipulated once and for all who the beneficiaries are and the proportions in which they will share the trust property.

***Examples of fixed trusts***

- *'I give all my estate to my Trustees to hold on trust for my wife for life remainder to my daughter.'*
- *'£100,000 to my Trustees on trust to divide the same between A, B and C equally'.*
- *'£40,000 on trust for my children.' (It is presumed that they will share equally, see* ***2.3.3.2****)*
- *'£20,000 on trust for X at 21.'*

Of course, there are some types of trusts which combine the two. For instance: 'I give all my estate to my Trustees to hold on trust for my wife for life remainder to such of my nephews and nieces and in such shares as my Trustees think fit' starts off as a fixed trust, but when the wife dies it converts into a discretionary trust for the nephews and nieces.

**Complete list test**

The test for certainty of objects in a fixed trust is the complete list test (*IRC v Broadway Cottages Trust* [1955] Ch 20). In other words, it must be possible to draw up a comprehensive list of each and every beneficiary. Otherwise, the trust fails.

'A complete list' sounds straightforward, but the practical application is not always easy. Two elements have to be present.

(a) *Conceptual certainty.* The settlor (or testator) must define the objects using clear concepts so that the trustees know what type of person they are looking for. For example, a trust 'to divide £50,000 between old friends equally' would be void. Insufficient criteria are laid down for the trustees to determine who is regarded as 'old' and who would be regarded as 'a friend'; the words do not have a precise, objective meaning. How friendly do they have to be? Does 'old' mean aged, or of long standing? 'Old friends' is conceptually uncertain.

(b) *Evidential certainty.* A complete list is possible only if you can identify each and every member of the class. If there is no evidence to say whether a particular individual qualifies as a beneficiary or not, a fixed trust is void.

The reason for the test is that without a complete list, the trustees cannot perform their duty to carry out the trust. In a fixed trust such as '£100,000 to trustees on trust to divide this sum equally between my most deserving relatives', unless the trustees know how many deserving relatives there are, they cannot distribute anything even to those who clearly qualify. As the £100,000 is to be divided equally, the amount taken by each beneficiary depends on whether there are, say, three or 10 deserving relatives. Thus, a complete and finite list is essential. Furthermore, the court needs a complete list of objects if it is asked to assist in a trust.

If the trustees are able to compile a list of beneficiaries in a fixed trust, difficulty in tracing a known beneficiary does not cause the trust to fail. In these circumstances, trustees can apply to the court for directions regarding the share of a beneficiary who cannot be found. Possibilities may be to pay their share into court or seek a court order allowing them to distribute as though the missing beneficiary were dead.

The same principles apply to commercial trusts. In *OT Computers Ltd v First National Tricity Finance Ltd* [2003] EWHC 1010 (Ch), the directors of the company feared that the company might become insolvent. They wanted to protect payments of customers' deposits and money due to suppliers. You may recall from **Chapter 1** that if a trustee becomes insolvent, money held on trust is not available for the creditors. Accordingly, the directors instructed the company's bank to open two trust accounts, one for the repayment of customer deposits and the other for the payment of money due to its 'urgent suppliers'. Although the trust for customers was valid, that for urgent suppliers failed through lack of certainty of objects; the term 'urgent' was too unclear.

#### 2.3.4.2 Certainty of objects – discretionary trusts

A discretionary trust is 'where someone is under a duty to select from among a class of beneficiaries those who are to receive, and the proportions in which they are to receive, income or capital of the trust property' (per Warner J in *Mettoy Pension Trustees Ltd v Evans* [1990] 1 WLR 1587).

Discretionary trusts have the advantage of flexibility. The trust will define a class of possible beneficiaries. Who is to benefit from within this class, and upon what terms, is not decided until the trustees select one or more of the possible beneficiaries. The trustees of a trust for the benefit of a defined group of family relations are thus able to respond to the changing circumstances of those individuals within the class of possible beneficiaries. Until selected, no object (a possible beneficiary) has an 'equitable interest' in the trust property. Until the trustees decide that an individual is to have a share of the trust income or capital, the individual merely has a hope ('a *spes*'), also described as an expectancy, that the trustees will choose them. The individual may never be chosen.

However, the trustees of a such a discretionary are only able to exercise their discretion in favour of an object from the class given to them by the settlor/testator. To give trust income or capital to someone outside that defined class would be a breach of trust and leave the trustees open to personal liability.

In the discussions which follow, the term 'powers of appointment' will be encountered. There is no need for a detailed study of these powers, but it will help to know a little about them.

**Background information on powers of appointment**

A power of appointment is an authority to deal with property in some way. The person who is given the power does not have to exercise the power.

***Example of a power of appointment***

*Gillian (called the 'donor' of the power) is making her will and cannot decide the proportion in which her property is to be divided between her children, Rebecca and Mary (the 'objects'). She therefore gives a power of appointment to her husband, Simon (called the 'donee' of the power) but adds that if no appointment is made then Rebecca and Mary will take in equal shares (called a 'gift in default of appointment').*

A power of appointment differs from a discretionary trust as the donee of a power is not obliged to distribute the property. The objects cannot complain to the courts if the donee does not exercise the power. In contrast, trustees of a discretionary trust are under a duty to distribute property in favour of members of the class of objects (but they have a discretion as to which members to choose). If the trustees do not perform their duty within the time specified in the trust instrument (or if none, within a reasonable time), the objects can get the court to intervene; the court could order a particular distribution or appoint new trustees.

Donees of a power may only appoint to people who are objects; they will breach their duties if they appoint to someone who is not an object. The test for certainty of objects for powers of appointment has always been the 'given postulant' test. The 'given postulant test' is a less stringent test than the complete list test which applies to fixed trusts (**see 2.3.4.1 above**). In *Re Gestetner's Settlement* [1953] 1 Ch 672, Harman J rejected the complete list test as inappropriate, on the grounds that:

- it was not necessary for the donee of a power to know of all the objects in order to appoint to one of them; and
- there is no obligation for the donee to do more than consider the merits of the persons in the specified class; there is no duty to distribute.

The correct test for determining whether the objects of a valid power of appointment were certain or not was the given postulant test - can it be said with certainty whether any given postulant (individual applicant) is or is not a member of the class of objects?

In *Re Gulbenkian's Settlement* [1970] AC 508, Lord Upjohn confirmed that the donees of the power did not need a complete list. All that was required for donees was that they were able to identify the sort of people who fell within the description of objects - the objects were to be regarded as sufficiently certain if the donor's description of the objects was clear enough to enable the donees to recognise, in general, the sort of people who were included.

**Certainty of objects test for discretionary trusts**

Before the House of Lords' decision in *McPhail v Doulton* [1971] AC 424, the test for certainty of objects for all trusts, fixed and discretionary, was the complete list test. Unlike donees of powers of appointment, all trustees had to be able to draw up a complete list of all the potential objects.

***McPhail v Doulton* [1971] AC 424**

In 1941, Bertram Baden signed a deed establishing the Matthew Hall Staff Fund. Baden intended that the fund provide benefits for the company's current and former employees as well as their relatives and dependents. The company in question had 1,300 current employees. When Baden died in 1960, his estate sought to challenge the validity of the deed and claimed the fund for the estate. Proceedings were started in 1962 (at this stage, the case is referred to as *Re Baden's Deed Trusts* as the application was for a determination by the court rather than adversarial). The issue in dispute became whether the relevant clause in the deed constituted a trust binding on the trustees to distribute or was a mere power with no such duty.

At first instance, and in the Court of Appeal, the clause was found to be a power, and the relevant test applied to determine certainty of objects was that derived from *Re Gestetner Settlements* - the given postulant test. On this basis, the clause in the deed was valid. (Had the clause been a trust, subject to the complete list test, it would have been invalid.)

The estate's appeal of the Court of Appeal determination was heard by the House of Lords in 1970, by which time the matter was referenced as *McPhail* (one of the PRs) v *Doulton* (one of the trustees). The House of Lords decided that the clause was a discretionary trust, not a power. However, their Lordships rejected the 'complete list' test for discretionary trusts and changed the certainty of objects test for discretionary trusts to the given postulant test.

The court concluded that the trustees of a discretionary trust (and the court if called upon to do so) did not need a complete list of the names of all objects to perform their duties. The settlor's or testator's intentions were clearly not for equal division of the trust fund. The trustees did not have to distribute to every object; they merely had to make a systematic survey of the class of objects.

The House of Lords held that what was required to pass the given postulant test was 'conceptual' or 'linguistic' certainty; in other words, the settlor must have laid down sufficient criteria in the description of objects so that it is objectively clear what sort of person will qualify.

However, evidential uncertainty - difficulty proving that someone falls within a conceptually certain class - will not cause the trust to fail. Further, difficulty in establishing the whereabouts of an object will not affect the validity of the trust.

After the House of Lords changed the test for discretionary trusts in *McPhail v Doulton*, the case was returned ('remitted') to the High Court to decide whether the trust satisfied the given postulant test. Despite the apparent simplicity of the test, it took further hearings in both the High Court and three judges of the Court of Appeal (*Re Baden's Deed Trust (No 2)* [1973] Ch 9) to decide that both 'relatives' and 'dependents' were terms which satisfied the given postulant test (albeit in respect of relatives their approaches and reasonings varied) and so the trust was valid. After over 10 years of litigation, the Court felt that 'the timetable of events [was] less than creditable to the process of law' and heavily criticised the parties and their lawyers alike. There was no further appeal.

A policy reason for relaxing the test was to avoid the wholesale invalidity of the larger discretionary trusts which were emerging at the time. Family trusts (such as 'a discretionary trust for my grandchildren or my brothers and sisters') easily satisfied the complete list test. However, discretionary welfare trusts for employees and their dependants and pension trusts for similar classes were liable to fail because of the difficulty in compiling a complete list of all objects. The House of Lords wanted to encourage these large-scale discretionary trusts, and indeed this is consistent with the policy of upholding trusts wherever possible in order to carry out the settlor's intention.

**Discretionary trusts - administrative unworkability and capriciousness**

Even if a discretionary trust has certain objects, the further issues of administrative unworkability or capriciousness could still invalidate it.

*Administrative unworkability*

It has long been accepted that the size of the anticipated class of objects does not impact on the validity of a power of appointment - powers of appointment for everyone in the world are permitted (*Re Hay's Settlement Trusts* [1982] 1 WLR 202). However, when it comes to discretionary trusts, in *McPhail v Doulton*, Lord Wilberforce said that if the class of beneficiaries was so hopelessly wide as not to form 'anything like a class' then the trust would be administratively unworkable. Reluctantly, so as not to prejudice future cases, he gave the example of such a class as 'all the residents of Greater London', while saying that 'relatives' would not be such a class. Thus, a discretionary trust 'for everyone in the world' has certain objects but would fail because the class is simply too big.

In *R v District Auditor, ex p West Yorkshire Metropolitan CC* (1986) 26 RVR 24, the Council was on the point of being abolished and created a discretionary trust of £400,000 for any or some of the inhabitants of West Yorkshire (about 2.3 million in number) to be benefited in any of a number of specified ways, eg helping youth, ethnic and minority groups. It was held that the trust was invalid because the size of the class of objects rendered it administratively unworkable.

The reason such large trusts are regarded as invalid is not entirely clear. There was a suggestion in the *West Yorkshire* case that the massive numbers would prevent trustees from performing their duties of surveying the class of objects properly and in turn prevent a rational, sensible distribution of the trust property.

*Capriciousness*

'Capricious' means irrational. According to Templeman J in *Re Manisty's Settlement* [1974] 2 All ER 1203, capriciousness arises when:

(a) the terms negative any sensible intention on the part of the settlor; and

(b) the terms require the trustees to consider only an accidental conglomeration of persons who have no discernible link with the settlor or any institution.

If this is the case, the discretionary trust (and a power) would be void.

### 2.3.5 The beneficiary principle

As a general rule, trusts must have ascertainable human beneficiaries. The very nature of a trust is that there is an equitable obligation binding on the trustee to deal with the trust property in accordance with the trust. In the absence of human beneficiaries, there is no one to ensure this happens. Thus, a trust for a purpose (an obligation to do something with the trust fund), as opposed to a trust for a human beneficiary, has no one to enforce the obligation. Purpose trusts are therefore, with exceptions, void.

***Re Shaw's Will Trust* [1957] WLR 729**

The will of playwright George Bernard Shaw left money to be used for the purpose of researching whether it would be more convenient for the English language to operate on the basis of a 40-letter alphabet, rather than the current alphabet. Although the trustees did initially attempt to undertake the research, the trust was ultimately declared void as there was no one to compel the trustees to carry out this 'obligation'.

There are two basic exceptions to this principle. First, if the purpose is regarded as charitable then this is valid. The trust is a public trust, and the Attorney-General will enforce the trust on behalf of the public. Secondly, there are some purpose trusts which, despite not being charitable, are nonetheless permitted. An example is a legacy in a will to maintain a much-loved pet. The pet cannot go to court to enforce the 'trust', yet the trust is permitted.

Purpose trusts will be considered in **Chapter 4**.

### 2.3.6 The rules against perpetuity

Trusts are often used to create future interests in property. The worry is that settlors or testators may wish to control what happens to their property for hundreds of years. For example, Tariq, motivated by a desire to keep his property in the family, makes a will leaving his estate on trust for his great-great-grandchildren when they attain 50. When Tariq dies, his children are aged 5 and 7. If the rule against perpetuities did not exist, such trusts would be valid; Tariq's estate would be held in trust for a very long time; it could be 150 years or more before Tariq's trustees would be able to distribute the property to the great-great-grandchildren and end the trust.

An actual example of this occurred in America with the will of Wellington Burt. The relevant wording meant that although Burt died in 1919, his descendants had to wait until 2011 in order to inherit his estate of approximately $100m.

There are policy reasons for limiting the ability of settlors to restrict the use of their property for an excessive length of time. In a market economy, property must be freely useable so that the market can allocate resources to the most profitable uses. Where property is held on trust for a lengthy period of time, money does not circulate in the economy. Also, beneficiaries are deprived of the freedom to use the property (in Wellington Burt's case, only 12 potential beneficiaries survived until 2011).

Consequently, the law will only tolerate trusts that last for an acceptable period. It achieves this aim by subjecting trusts to the rules against perpetuity.

2.3.6.1 Rule against remoteness of vesting

This rule is relevant to contingent interests and discretionary trusts. A contingent interest is void unless it vests (ie the contingency will be satisfied) within 'the perpetuity period'. At common law, there was a formula for determining how long this was, ie 'lives in being plus 21 years'. This historical formula was, for all practice purposes, superseded by a statutory period under the Perpetuities and Accumulations Act 1964. Under this Act, the trust instrument could specify a perpetuity period of up to 80 years. At that time, the main practical application of this was that discretionary trusts, where the trustees have a power to choose whom from a class of beneficiaries is to benefit, were limited to lasting for 80 years. At the end of this period, if any money remained to be distributed, the trustees had to make an absolute distribution.

The Perpetuities and Accumulations Act 2009, which came into force on 1 April 2010, now permits a 125-year perpetuity period. This longer period applies to wills which were executed and came into effect on or after that date and to (non-will) trusts which came into effect on or after that date.

2.3.6.2 Rule against inalienability

This rule applies to trusts for non-charitable purposes. A trust for non-charitable purposes will be void from the outset if the trust capital is not freely alienable (used) within the relevant perpetuity period.

This rule and the relevant period will be considered in context when we look at non-charitable purpose trusts in **Chapter 4**.

## 2.4 Formalities for a lifetime express declaration of trust

The final question to consider when looking at how the settlor declares the trust is whether any written formalities are required. First, it is necessary to distinguish trusts of personalty and trusts of land.

### 2.4.1 Personalty

If settlors wish to declare a trust over personalty during their lifetimes, there are no written formalities to observe. The declaration can be oral. Thus, a settlor could state in a conversation, 'from now on I am holding my ICI shares on trust for Bob', and this would be a valid trust. If the settlor wished Karen to act as trustee, they would have to transfer the shares to Karen in the proper manner to 'constitute' the trust. However, the declaration that Karen is to hold on trust for Bob could be made orally.

Although the law accepts oral declarations of trust over personalty, in practical terms writing is clearly desirable for evidential purposes.

### 2.4.2 Land

However, there are different rules when a settlor seeks to declare a new trust over land (or any interest in land). In this circumstance, s 53(1)(b) of the Law of Property Act 1925 will apply, requiring that a 'declaration of trust respecting any land, or any interest therein must be manifested and proved by some writing signed by some person who is able to declare such trust or by his will'. This means that:

(a) the declaration of trust must be evidenced in writing (rather than be in writing). The declaration itself can be written or the declaration can be oral and confirmed in writing. For example, s 53(1)(b) is satisfied if the settlor tells X orally, 'from now on I am holding my farm, Blackacre, on trust for you', and later that day writes to their solicitor telling the solicitor what they have done. The letter to the solicitor is written evidence that will satisfy s 53(1)(b);

(b) the written evidence must contain the terms of the trust; and

(c) the written evidence must be signed by the person able to declare the trust. The person able to declare the trust will usually be the settlor.

The written evidence need not be a deed or other formal document. A signed letter or memorandum will suffice, as will an email (accepted as a written document in case law) provided the settlor has 'deliberately subscribed' their name to the end of the email (*Hudson v Hathway* [2022] EWCA Civ 1648).

There is no indication in the statute as to the consequence of non-compliance with the requirement for written evidence of the declaration. It is presumed that the absence of signed writing merely makes the trust unenforceable by the beneficiaries against the settlor (and they would not be able to bring an action in court).

**Figure 2.5** Summary - considering the declaration of trust

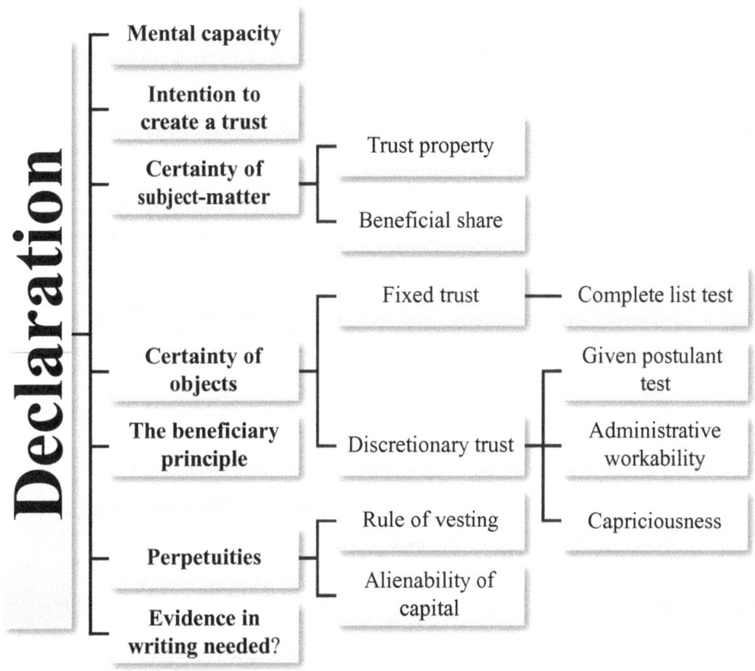

## 2.5 Consequences of issues with the declaration of trust

There are a number of ways in which a declaration of trust could fail, so impacting on the validity of the attempted disposition. However, the consequences of the failed attempted trust depend on the reason for the failure. **Table 2.1** outlines the possible consequences.

**Table 2.1** Consequences of a failed declaration of trust

| Issue with declaration of trust | Consequence |
|---|---|
| Settlor lacks mental capacity | Attempted trust void |
| Settlor/testator lacks intention to create a trust | No trust – recipient of property takes absolutely |
| Attempted trust does not describe the whole of the trust property with certainty | No trust as property not transferred and so reverts back to the settlor (or their estate) on resulting trust |
| Attempted trust does not define beneficial interests with sufficient certainty | Trust property which has been validly transferred will be held on resulting trust for the settlor (or their estate) |
| Attempted trust lacks certainty of objects | Trust property which has been validly transferred will be held on resulting trust for the settlor (or their estate) |
| Attempted trust is administratively unworkable | Trust property which has been validly transferred will be held on resulting trust for the settlor (or their estate) |
| Attempted trust is capricious | Trust property which has been validly transferred will be held on resulting trust for the settlor (or their estate) |
| Attempted trust offends the rule against perpetuity | Trust property which has been validly transferred will be held on resulting trust for the settlor (or their estate) |

What constitutes the valid transfer of trust property will be considered in **Chapter 3**. There will be further discussion of resulting trusts in **Chapter 6**.

**ACTIVITY Review your understanding – declarations of trust**

Analyse the following scenarios. In each case, consider whether the declaration of trust is valid:

(1) A valid will contains the following provisions:

(a) 'I give £10,000 to my trustees be divided between my most deserving cousins.'

(b) 'I give £15,000 to Rebecca in the hope and belief that she will share it with her two daughters, Daisy and Alice.'

(c) 'I give the residue of my estate to my trustees to distribute among such cat-lovers in the North-West and in such shares as my trustees think fit.'

(2) Casper wrote a letter to his 20-year-old nephew, Jonas, saying, 'I am holding one of my commercial properties, the shop on Cliff Road in Newton, and £20,000 for you. I will transfer the shop and the money to you if you attain the age of 25.' He signed the letter 'Uncle Casper'.

**COMMENT**

(1) (a) The testator attempted to create a fixed trust in this clause. It is a fixed trust because the money is to be divided between the objects and the presumption is that they will share equally. There is evidence of intention in the obligation imposed on the trustees to divide the £10,000 (the subject-matter). However, in order to be valid there must be certainty of objects. The certainty of objects test for fixed trusts is the complete list test (*IRC v Broadway Cottages*). The clause is likely to be void as, while the term 'cousins' may be both conceptually and evidentially certain so that it would be possible to come up with a full list of them, it would not conceptually be possible to identify which of them is 'deserving'. The trust would not be valid and the £10,000 will form part of the residue of the estate.

(b) Here, there appears to be a valid gift of the £15,000 to Rebecca (there is certainty of intention, subject and object). The question here is whether Rebecca has to share the money with Daisy and Alice. Has the testator actually created a trust over the £15,000? The objects of any trust are clear (Rachel and her two daughters), but the subject-matter is not certain – how much is each beneficiary to receive? Also, there is insufficient certainty of intention to create a trust as the words 'in the hope and belief' fall short of imposing an obligation on Rebecca to distribute the fund. The words are precatory (*Adams v Kensington Vestry*), and Rebecca can do as she likes with the money.

(c) The testator has tried to create a discretionary trust. There is an intention to create a trust as there is a duty on the trustee to distribute the money by the words 'to distribute'. The trust property is the residue of the estate which is certain. However, there are issues with the intended objects of the trust. Is the description of the objects, 'cat-lovers in the North-West', objectively certain? Can it be said with certainty whether any given individual is or is not a member of the class of objects (the given postulant test – *McPhail v Doulton*)? Are the objects described with sufficient conceptual certainty? Possible issues:

- 'Cat-lovers' is probably conceptually uncertain as it is not capable of objective definition; how deeply must people love cats in order to qualify?
- 'North-West' could also be regarded as uncertain as it is not possible to objectively identify the geographical area.

Even if the court regarded the definition of objects as certain, the trust may fail on the ground that it is administratively unworkable. The number of cat-lovers in the North-West may run into millions (*R v District Auditor, ex p West Yorkshire Metropolitan CC*, where the trust was for 2.3 million inhabitants of West Yorkshire). Whether or not the intended trust would be considered capricious is likely to depend on the testator's position on and/or relationship to cats.

The provision is unlikely to be valid. (As the residue of the will has failed, the remainder of the estate will fall to be distributed under the intestacy rules to the deceased's relatives in accordance with a specified order of entitlement. The identity of the statutory next of kin will be determined by the circumstances of the deceased at the time of their death.)

(2) (a) The Cliff Road shop – Casper did not say that he was holding 'on trust' for Jonas. However, the words he used indicate that he intended to declare himself a trustee for Jonas. He did not intend an outright gift because he contemplated retaining some title to the property ('I am holding') and making a transfer of the

property (certain subject-matter; although Casper appears to have more than one commercial property, he has identified which one from the portfolio) to Jonas (a clear object, able to enforce any trust) in the future (on Jonas's 25th birthday, which is within the perpetuity period). In order for a declaration of trust over land to be enforceable, the declaration must be evidenced in signed writing (LPA 1925, s 53(1)(b)). The letter would suffice. Casper has effectively declared a trust and will have to transfer the Cliff Road shop to Jonas when he is 25.

(b) £20,000 – Trusts over personalty do not require any formality. However, all trusts require the three certainties to be present (and the beneficiary principle and perpetuities to be satisfied). There is certainty of intention in Casper's words and there is certainty of object and satisfaction of the beneficiary principle (Jonas). However, here certainty of subject-matter may be an issue. If Casper has not segregated the £20,000 from his other money, placing it in a separate bank account, then the attempted trust will fail due to uncertainty of subject-matter (*Mac-Jordan Construction Ltd v Brookmount Erostin Ltd*). There will be no trust of the £20,000 and Casper will be under no obligation to transfer that amount to Jonas when he is 25.

## SUMMARY

- It is important to understand the reasons why people might wish to gratuitously benefit another person or a group of people and the ways in which they can do this both in their lifetime and in their will and how they might achieve this.
- Why a person might choose to create a trust, rather than make an outright gift, and the type of trust they might select will depend on their aims and the particular circumstances.
- When looking to create a valid express trust, it is necessary to address the two required and separate stages – the declaration of the trust and the constitution of the trust.
- In this chapter, we have focused on the elements of the declaration of trust:
  - capacity – understanding of the nature and effect of what is being proposed;
  - the three certainties – the intention to create a trust being clearly evidenced by words or conduct, the subject-matter of the trust (the trust property) and the beneficiaries' interest in that subject-matter being similarly clear, and the intended objects or beneficiaries of the trust being objectively defined;
  - the beneficiary principle – the need to have a beneficiary capable of enforcing the trust;
  - the rules of perpetuity – ensuring that any trust does not last too long.
- There are differing rules associated with all these components, and compliance with all these rules contributes to the validity of the declaration.
- It is necessary to distinguish fixed trusts from discretionary trusts as some of the tests used to determine compliance are considered and applied differently.
- It is important to understand why these rules exist and the effect on the declaration if they are not satisfied.
- If being asked to draft a declaration of trust or to consider the validity of what someone else has drafted, it is necessary to be able to discuss and apply all the relevant rules to the given circumstances, so as to be able to draft a valid declaration for a client or to express a view on whether a declaration is valid. A structured approach to any analysis is vital.

# 3 Creating Express Trusts - The Constitution of the Trust

**LEARNING OUTCOMES**

By the end of this chapter, you should be able to:

- appreciate how to validly constitute trusts intended to be effective on death;
- recognise the circumstance when the transfer of the legal title is not required to constitute a trust;
- explain and apply the relevant rules for the transfer of the legal title to different types of property;
- identify the circumstances when equity might rescue a failed intended lifetime transfer of the legal title; and
- understand why and how a beneficiary may wish to dispose of their existing equitable interest and how they must effect that disposal.

## 3.1 Introduction

A fundamental element of our ownership of property is our right to give it away. In **Chapter 2**, we discussed reasons why a person might wish to do just that. We also examined the various ways that property could be gifted. Much depends on when any benefit is to be given away - during lifetime (*inter vivos*) or only on death - and the chosen vehicle for how the benefit is to be given - outright gift or a form of trust.

There are various rules which need to be complied with to ensure that any proposed trust, whether lifetime or on death, is effectively made. In **Chapter 2**, we addressed those rules in relation to declaring a trust.

A second but just as vital component of achieving an effective trust is the need for the subject-matter of the trust (the property being given away) to be transferred from the settlor in the correct manner. In this chapter, we consider what is required to 'constitute' a trust and how the relevant requirements are again dependent on when in time the trust is to take effect and the chosen vehicle for how the benefit of the trust is to be received.

## 3.2 Constitution of trusts only to be effective on death

Where a trust is only to take effect on death, obviously, a declaration of self as trustee will be unavailable. For a proposed trust involving third party trustees, any declaration of trust must comply with all the conditions discussed in **Chapter 2**, and it is necessary to consider a transfer of the legal title to those trustees of the property to be held on trust. However, the constitution of the trust only to be effective on death is straightforward. If the valid declaration is contained in a valid will, it is the legal effect of the will which transfers the legal title to the trustees (via the estate's personal representatives - the PRs). The only requirement is that the testator possesses the subject-matter of the trust when they die. If they have sold it or given it away during their lifetime, the intended trust will fail (by *ademption*).

In order to make a valid will, the testator must comply with s 9 of the Wills Act 1837. The will must be in writing, signed by the testator in the joint presence of two witnesses, who must then witness the testator's signature by signing the will in the testator's presence. When the testator dies, the PRs (called 'executors' as appointed by the will) receive the legal title to their property by operation of law.

Many of the functions and duties of the PRs are similar to those of trustees. For example, many of the statutory powers that apply to trustees (**Chapter 7**) also apply to PRs.

Where the deceased left a will leaving property to be held on trust, both PRs and trustees will be involved in the estate of a person who has died. When the administration of the estate has been completed, the PRs cease to hold the subject matter of the trust as PRs. At that point, they must 'assent' (transfer using the appropriate method) the trust property to the trustees appointed by the deceased in the will. Often, the same people are appointed as both PRs and trustees. Where this happens, they must assent from themselves (as PRs) to themselves (as trustees). If the trust property is *land*, the assent must be in signed writing.

## 3.3 Constitution of lifetime trusts with settlor as trustee

With this method of giving benefit to another, the settlor already has the legal title to the subject-matter of the trust. From the moment the settlor declares the trust, the settlor retains the legal interest but in a trustee capacity. No transfer of property is needed, and the trust is automatically 'constituted'. The equitable interest passes to the beneficiary. However, as with the trust only to be effective on death (**3.2** above), there must be a valid declaration of trust for this trust to be effective.

## 3.4 Constitution of lifetime trusts with third party trustees

Where a settlor wishes to provide benefit by means of a trust with third parties (such as family members or professionals) as trustees, in order for the trust to be effective the settlor must (in addition to making a valid declaration of trust) transfer the proposed trust property to the trustees. In this context, the term 'property' is not limited to houses and flats. 'Property' means anything a person can 'own'. Any type of property can form the subject-matter of a trust. However, 'property' is a vital component of any trust; without subject-matter there is no trust.

### 3.4.1 Types of property

#### 3.4.1.1 Real property ('realty')

Real property is freehold land. For historical reasons, this term does not include leasehold land.

#### 3.4.1.2 Personal property ('personalty')

Personalty is all property except freehold land. For example:

(a) *Chattels* ('things in possession'). Tangible things, eg jewellery, cars, furniture, paintings, animals, etc.

(b) *'Things in action'.* Intangible things which must be recovered by bringing a claim in court, not by taking physical possession, eg debts, life assurance policies, copyrights, company shares, bank accounts, etc.

(c) *Leasehold land.*

3.4.1.3 Digital assets

As yet without statutory definition, the term 'digital assets' (property or records in a digital form) covers a wide range of asset types ranging from high value property, for example cryptocurrency or non-fungible token (NFT) holdings, to property of a more personal or sentimental nature (Facebook, Instagram, iTunes accounts).

In relation to cryptocurrencies, at the end of 2019, a legal statement from the UK Jurisdiction Taskforce (the UKJT) ('Legal Statement on Crypto-assets and Smart Contracts') concluded that cryptocurrency such as Bitcoin could be treated, in principle, as property. Previous case law had given rise to doubts about the status of such assets as cryptocurrency was technically neither a 'thing in possession' nor a 'thing in action'. Since the UKJT endorsement of cryptocurrency as property, court cases in England and Wales involving equitable remedies (for instance, freezing orders and interim injunctions) have resulted in orders being given to protect cryptocurrency assets before judgment (see *AA v Persons Unknown* [2019] EWHC 3556 (Comm); *Fetch.ai Ltd v Persons Unknown* [2021] EWHC 2254 (Comm)).

In July 2022, the Law Commission issued a consultation paper which recommended that there should be recognition for a new category of personal property in English Law - 'data objects' (alongside 'things in possession' and 'things in action'). The intention was to provide digital assets, as intangible pieces of information, with legal status and to give greater consistency and protection to users. The consultation closed in November 2022 and the Commission's report was published in June 2023; a supplemental report and draft Bill on digital assets was published in July 2024. The final report concluded that the flexibility of the common law in England and Wales allows for a distinct category of personal property that can accommodate digital assets, recommending legislation to confirm this.

3.4.1.4 Expectancies

An expectancy is not property; there is no proprietary interest. It is a mere hope of ownership of property in the future, such as a legacy under the will of a person still alive. As a will is ineffective until the testator dies and as the testator could change their will in the meantime, any beneficiary named in a current will owns nothing until the testator dies.

As to the transfer of an expectancy, the law takes the pragmatic view that you cannot give away that which you do not own. A purported transfer of the 'property I may receive under my brother's will' would be ineffective. It is, however, possible to conclude a binding contract to transfer such future property.

### 3.4.2 Transfers of the legal title

According to Turner LJ in *Milroy v Lord* (1862) 4 De GF & J 264, to be effective the transfer of the trust property to the trustees must be done 'according to the nature of the property comprised in the settlement'. As already discussed, there are many distinct types of 'property'. How does a current legal owner effectively transfer property from themselves to another to constitute their intended trust?

3.4.2.1 Land (or any legal interest in land)

Where the intended trust property is land, the transfer of that legal interest is a three-stage process.

(1) According to s 52(1) of the Law of Property Act 1925, a settlor, as transferor of the legal title, must execute a deed in favour of the trustees (the transferee). Failure to execute a deed renders the attempted transaction void. Section 1 of the Law of Property (Miscellaneous Provisions) Act 1989 determines what constitutes a deed - a document stated to be a deed or stated to be signed as a deed; with the person making the deed signing the document in the presence of a witness who also signs it.

Where the land is registered (which most land now is), the 'deed' used is the Form TR1, as issued by Land Registry.

(2) The deed must be sent to Land Registry to register the transferee as the new legal owner. The signed deed can be sent to the Land Registry direct by the transferor, or the transferor can give the signed deed to the transferee for them to forward to the Land Registry.

(3) The Land Registry registers the transferee as the new legal owner of the land. Legal title is not transferred until the registration is completed.

#### 3.4.2.2 Shares in a company

Shareholders are the owners of companies. Each shareholder owns a number of shares in the company. In a large public company, such as British Telecom, this is likely to be an extremely small proportion of the total number of shares. In a private company, there may be only two or three owners. The principles governing registration and transfer are the same for both types of company.

The person who has the legal title to the shares is the person registered as the shareholder of those shares in the Register of Members which the company is obliged by statute to keep (Companies Act 2006, ss 112 and 113). There are two parallel methods of transfer of the legal ownership.

*(a) Shares outside the CREST system*

Shares in private companies ('Ltd' companies) will be outside the CREST system. Here the shareholder will have a share certificate as evidence that they are so registered. Possession of a share certificate is merely evidence of ownership. It is the registration which constitutes legal ownership.

The method of transfer of the legal title to these types of shares is:

(i) the transferor signs the form of transfer (a 'stock transfer form', prescribed by the Stock Transfer Act 1963, s 1);

(ii) the signed stock transfer form is sent to the company along with the existing share certificate (the transferor could send the completed stock transfer form and 'old' share certificate direct to the company on the transferee's behalf or could provide both documents to the transferee for submission by them to the company); and

(iii) the new shareholder is then registered in the Register of Members, and the legal title passes to them when registered. The company sends the new shareholder a certificate in their name.

*(b) Shares within the CREST system*

Under the CREST computerised share transfer system, owners of shares in public quoted companies may, if they wish, dispense with share certificates. Their shareholdings are recorded electronically by an organisation (eg stockbroker, nominee company) which is a member of the CREST system. Transfers are recorded electronically on the instructions of the shareholder without the need for them to sign a stock transfer form. Registration, and therefore transfer of legal title, is immediate. However, where a public quoted company has not dispensed with share certificates as evidence of ownership, the paper-based system of transfer will continue to apply.

#### 3.4.2.3 Money

*(a) Bank notes*

Bank notes issued by the Bank of England are a form of 'bearer' instrument. This means that the possessor, or 'bearer,' has the rights conferred by the instrument. Transfer of those rights is achieved by delivery of the note to the transferee. No writing is necessary. The wording on bank notes, 'I promise to pay the bearer on demand the sum of TEN pounds', signed by the Chief Cashier, indicates this. If you held them to their promise, they would probably just give you another note, containing the same promise.

*(b) Cheques signed in favour of a transferee*

A cheque is merely a revocable instruction ('mandate') to the transferor's bank to pay the amount of money indicated to the donee upon presentation of the cheque. The transferor can revoke this mandate by 'stopping the cheque' before the donee has presented it to the transferor's bank. The position would be the same if the transferor died before the donee presented the cheque.

The use of debit cards operates in a comparable way to cheques. They are a mandate to the bank to pay. However, unlike cheques, which must presented for clearance, the instruction given to bank via a debit card is immediate.

*(c) Electronic transfers*

An electronic transfer is the movement of money from one bank account (that of the transferor) to the account of another (the transferee) using computer-based technology. The transfer takes place on the authorisation of the transferor, but independently from any interaction with bank employees and without the need for paper documents to be completed.

3.4.2.4 Chattels

Transfer of the title to chattels (technically known as 'choses in possession'), such as jewellery or furniture, is by physical delivery of the asset to the transferee, or by a deed. An example of the latter method occurred in *Jaffa v Taylor Gallery Ltd* (1990) *The Times*, 20 March, where the transfer of a picture to trustees was valid without physical delivery, as the deed setting up the trust vested title in them. One of the trustees lived in Northern Ireland and, as the judge commented, it would be impossible (and absurd) to require the painting to be physically handed over to all the trustees.

3.4.2.5 Digital assets

Given the rapid growth in the use of digital technology and the internet, the ability to give away and transfer digital assets is becoming an area of great interest both in terms of lifetime giving and general estate planning (for instance, see 'Digital Assets: A Call to Action', a 2021 report by the Society of Estate and Trust Practitioners in partnership with Queen Mary University of London Centre for Commercial Law Studies).

In light of the rapid developments, in its 2019 statement on crypto assets, the UKJT (see **3.4.1.3**) reflected on how ownership of these types of assets is determined and how ownership is transferred. Seeking to address the question of whether such crypto-assets could be given away or held on trust, the UKJT discussed various methods of transfer depending on the nature of the currency and the issues that might be raised in light of the intangible nature of the currency as essentially digital files. The UKJT made reference to a case in Singapore which accepted that Bitcoins could be the subject matter of a trust (*B2C2 v Quoine Pte Ltd* [2019] SHGC(1) 03) to support its conclusions.

Further developments in this area are anticipated as more and more people become involved with these high value assets and seek to give them away in their lifetime or on their death.

## 3.5 Defective transfers of the legal title and the role of equity

Legal title to the property must be transferred to the transferee (the third party trustees) using the method appropriate to that type of property. By way of reminder, **Figure 3.1** summarises the 'appropriate methods' as dealt with in **3.4.2** above.

**Figure 3.1** Summary – transferring the legal title

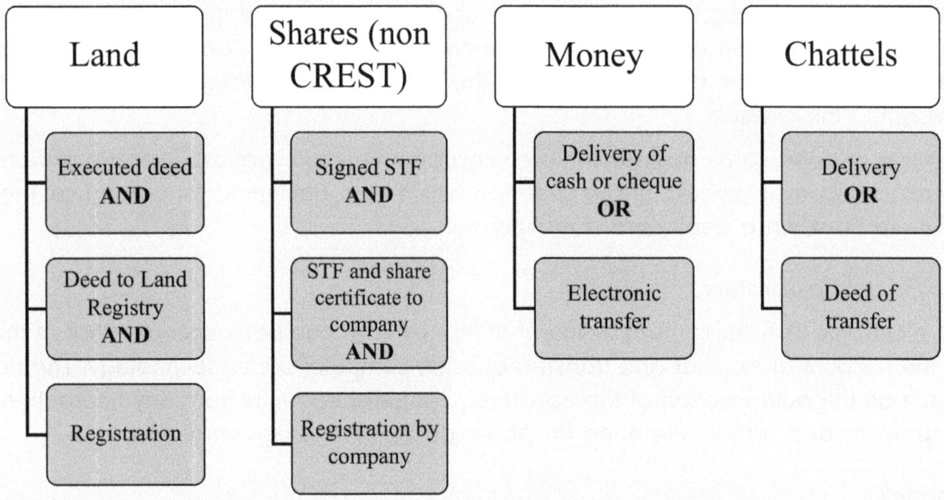


In the absence of fraud, a settlor who had validly transferred the trust property to the trustees (unless they have retained a power of revocation, which, while possible, is rare given the tax consequences) will be unable to demand the property be returned to them. If accompanied with a valid declaration (**Chapter 2**), the trust will be fully constituted.

If, however, any required element for the legal transfer process is missing, the proposed transaction will be defective. It will be as if the intended disposition never occurred; the trust is not constituted.

As discussed in **2.3.2**, Turner LJ in *Milroy v Lord* (1862) 4 De GF & J 264 said, 'If the settlement is intended to be effectuated by one of the modes ... the Court will not give effect to it by applying one of the other modes.' In *Richards v Delbridge* (1874) LR 18 Eq 11 an attempted transfer of an interest in land was ineffective because it was not by deed. It was argued that the ineffective gift should be regarded as a declaration of trust by the donor in the donee's favour. The Court of Appeal rejected this as it was clear that a gift rather than a trust was intended. The intended donee could not sue for the intended gift on the basis of the pretence that the donor intended to create a trust in favour of the disappointed recipient. You will recall in **1.3.3** the equitable maxim 'equity will not perfect an imperfect gift'.

If it can be shown that there was a contract between the transferee (or the beneficiaries) and the intended transferor, then they could sue on the contract. This would require evidence that they had provided some reciprocal value ('consideration') for the transaction. This is very unlikely in the context of an intended trust, the whole nature of which is meant to confer a gratuitous benefit. Donees of gifts and beneficiaries of a trust are regarded as a 'volunteers' and 'equity does not assist a volunteer' (**1.3.3**).

In the face of a defective transfer, there appears to be little that can be done to salvage the transaction. However, in certain circumstances, equity may provide exceptions to the basic principles, and it is not always popular for so doing.

### 3.5.1 'Every effort' test

As stated by Turner LJ in *Milroy v Lord* (1862) 4 De GF & J 264:

> in order to render a voluntary settlement valid and effectual, the settlor must *have done everything* which, according to the nature of the property comprised in the settlement, was necessary to be done in order to transfer the property and render the settlement binding upon him. [emphasis added]

This has given rise to the equitable principle known as the 'every effort' test. Where the transferor (the settlor) has failed to transfer legal title, the transfer may, however, be regarded as complete in equity if the transferor has put the property beyond their recall, ie they have done everything in their power to transfer the legal ownership to the trustees; the only outstanding matters to effect the legal transfer are the actions of third parties, whose involvement in the transfer process is required. The test was applied in *Re Rose* [1952] Ch 499.

***Re Rose* [1952] Ch 499**

On 30 March 1943, Rose executed the appropriate form of transfer, transferring 10,000 shares in a company to his wife. He handed the transfer and share certificate to his wife, the documents were sent to the company, and his wife was registered as the new shareholder on 30 June 1943. Rose subsequently died, and the Inland Revenue claimed estate duty on the gift.

If the date of the gift was before 10 April 1943, no duty was payable. The actual date of the gift was therefore crucial.

When was the gift perfected? The court found that this was on 30 March 1943, the date of the transfer, even though the legal title did not pass until Mrs Rose was registered as shareholder on 30 June 1943. Rose had done everything required of him - signed a stock transfer form, and sent it and his share certificate, enabling the donee to apply for registration as the new legal owner - the transfer was valid in equity and Rose was regarded as a trustee for his wife (the donee) in the period before she was registered by the company registrars (at which point the legal title would pass). There was no express trust (so circumventing 'equity will not assist a volunteer'). The court implied a trust to recognise the relative positions of Mr and Mrs Rose.

The principle was further applied in *Mascall v Mascall* (1984) 50 P & CR 119, a case which concerned a gift of registered land. Here the transferor handed over a deed of transfer to the transferee, which was sufficient to enable the transferee to become registered by the Land Registry as legal owner. The transferor later changed his mind about the transfer and tried, unsuccessfully, to recover the land.

Brown-Wilkinson LJ explained:

> The basic principle underlying all the cases is that equity will not come to the aid of a volunteer. Therefore, if a donee needs to get an order from a court of equity in order to complete their title, they will not get it. If, on the other hand, the donee has under their control everything necessary to constitute their title completely without any further assistance from the transferor the donee needs no assistance from equity and the gift is complete. It is on that principle, which is laid down in *Re Rose*, that in equity it is held that a gift is complete as soon as the settlor or donor has done everything that the donor has to do, that is to say, as soon as the donee has within their control all those things necessary to enable them, the donee, to complete their title.

### 3.5.2 Defective transfers and unconscionability

As discussed in **Chapter 2** (see **2.2**) the two methods of creating express lifetime trusts, as explained by Turner LJ in Milroy v Lord *Milroy v Lord* (1862) 4De GF & J 264, are:

- a transfer to trustees to hold on trust for the person to be benefited - the settlor declares a valid trust (as in **Chapter 2**) and then transfers the trust property to the trustees in the appropriate way to 'constitute' the trust (as discussed above in **3.4**) with the every effort test applying to such a transfer if necessary and applicable; and

- a declaration of self as trustee for the person to be benefitted – a valid declaration is needed. However, no transfer is required as the settlor already has the legal title.

However, when considering the case of *Choithram (T) International SA v Pagarani* [2001] 2 All ER 492, the court was asked to consider a case which did not fit neatly into the *Milroy v Lord* classification. Trying not to 'officiously defeat' (per Browne-Wilkinson LJ) what the settlor had wanted to achieve, controversially the Privy Council came up with the concept of it being unconscionable, in the specific circumstances, for a settlor to resile from a trust which had not been fully constituted.

***Choithram (T) International SA v Pagarani* [2001] 2 All ER 492**

Pagarani (referred to as 'TCP' in the judgment) had created the Choithram International Foundation ('the CIF'). He was one of the seven trustees of this foundation. He purported to transfer 'all his wealth' by way of gift to the CIF. His wealth comprised shareholdings in various companies. Legal title to shares passes when all the trustees are registered at the company, although equity regards the transfer as complete under the every effort test when the settlor has handed over the stock transfer forms and share certificates to the trustees (or the company registrars). TCP did not complete or hand over any stock transfer forms or share certificates. He just made an oral statement that he was giving all his wealth to the Foundation and orally instructed the companies' accountant to transfer all his wealth in the companies. TCP then died. The judges at first instance held that TCP's actions were not valid to make an effective gift or trust.

At the Privy Council, it was noted that the particular facts of the case did not fit 'squarely' within the *Milroy v Lord* methods of making a gift or creating a trust. It therefore interpreted TCP's words of gift as meaning a transfer to the CIF to hold on the trusts declared in the trust deed which had just been executed. The CIF had no separate existence; it just comprised a body of the seven trustees and so this was the natural inference. TCP had effectively declared himself a trustee of the property (declarations of trust over personalty can be oral). The fact that the shares were already vested in him as trustee was sufficient to constitute the trust. As he was one of the trustees of the CIF, the shares were vested in one of the trustees. He was under a duty to transfer them into the names of all the trustees. His conscience was affected as soon as he validly declared the gift and he (or his estate) could not subsequently resile from it as this would be unconscionable. The trust was, therefore, valid.

Even more controversially than *Choithram v Pagarani*, the issue of unconscionability was further considered in *Pennington v Waine* [2002] 1 WLR 2075.

***Pennington v Waine* [2002] 1 WLR 2075**

AW owned shares in a private company. She informed one of company's auditors that she wished to transfer some of their shares to her nephew so that he could become a director of the company. The company already held AW's share certificate, so she merely signed a stock transfer form and sent it to the auditor who placed it on the company's file at his office. The auditor informed the nephew what had happened and why and that no action was required on the nephew's part other than to sign a form agreeing to be a director, which the nephew did and returned. AW subsequently died and the issue became whether the gift was complete in equity even though no documents had been delivered to the donee, nor the stock transfer form to the company.

Citing *Choithram* in its wish not to 'officiously defeat' AW's intended gift, the Court of Appeal held that while she had not delivered the documents to the donee or the company and so had not satisfied the every effort test, she had reached the stage where it would have been unconscionable for her to have recalled the gift. The gift was complete in equity.

There was considerable unfavorable critical comment on this case at the time given the level of uncertainty it created. In *Choithram*, the settlor's valid declaration of trust, while being one of multiple trustees, was clearly the trigger for the settlor's conscience being effected. However, in *Pennington,* Lady Justice Arden said there was no definitive list of factors that would make it unconscionable for a donor to back out of their gift. Whether unconscionability arose would be dependent on the circumstances of the gift (and she provided details as to the factors relevant in the case).

The High Court decision in *Curtis v Pulbrook* [2011] EWHC 167 (Ch) subsequently suggested that *Pennington* was decided on the basis of detrimental reliance. AW was bound because the nephew acted to his detriment by becoming a director of the company, relying of the gift of the shares to do so. On this view, *Pennington* is simply an example of proprietary estoppel (see **Chapter 6**), well established as being outside the idea that equity will not aid a volunteer nor perfect the incomplete gift.

### 3.5.3 The rule in *Strong v Bird*

The rule in *Strong v Bird* (1874) LR 18 Eq 315, on the other hand, is a long-accepted exception to the maxims 'equity will not perfect an imperfect gift' and 'equity will not assist a volunteer'. The rule applies on the death of the intended transferor and has the effect of making a lifetime gift perfect or a lifetime trust properly constituted. The donee of a gift or the trustees can claim the property in priority to those entitled to the rest of the estate which the transferor has left on death, ie their heirs.

For the rule to apply, the following four conditions must be met:

(a) The transferor intends to create a trust with third party trustees (or make an outright gift), but the intended disposition is invalid because the transferor failed to comply with the appropriate formality for transferring the legal title to the relevant property. For instance, where the disposition involves the transfer of land, a deed in accordance with s 52 of the Law of Property Act 1925 has not been executed. Other examples might be the failure to complete a stock transfer form for company shares, failure to deliver a chattel or execute a deed of transfer.

(b) The intention of the transferor must be to make an immediate disposition (ie create the trust or make a gift), not one conditional on an event in the future. Thus, in *Re Freeland* [1952] 1 Ch 110, a stated intention to give a car to a donee 'as soon as I can get it on the road' was not to be an immediate disposition, and so the rule did not apply.

(c) There must be evidence not only of an intention to make an immediate disposition of their property but of that intention continuing up to the transferor's death. It must be evidenced that, when they died, the transferor still had the belief that they no longer owned the property; it had effectively been given to the intended recipient. However, if, in the meantime, the transferor deals with the property in some way which suggests it is still owned by them, this will prevent the intention from continuing. For instance, in *Re Gonin* [1979] 1 Ch 16, a mother allegedly attempted to give a house and garden to her daughter but failed to sign a deed. Subsequently, she sold part of the garden, thus indicating she still considered herself the owner. This (along with other factors) prevented the rule from applying.

(d) The transferor dies, and the donee or an intended trustee (or one of them) is appointed the transferor's personal representative. The legal title to the property vests in the donee or the intended trustee by operation of law on the transferor's death (see **3.1**). The transfer of the legal title is finally accomplished; the trust is now constituted (the gift now perfect).

**Figure 3.2** Summary - considering the constitution of the trust

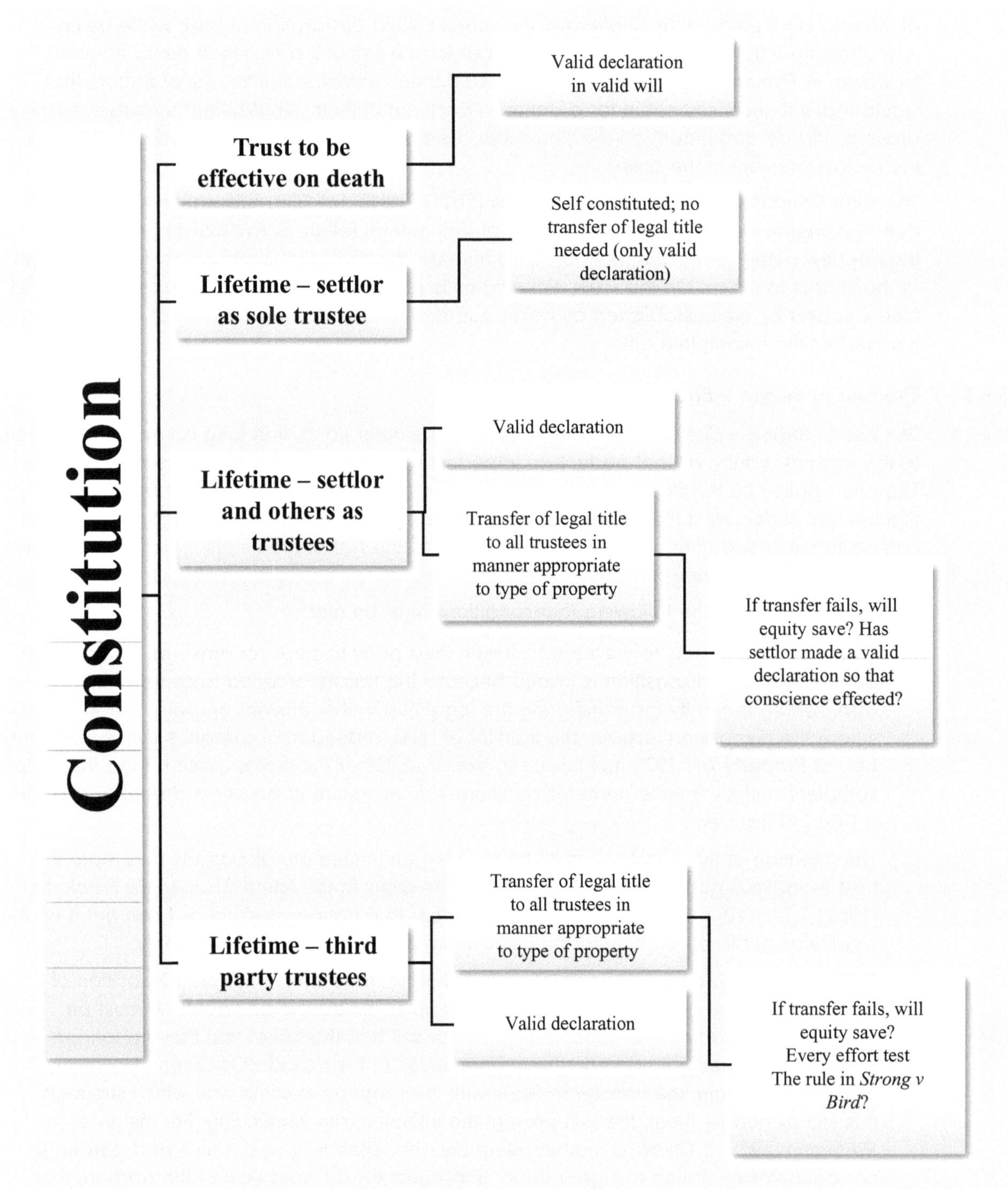

not doing

## 3.6 Lifetime transfers of equitable interests

In this instance, there is already a trust in existence; validly declared and already constituted. The trust property, whether land or personalty, is already held by the trustee upon trust for the beneficiary; the legal and equitable interests are separated (**Chapter 1**). We considered 'vested' equitable interests in **1.7.1**. A key point to remember is that a vested equitable interest is a proprietary interest - a 'piece of property'- in its own right. A beneficiary of such an interest may want to give it away or sell it or otherwise dispose of it.

***Example***

*Trustees are holding the trust property (say some land and a portfolio of financial investments) on trust for A for life (receiving the income earned by the trust property - any rent earned from the land and dividends from the investments during their lifetime), remainder to B (a postponed interest, until A's death, in the capital).*

*The postponement of B's interest may give a clue as to why B might want to transfer their interest in remainder to someone else. B may need money now and is unable to wait until A dies. B may, therefore, sell the equitable interest to C, who in turn becomes entitled to the same interest in the trust as B had, ie the right to the capital on A's death. How much C is willing to pay depends on the anticipated life expectancy of A. The older (or more ill) A is, the sooner the interest is likely to fall into possession, and the more C will have to pay. This is known as an 'actuarial' valuation.*

*Rather than sell, B might raise a loan on the security of the interest and assign the interest to the creditor for the duration only of the loan. Another common possibility is a gift of the remainder to B's children or grandchildren. There can be tax advantages in doing this.*

### 3.6.1 Dispositions of equitable interests

Whatever the reason for the transfer, if the equitable interest is to be transferred *separately* from the legal title, then, by s 53(1)(c) of the Law of Property Act 1925, it must be in writing; otherwise the purported transfer is void.

Section 53(1)(c) reads as follows:

> [A] disposition of an equitable interest or trust subsisting at the time of the disposition, must be in writing signed by the person disposing of the same, or by his agent thereunto lawfully authorised in writing or by will.

There are a number of points to note when considering the statutory provision:

(a) Section 53(1)(c) applies to dispositions of *subsisting* equitable interests, ie ones which are already in existence at the time of the disposition. Therefore, it is only relevant when a beneficiary under an existing trust wishes to dispose of their *existing* equitable interest (so a legal owner of property who wishes to declare themselves a trustee of the property (as in **2.2.2**) does not have to comply with s 53(1)(c) as this is the creation of a *new* equitable interest).

(b) The actual disposition has to be in writing (and not merely evidenced in writing); otherwise it is void.

(c) The written disposition can be signed by the person disposing of the interest (the transferor) or by their agent if the transferor has given the agent written authorisation to sign for them.

Section 53(1)(c) has its origins in the Statute of Frauds 1677, which as the name suggests, was intended to prevent fraudulent transactions in equitable interests. The trustees need to know who the owner of the beneficial interest is to be able to hold on trust for the correct person. Any dealing with the equitable interest, therefore, has to be in writing (although there is no obligation to actually notify the trustees of the transaction).

The type of transaction caught by s 53(1)(c) has been the subject of much litigation, so it is necessary to look at the various methods by which a disposal of a subsisting equitable interest might occur.

(a) *Method 1.* A trustee holds property on trust for a beneficiary (B) and B wishes to transfer their equitable interest to X. B can assign their equitable interest to X direct. Such an assignment of B's equitable interest must be done in signed writing to satisfy s 53(1)(c) (see **Figure 3.3**).

**Figure 3.3** Method 1 – disposal by B direct to X

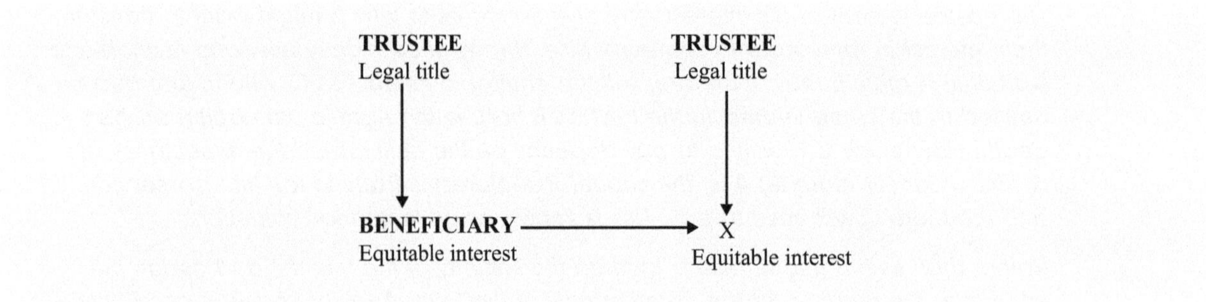


(b) *Method 2.* B can orally direct T to hold the trust property on trust from now on for X (see **Figure 3.4**).

**Figure 3.4** Method 2 – disposal by B to X following oral direction to trustee

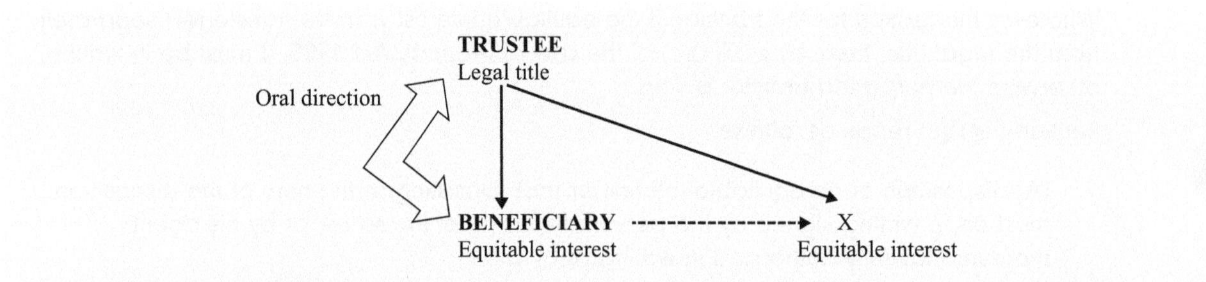


This was the method considered in *Grey v IRC* [1960] AC 3.

***Grey v IRC* [1960] AC 3**

In 1949, Hunter transferred assets to trustees to hold on trust for his six grandchildren. Subsequently, in 1955, he transferred 18,000 shares in a company to the same trustees, telling them to hold them on bare trust for himself. In an attempt to avoid stamp duty (which would be payable on a written transfer of his equitable interests to the grandchildren), he then orally directed the trustees of the 1955 bare trust henceforth to hold the shares on trust for the grandchildren under the terms of the 1949 trust rather than for him. The trustees subsequently executed a document confirming the directions, and the Inland Revenue (as it was then known - now HMRC) assessed these documents to stamp duty.

The court found that the oral direction given to the trustees amounted to a 'disposition of an equitable interest or trust subsisting at the time of the disposition'. Hunter was seeking to divert his beneficial ownership of the shares to his grandchildren. As the disposition was not in signed writing, it was ineffective to transfer Hunter's equitable interest at the time of the oral direction to the trustees. The transfer of the equitable interest took place when the trustees executed the confirming document, upon which stamp duty was payable.

(c) *Method 3.* B can orally direct T to transfer the trust property to X. Here B is seeking to transfer their equitable interest in the trust property along with the legal title. The end result is that X becomes the legal and equitable owner of the trust property, effectively bringing the trust to an end (see **Figure 3.5**).

**Figure 3.5** Method 3 - disposal by trustees to X and by B to X

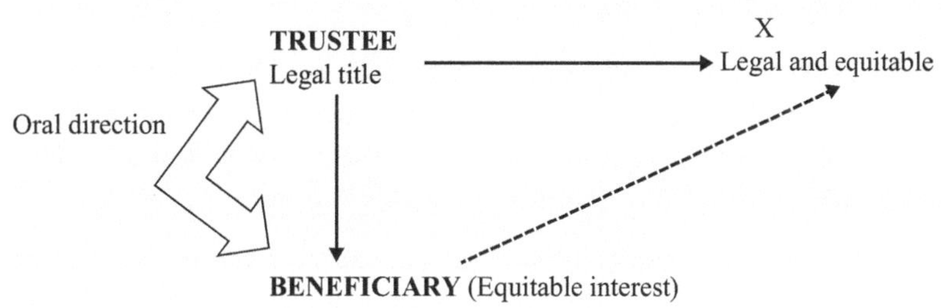


This method was analysed in *Vandervell v IRC* [1967] 2 AC 291 and its progeny, *Re Vandervell (No 2)* [1974] Ch 269.

***Vandervell v IRC* [1967] 2 AC 291**

Vandervell ('V'), a wealthy industrialist, wanted to donate £150,000 to the Royal College of Surgeons ('the College'). To achieve this end, he decided to transfer 100,000 shares in the family business to the College, until those shares had supplied the £150,000 by way of dividends. Thereafter, a separate company (a family trust) was given an option to purchase the shares from the College for £5,000. V's shares in the family business were held by a bank for convenience. The bank, therefore, held the legal title, and V held an absolute equitable interest under a 'bare trust'. V instructed the bank (as absolute owner he was entitled to do this) to transfer the shares to the College, which it duly validly did, and the dividends were then paid to the College. If V still retained an interest in the shares, he would be liable for tax on the dividends. This in turn depended on whether he had transferred his equitable interest to the College. The Revenue argued that V had not disposed of his equitable interest in writing as required by s 53(1)(c).

The court indicated that s 53(1)(c) was only relevant when 'dealings with the equitable estate are divorced from dealings with the legal estate'. In a bare trust, when the beneficiary directs the trustee to transfer the legal estate to a third party with the intention that the third party takes the equitable interest as well, s 53(1)(c) does not apply. The transfer of the legal title also effects the transfer of the equitable interest. There is no need to discuss the separate transfer of the equitable interest.

It is important to be clear of the nature of the subject matter of the proposed transaction. Is it the legal title, or an equitable interest? For instance, in *Zeital v Kaye* [2010] EWCA Civ 159, X held a company share on a bare trust for Y. Y intended to give the share to Z, and a stock transfer form completed by Y in favour of Z was handed over to Z. The court found that as Y held an equitable interest, the correct way to transfer this interest was in writing, complying with s 53(1)(c) of the LPA 1925. The stock transfer form (which would have been suitable had Y held the legal title) did not constitute the necessary writing.

**ACTIVITY Review your understanding – constitution of trusts**

Analyse the following scenarios. In each case, consider whether the intended trust has been validly constituted.

(1) Peter called his sister Janet asking her to hold Peter's shares in AB Enterprises Ltd on trust for her son, Benjamin, and hand them over to him when he is 21. Benjamin is currently 17. AB Enterprises Ltd is a private company. Janet agreed and has received a share certificate and a signed stock transfer form from Peter. However, she has not yet sent the documents to the company and Peter has asked for them to be returned as he needs to sell the shares.

(2) Last month, Rohit wrote to his nephew Sadiq (aged 18) and said 'You are to have my townhouse in Liverpool if you attain 25. In the meantime I plan to hold it on trust for you and I am going to ask your father, Ashok, to be a trustee with me. Yours, Uncle Rohit.' The townhouse is still registered in Rohit's sole name.

(3) Six weeks ago, Kwame wrote a letter to his daughter Amara explaining that he wanted her to have his valuable Chadwick sculpture to hold on trust for her two children. The letter said, 'Pick it up whenever you can.' Amara has not been able to collect the sculpture and Kwame died suddenly last week. Amara is named executrix in Kwame's will. The sculpture has been on loan to a local museum for the last month.

**COMMENT**

(1) Legal title to shares does not pass until the transferee is registered as shareholder so the trust has not been legally constituted. However, the transfer is complete in equity once the transferor has done all they can do to transfer the shares (*Milroy v Lord*). In *Re Rose* the court held that this stage is reached when the transferor hands over the stock transfer form and share certificate, putting them beyond recall. This has occurred here as Janet, as trustee, is able register herself as the new legal owner without any further assistance from Peter. While Peter is still registered as the legal owner, he cannot recover the shares as his intended trust has been constituted in equity. He merely holds the legal title on trust (for Janet as a trustee for Benjamin) until the registration has taken place.

(2) Rohit tried to create a trust of the Liverpool townhouse with himself and Ashok acting as trustees for Sadiq. The trust needed to be constituted – legal title to the trust property being transferred in the proper manner to all the trustees. In this case, the trust property is land, so Rohit needs to execute a transfer deed (LPA 1925, s 52) and have it registered at the Land Registry. A letter is not a deed (a document complying with LP(MP) Act 1989, s 1) and Rohit remains the sole registered owner. However, the trust property is already vested in Rohit, and by signing the letter to his nephew, he has done enough to validly declare himself a trustee of land, satisfying s 53(1)(b) of the LPA 1925. In *Choithram v Pagarani,* the trust was constituted in equity because it would have been unconscionable for the settlor to have resiled from the trust by relying on the

technicality that the property had not been vested in the names of all the trustees. Rohit is under a duty to transfer legal title into the names of both trustees to complete the transfer of the legal title and constitute the trust.

(3) Transfer of legal title to chattels, such as the sculpture, passes by delivery or a deed (*Jaffa v Taylor House Gallery*). As the letter does not constitute a deed, so legal title to the sculpture had not been transferred to Amara as trustee by either method before Kwame died. On this basis, the intended trust was not constituted. However, as Kwame's executrix, Amara has acquired legal title to the sculpture (along with the rest of his estate) by operation of law. In *Strong v Bird,* it was held that this would be sufficient to complete the transfer if further conditions were met. The transferor must have intended an immediate, unconditional transfer (which appears satisfied) and the transferor must not have changed their mind before they died. Here, Kwame has acted as if he retained ownership of the sculpture as it was loaned to the museum, so this condition is not satisfied. The trust is, therefore, not constituted and the sculpture will form part of Kwame's estate.

## SUMMARY

- It is important to recognise that for a trust to be validly created it is necessary to ensure that the legal title to the subject-matter of the trust is effectively transferred. How this transfer is successfully achieved depends on when and how the benefit of the trust is intended to take effect.
- Where, in their lifetime, a settlor validly declares themselves to be a trustee, no transfer of the legal title is needed as it already rests with the settlor.
- For dispositions only to come into operation on death, a valid declaration of trust has to be included in a valid will. The personal representatives obtain legal title to the deceased's estate by operation of law, and they are responsible for completing the transfer of property to be gifted or held on trust.
- When dispositions are planned to take effect during someone's lifetime, legal title to the subject-matter of the trust must be transferred either to the donee of the gift or to the proposed third party trustees. Here it is important to recognise that there are many different types of property which can form the subject-matter of a trust (or an absolute gift).
- Knowing how the transfers of the legal title to diverse types of property are effectively accomplished is vital so as to ensure that a trust is validly constituted. Without a successful transfer, a settlor's intention to create a lifetime trust will fail.
- Equity can, in certain circumstances, be used as a means of salvaging what, on its face, is an attempted lifetime disposition of the legal title to property which has failed. Recognising when these circumstances may (nor may not) arise will be useful to fully understand whether or not a trust, while not legally valid, might be valid in equity and the consequences of this.
- Knowledge and understanding of the nature of equitable interests enhances an appreciation of why a beneficiary might wish to dispose of their equitable interest under an existing trust and what a beneficiary is required to do to validly complete the disposal of their separate interest.

# 4 Trusts for Purposes

**LEARNING OUTCOMES**

By the end of this chapter, you should be able to:

- distinguish between trusts for individuals and trusts for purposes;
- explain the difficulties arising from trusts for purposes;
- understand the criteria to determine whether a trust for a purpose could be classed as charitable or not;
- recognise the circumstances in which non-charitable purpose trusts may be valid; and
- appreciate the problems surrounding gifts to non-charitable clubs and societies and how they are commonly resolved.

## 4.1 Introduction

A trust only exists if the trustees are under a duty to carry it out, and there can be no duty unless there is someone to enforce it. In short, if there are no beneficiaries, there are no enforcers; hence the 'trustees' are not subject to a duty and there is no valid trust. This is the basis of the 'beneficiary principle' (*Morice v Bishop of Durham* (1804) 9 Ves 399).

This principle causes a particular problem when the person creating the trust wants the trust property to be used not to benefit particular people, but instead wants the trust property to be used to do something: the dedicated dog owner wants to create a trust in their will to look after their canine pet; a lifelong political party supporter wants trustees to use their money to further the interests of their party. All these are purposes and have no obvious benefit to a particular beneficiary with legal capacity. On this basis, it would appear that these trusts would not be valid because of the lack of anyone able to enforce the obligations the settlors or testators wanted to impose on the trustees.

## 4.2 Objections to purpose trusts

In the context of discussing express trusts, there are a number of factors which contribute to the basic principle that purpose trusts are void for want of a beneficiary.

### 4.2.1 The beneficiary principle

The beneficiary principle dictates that trusts need legally competent beneficiaries. This would normally be humans or properly constituted corporate entities. Without such beneficiaries, who could ensure that the trust was being administered in accordance with its terms, who could bring court action against trustees in the event of a breach?

In the words of Sir William Grant in *Morice v Bishop of Durham*:

> There can be no trust, over which this Court will not assume control; for an uncontrollable power of disposition would be ownership, and not a trust. Every trust ... must have a definite object. There must be somebody in whose favour the Court can decree performance.

As seen in **Chapter 2**, George Bernard Shaw's proposed trust to research a 40-letter alphabet failed (*Re Shaw's Will Trust* discussed in **2.3.5**) because of its non-compliance with the beneficiary principle.

### 4.2.2 Lack of certainty

The concept of certainty is important when looking at trusts. Purpose trusts are not immune to this issue as often the intended use of the trust fund is not described with sufficient clarity. In this circumstance, how will the trustees know what they are to do with the trust fund and, more importantly, how would a court know if trustees were acting in accordance with the terms of the trust?

***Re Astor's Settlement Trusts* [1952] 1 All ER 1067**

A 1945 settlement created by Viscount Astor (owner of the *Observer* newspaper at the time) contained a trust which required the trustees to use the income of the trust fund (for a period which satisfied the rule of perpetuities) for the purposes of establishing (inter alia):

- the maintenance of good understanding, sympathy and co-operation between nations;
- the preservation of the independence and integrity of newspapers; and
- the promotion of the freedom of independence and integrity of the Press.

In addition to being void on the grounds of the beneficiary principle, the trust was also declared void on the grounds of uncertainty. The trust gave no guidance as to how the purposes were to be performed. This uncertainty would not only paralyse the trustees but would also prevent the court from controlling the trust and carrying out the purpose if the trustees should fail to do so.

### 4.2.3 Perpetuities

Purpose trusts are also impacted by an aspect of the rules against perpetuity, discussed in **2.3.6** as another required element of a valid trust. The rule against inalienability of trust capital is a separate perpetuity rule (the rule against remoteness of vesting is not relevant here because the whole idea of a purpose trust is that the property is not intended to vest in a beneficiary).

The issue relates to the potential for the capital of the trust fund being tied up for too long. British law frowns upon attempts to restrict the use of property held in trust for excessive periods of time. Policy demands that people own money outright and are therefore able to spend and invest it freely.

The capital of a trust fund can comprise different types of property – shares, money, land (all of which will be invested to produce income in the form of dividends, interest, rent). The rule against inalienability of trust capital states that a purpose trust will be void if it causes the capital to be unavailable for a period longer than the perpetuity period, which for this rule is currently 21 years.

The Perpetuities and Accumulations Act 2009 does not affect the rule against inalienability (Perpetuities and Accumulations Act 2009, s 18).

To comply with the rule, either:

(a) the trust must state that it is to last for no more than 21 years; or

(b) the trustees must be able spend all the trust capital on the purpose and thereby end the trust at any time.

### 4.2.4 Capriciousness

Some trusts are attempted for purposes which are quite whimsical. The court is unwilling to allow trusts which it regards as capricious or serving no useful purpose. For instance, in *Brown v Burdett* (1882) 21 Ch D 667, the court would not uphold a trust where the testatrix left her house on trust to block up the windows and doors for 20 years. There were also comments about the capriciousness of George Bernard Shaw's trust in *Re Shaw's Will Trust* (see **2.3.5**).

## 4.3 The charitable exception

All of the objections detailed in **4.2** support the basic principle that purpose trusts are void. However, this principle is not an absolute. There are exceptions which allow a valid purpose trust to be created. The most significant of these exceptions is the creation of trusts for charitable purposes.

### 4.3.1 Advantages of charitable purpose trust status

The Joseph Rowntree charitable Trust (the 'JRCT') is governed by a declaration of trust dated 6 November 1939, and its stated charitable objects are 'income to be applied for such charitable purposes or objects and in such manner as the trustees shall in their uncontrolled discretion think fit'. Considering the basic trust principles already discussed, this trust should not be valid – it offends the beneficiary principle as there are no ascertainable beneficiaries with a sufficiently tangible benefit to be able to go to court to enforce the trust; it offends the rule against inalienability – there is no time limitation and only the income is to be used so capital has been tied up for longer than 21 years; the objects or purpose of the trust are uncertain. However, the JRCT is a registered charity (registered number 210037) and provides a good illustration of the benefits which can be achieved with charitable trust status.

#### 4.3.1.1 The beneficiary principle

Charitable purpose trusts are not subject to the beneficiary principle. This is because they are enforced by the Crown through its officer, the Attorney-General. The Charity Commission (the Commission) takes on the Attorney-General's role of supervising and monitoring charitable trusts. To ensure that the Commission is aware of all charities, trustees of charitable trusts are under a duty to register them with the Commission. Registration raises a conclusive presumption of charitable status.

From the Commission's register (available online) it is possible to review the history and current financial status of all charities registered with it. For instance, information about the JRCT is available at https://register-of-charities.charitycommission.gov.uk/charity-search/-/charity-details/210037/governing-document.

#### 4.3.1.2 Certainty

Charitable trusts are not subject to the certainty of purpose rule. Even if a charity's purpose is expressed in vague terms, provided the purpose is charitable (see **4.3.2**) it will not be void. The trustees can seek guidance from the Commission on how to apply the money.

4.3.1.3 Perpetuities

Charitable trusts are not subject to the rule against inalienability of capital (discussed at **4.2.3**). There is no 21-year time limit to the holding of the capital of a charitable purpose trust. As can be seen from the JRCT, charitable purpose trusts can last a long time.

4.3.1.4 Lapse

Charities enjoy privileged status through the concept of 'cy-pres'. Where there is a gift or trust in a will to a named individual, this gift or trust will lapse should the potential beneficiary die before the testator (see **2.3.4**). This principle does not apply to a charity. If the named charity no longer exists at the time of the testator's death, there is a scheme with the Commission which enables the proposed gift to be redirected to another charity with similar objects.

4.3.1.5 Tax benefits

Charitable trusts enjoy significant tax benefits, available both to the person creating the charitable trust and to the trust itself once it has been properly set up with the Commission. For the person creating the trust, there can be substantial inheritance tax savings (a possible full exemption from the tax itself, or a reduction of the IHT rate payable by an estate where 10% of the net estate is left to charity and/or charitable purposes). In addition, once established, charities themselves enjoy tax reliefs given to them by the Government. For instance, donations from UK taxpayers benefit from Gift Aid – the charity can reclaim the income tax on the contribution so increasing the value of donation given; investment of the charity fund is exempt from tax (income tax and capital gains tax).

Given the tax reliefs available to charities and the governmental funding of the Commission, taxpayers fund charities, even if they do not contribute directly to one of them. Because of this taxpayer involvement in the funding of charities, trusts can only be charities if they have a sufficient element of public benefit; this justifies paying the cost of enforcing them from public funds.

### 4.3.2 What makes a purpose trust charitable?

Having a sufficient level of public benefit is only one requirement for a valid charitable purpose trust. **Figure 4.1** details the three essential elements to achieve charitable status.

**Figure 4.1** Requirements to achieve charitable status

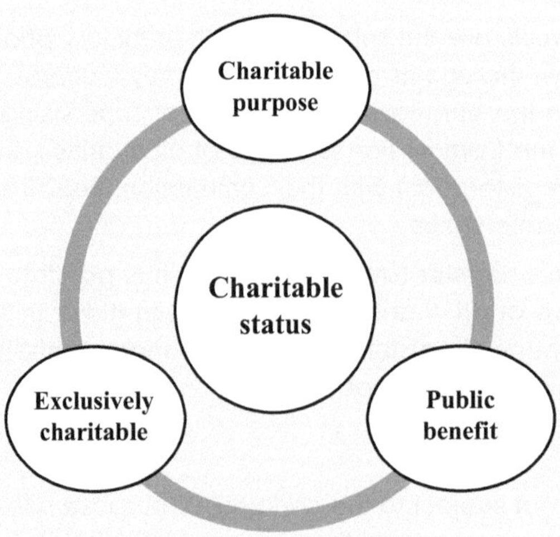

For centuries, the definitions of 'charitable purpose', 'exclusively charitable' and 'public benefit' were found in case law based on the 1601 Preamble to the Statute of Charitable Uses. It became increasingly difficult for non-lawyers (and even lawyers) to trawl through that case law to discover whether a particular trust was charitable or not. In the interests of transparency, the Charities Act was passed in 2006, which set out the purposes which were regarded as charitable as well as matters relating to public benefit. This Act and other charities legislation were consolidated by the Charities Act 2011 (as amended by the Charities Act 2022). Previous case law is still used to interpret the Act's provisions (Charities Act 2011, s 2(5)) and the Commission provides extensive guidance on how it interprets the statutory provisions.

### 4.3.3 Charitable purposes

A charitable purpose is a purpose which falls within s 3(1) of the Charities Act 2011 and is for the public benefit (Charities Act 2011, s 2(1)).

4.3.3.1 Purposes within s 3(1) of the Charities Act 2011

Section 3(1) of the Charities Act 2011 details 13 broad areas of potential charitable activity ('heads' of charitable purposes). The Commission is keen to point out that the items contained in s 3(1) are merely descriptions, providing an indication of areas of activity which have been or could be recognised as charitable. The s 3(1) list includes:

(a) the prevention or relief of poverty;

(b) the advancement of education;

(c) the advancement of religion;

(d) the advancement of health or the saving of lives;

(e) the advancement of citizenship or community development;

(f) the advancement of the arts, culture, heritage or science;

(g) the advancement of amateur sport;

(h) the advancement of human rights, conflict resolution or reconciliation or the promotion of religious or racial harmony or equality and diversity;

(i) the advancement of environmental protection or improvement;

(j) the relief of those in need by reason of youth, age, ill-health, disability, financial hardship or other disadvantage;

(k) the advancement of animal welfare;

(l) the promotion of the efficiency of the armed forces of the Crown, or of the efficiency of the police, fire and rescue services or ambulance services;

(m) any other [charitable] purposes.

In 2013, the Commission provided guidance of how the different 'heads' of charitable activity might be approached to ensure that a proposed purpose falls within one of the s 3(1) descriptions and, just as importantly, is for the public benefit (available on the Commission website):

(a) *The prevention or relief of poverty* is not merely a matter of providing financial assistance. In *Re Coulthurst* [1951] Ch 661, the court described poverty as being the circumstances where 'persons ... have to go short in the ordinary acceptation of that term, due regard being had to their status in life'. In its guidance, the Commission refers to poverty as 'financial hardship' (which does not necessarily mean poor) or 'lack of material things'. On this basis, it is possible to seek to 'prevent or relieve poverty' by the provision of monetary grants or household items such as bedding, furniture, domestic appliances; paying for essential services, offering training or recreational support or facilities.

(b) *The advancement of education* goes beyond classroom education; in fact, education does not need to take place in a learning institution of whatever level; museums, libraries and zoos could also be charitable for the advancement of education. According to the Commission guidance, education is to 'promote, sustain and increase individual and collective knowledge and understanding' and accordingly the types of organisations capable of advancing education are wide-ranging. Research would also be included, but the research must add educational value rather than merely be research for research's sake. George Bernard Shaw's trust to research into the 40-letter alphabet was not charitable for the advancement of education on this basis (*Re Shaw's Will Trust* [1957] WLR 729).

(c) *The advancement of religion* relates to the promotion of a system of beliefs which may or may not involve the worship of a god or gods (Charities Act 2011, s 3(2)(a)). This allows for Buddhism and Druidism to be classed as religion and can also include 'atheism' (a belief in no god at all) and 'agnosticism' (a belief that neither affirms or denies the existence of a God or gods). However, the definition does not extend to the Church of Scientology (the Church's application for charitable status in England and Wales was rejected by the Commission in 1999 and has not been appealed). Advancement of the system of beliefs could manifest itself in provision of spaces of worship, outreach work, devotional activities and educational programmes about the belief system. What is needed are activities which make a connection with the public, however minimal. In *Gilmour v Coates* [1949] AC 426 money given for the purposes of a cloistered priory involved in devotional activities within the priory only was not charitable.

(d) *The advancement of health and saving lives* covers prevention against and relief from illness as well as the promotion of health. It also spans both conventional health provision and alternative methods of healing, although the Commission indicates that the benefits of any alternative therapy must be sufficiently evidenced. As with education, the Commission's guidance on what activities could be charitable within this head of charitable purpose are wide-ranging, from the provision of treatment and facilities, medical research, to rescue services and disaster assistance.

(e) *The advancement of citizenship or community development* is focused on community services as it relates to organisations which maintain and/or improve the support of social and community infrastructure. According to the Commission, this would cover organisations such as the Scouts or the Guides, promoting civic responsibility, or promoting volunteering and the voluntary sector.

(f) *The advancement of the arts, culture, heritage and science* was previously considered charitable under the advancement of education. Given separate status under the Charities Act 2011, this head of charitable purpose covers the promotion of art at a national, local, professional or amateur level across different media and materials. The art does, however, have to satisfy an analysis of its merit. In *Re Pinion (Dec'd)* [1965] Ch 85, a testator's attempt to have his house opened as a museum after his death was not charitable on the basis that the contents of the house had no artistic value or merit. Heritage relates to national or local history, cultural traditions, preservation of historic land and buildings.

(g) *The advancement of amateur sport* involves the promotion of health by the undertaking of physical or mental skill and exertion at an amateur, community level. The Commission's guidance makes reference to the support of 'healthy recreation' and open access to facilities; on this basis not all sports are recognised as meeting the criteria for charitable status under this head (see RR11 Charitable Status and Sport: available on the Commission website). It is possible for community amateur sports clubs to be recognised with HMRC for special tax treatment. Such clubs cannot be registered as charities as well.

(h) *The advancement of human rights, conflict resolution or reconciliation or the promotion of religious harmony or equality and diversity* addresses a number of different areas - for instance when considering human rights, the Commission accepts that raising awareness of human rights at home and abroad, monitoring of human rights abuses, obtaining redress for and relieving the needs of victims are all relevant activities. Conflict resolution involves identification of causes of conflict as well as resolution by mediation or other means. Organisations which promote good relations, equality and diversity between different racial, religious, social or sexual groups are likely examples of this purpose.

(i) *The advancement of environmental protection or improvement* is about preserving and conserving the natural environment and promoting sustainable development. It also encompasses activities which seek to safeguard a particular species or wildlife in general. However, as with arts, culture and heritage, the preservation of a particular species or habitat must pass a merit assessment; it must be shown to be worthy of conservation.

(j) *The relief of those in need, by reasons of youth, age, ill-health, disability, financial hardship or other disadvantage* is a wide-ranging head of charitable purpose and can cover providing relief - advice, equipment, accommodation, care - to anyone in need as a result of any of the stated issues.

(k) *The advancement of animal welfare* is concerned with the prevention or elimination of cruelty to animals and the general prevention and relief of animal suffering.

(l) *The promotion of the efficiency of the armed forces of the Crown, or the efficiency of the police, fire, rescue services and ambulance services* concerns the active promotion of the efficiency of the relevant services as a means of defending the country or protecting the public. It ranges from organisations offering specialist training to facilities for and research of military or service history.

(m) *Any other charitable purposes* recognises that the s 3(1) list is not fully comprehensive. It allows for new charitable purposes to be recognised in the future, responding to changes in social conditions. A new charitable purpose would be considered by analogy either to the s 3(1) purposes or to previous case law (Charities Act, s 3(1)(m)(ii) and (iii)).

#### 4.3.3.2 Not a charitable purpose

A political purpose is one which seeks to further the interests of a particular political party; or procure changes in the laws of the UK; or procure changes in the law of a foreign country; or procure a reversal of government policy or decisions of governmental authorities in this country or abroad (Slade J in *McGovern v Attorney General* [1982] Ch 321).

A trust that has such a political purpose as one of its aims will not be able to achieve charitable status as such purposes have been deemed to be non-charitable. In *Hanchett-Stamford v Attorney General* [2009] Ch 173, an organisation seeking to prevent cruelty to animals used in film productions was denied charitable status because its objective could only be realised by a change in the law.

The support of this principle relates to the issues which could arise if courts were asked to decide whether the change in the law advocated for would or would not be for the public benefit, an assessment which is particularly difficult where the proposed change is to be carried out abroad in a country where the culture and/or religion etc is different to the United Kingdom. There is also a perception that judges must decide on the basis that the law is right as it stands rather than usurping the function of the legislature.

This basic principle does not prevent charities from engaging in political activities (for instance, raising public support, lobbying parliament, organising demonstrations, publishing political commentary) provided those activities are ancillary or incidental to the main charitable purposes, lawful, and an effective use of the charity's resources. For instance, in *Baldry v Feintuck* [1972] 1 WLR 552, a university's student union, an educational charity, was prevented from making a financial donation to a political campaign arguing against the discontinuance of the free supplies of milk as the payment was for a political purpose outside the educational purposes for which the union had been established.

### 4.3.4 Exclusively charitable

To be a charitable purpose trust, it must be exclusively charitable (Charities Act 2011, s 1). If the stated purposes of the trust include anything which is not charitable then the whole trust will not be regarded as charitable.

***McGovern v Attorney General*** **[1982] Ch 321**

Amnesty International sought charitable status for a trust which it had established in 1977. The trust's purposes included, inter alia, the relief of needy persons who were or recently had been prisoners of conscience and their families, attempting to secure the release of prisoners of conscience, procuring the abolition of torture or inhuman treatment or punishment, the promotion of research into the observance of human rights and the dissemination of the results of such research. It was accepted that some of the trust's purposes could be charitable (the relief of needy persons, the relief of human suffering and distress). However, seeking to secure the release of prisoners of conscience and procuring the abolition of torture were both attempts to change government policy or administrative decisions, and so were political, non-charitable, objects. The trust as a whole was, therefore, invalid as not being for exclusively charitable purposes; the court upheld the Commission's decision to refuse charitable status.

Another circumstance where exclusivity of charitable purpose could arise relates to how profits earned from charitable activities are dealt with. A trust created to establish a nursing home for the care of the elderly would have a charitable purpose under s 3(1)(j) of the Charities Act 2011. However, if, after the payment of staff salaries and nursing home expenses, any profits were to be paid to the owners of the home, this would be non-charitable – the money is accruing to individuals rather than being ploughed back into the charitable purpose. Consequently, the trust would be completely non-charitable despite its caring for the elderly activities.

### 4.3.5 Public benefit

The requirement for the proposed trust purpose to have sufficient public benefit (Charities Act 2001, s 4) is why charitable trusts are sometimes called 'public' trusts.

Before the passing of the 2006 and the 2011 Charities Acts, a charitable purpose was presumed to be for the public benefit. However, this position has now changed. Section 4(2) of the Charities Act 2011 provides that there is no presumption of public benefit; it must be proved.

There is no definition of what is meant by 'public benefit' in the 2011 Act. All the Act says is that 'reference to the public benefit is a reference to the public benefit as that term is understood for the purposes of the law relating to charities in England and Wales' (Charities Act 2011, s 4(3)). As with charitable purposes, the Commission has published guidance on its understanding of the case law relating to public benefit ('Public benefit: the public benefit requirement'; available on the Commission's website).

There are two aspects of public benefit, namely the 'benefit aspect' and the 'public aspect'.

#### 4.3.5.1 The benefit aspect

There are two elements to this consideration. The purpose(s) must be beneficial, and any detriment or harm resulting from the purpose(s) must not outweigh the benefit. If either of these is not obvious, the Commission will require evidence. The Commission states that a charitable purpose 'must be beneficial in a way that is identifiable and capable of being proved by evidence where necessary (rather than on personal opinion)'. While the Commission accepts that some purposes are clearly beneficial, others, for instance the artistic merit of an art collection or the healing benefits of a proposed therapy, are not so clear and this is where evidence of benefit is required. It is, however, not necessary for the benefit to be quantified or measured.

Where a charitable purpose has a benefit, but it may also cause detriment or harm (or vice versa), there is a need to consider the balance between the two, again based on evidence rather than personal views.

***National Anti-Vivisection Society v IRC* [1948] AC 31**

Historically, the courts had held that gifts to anti-vivisection organisations were charitable (as prevention of cruelty to animals). However, the National Anti-Vivisection Society was denied charitable status by the House of Lords on two grounds, one of which was that the benefit to the public derived from the research which involved the experimentation on animals outweighed the harm caused to the animals that were used. The other ground related to the Society's objects being to bring about a change in the law and so political (see **4.3.3.2**).

### 4.3.5.2 The public aspect

The purpose(s) must be of benefit to the public in general or to a sufficient section of the public and must not give rise to more than incidental personal benefit.

There is no problem where the benefits are offered to the whole public, such as trusts for medical research, a museum or school which is open to all. These trusts involve sufficient public benefit even if only a small number take advantage of the benefit and even if, say, the location of the school means that only the children living in a particular village will attend.

Where the benefit is restricted to a section of the public, the numbers involved must not be negligible and there are certain considerations as to what is a sufficient 'section of the public' to satisfy the public benefit requirement.

(a) *Restrictions on benefit.* The opportunity to benefit must not be unreasonably restricted. Any restrictions must be legitimate, proportionate, rational and justifiable given the nature of the organisation's charitable aims. There are no objections if the benefits are restricted according to charitable need (eg youth, age, poverty, disability). A children's home could be charitable even though its use is restricted to those under the age of 18. Similarly, geographical restrictions are acceptable if they are related to the aims of the purpose. For instance, a village hall which only benefits the inhabitants of the village and the provision of facilities to a local hospital would both be considered as having sufficient public benefit. Restricting benefits with reference to some personal characteristic such as religion or gender is acceptable if related to the charitable aim. For example, a charity concerned with women's health problems is acceptable even though the benefits are restricted to females. Contrast a village hall for use only by females where the restriction to the female gender is not a rational consequence of the charitable aim.

(b) *Unreasonable restrictions.* Where the purpose has a clear benefit for everyone, for instance, research into finding a cure for a particular disease, it would not be considered reasonable to limit that benefit to a particular area. Similar, imposing too many limitations on the persons able to benefit from the purpose would also not be reasonable.

***IRC v Baddeley* [1955] AC 572**

Here a trust for the promotion of the religious, social and physical training of residents of West Ham who were or were likely to become Methodists was held not to be charitable. Viscount Simmonds distinguished 'a form of relief extended to the whole community yet by its very nature advantageous only to the few, and a form of relief accorded to a selected few out of a larger number equally willing and able to take advantage of it'. The trust in question fell within the second category. Restricting the benefits to a particular area would not have been objectionable, but further limiting the trust to Methodists within that area made the group a class within a class, and they were not a sufficient section of the public to satisfy the public benefit requirement of charitable trusts.

Trusts where the purpose is to benefit named individuals would not be charitable.

(c) *Personal nexus*. The benefit must not be restricted to those people who have a 'personal nexus'. Personal nexus arises through a familial relationship to given individuals (*Re Compton* [1945] Ch 123), or to employment by a common employer (*Oppenheim v Tobacco Securities Trust Co Ltd* [1951] AC 297). This is regardless of the actual numbers involved. It should, however, be noted that the personal nexus limitation does not arise where the purpose of the trust is to relieve poverty. In *HM Attorney-General v Charity Commission for England and Wales* (www.tribunals.gov.uk, FTC/84/2011), the Upper Tribunal Tax and Chancery confirmed that trusts to relieve poverty among relations, employees of the same employer and members of a club or society were charitable despite doubts expressed by the Commission. In fact, trusts for the relief of poverty are charitable even though the benefit is restricted to a small class of objects such as the settlor's 'poor relations' (*Re Scarisbrick* [1951] Ch 622). It is also thought that personal nexus does not apply if the purpose of the trust is the advancement of religion.

(d) *Charging fees*. Charities are allowed to charge fees for the benefits which they provide but, if they do, they must be careful not to jeopardise their ability to meet the public benefit requirement by excluding a considerable number of people who cannot afford to pay the fees, for instance, limiting the provision of health care only to the very wealthy by charging high fees. If a substantial number are excluded, there must be other material ways related to the charity's aim in which the less wealthy can benefit. For example, an opera house might provide concessions and cheaper seats, publish cultural, educational material on the internet, arrange television and cinema broadcasts and support arts groups.

In *Independent Schools Council v Charities Commission for England and Wales* [2011] UKUT 421, the Independent Schools Council challenged part of the Commission's Guidance on Public Benefit and sought guidance on how private schools could satisfy the public benefit test. The Upper Tribunal said that schools whose sole object was the education of children whose families could afford to pay the fees would not be charitable. The reason was that a trust which excludes the poor from benefit cannot be a charity. In this context, 'poor' did not mean destitute but included people of modest means. In order to be charitable, the school must make more than a de minimis or token provision for the less well-off. Such provision should focus on direct benefits which could include (in descending order of importance) scholarships and bursaries, arrangements allowing students from local state schools to attend classes in subjects not otherwise available to them, the sharing of teachers or teaching facilities with local schools and the sharing of sports fields, swimming pools etc. Once the de minimis threshold was satisfied, it was a matter for the trustees to decide what action to take in the circumstances of the particular school. It was not for the Commission or the court or anyone else to impose its view about what would be reasonable.

## 4.4 Non-charitable purpose trusts

While charitable purpose trusts are the most notable exception to the basic principle that purpose trusts are void for want of a beneficiary to enforce the trust obligations (*Morice v Bishop of Durham* (1804) 9 Ves 399), the courts have accepted that there are other limited exceptions to this beneficiary principle.

### 4.4.1 Trusts of imperfect obligation

In *Re Astor's Settlement Trust* [1952] 1 All ER 1067, Roxburgh J identified two types of trust which fell within this category of exception:

(a) trusts for the care or maintenance of specific animals; and

(b) trusts for the maintenance of graves and funeral monuments.

*Re Dean* (1889) 41 ChD 552 (a trust to provide income for the upkeep of the testator's eight horses and hounds) and *Pettingall v Pettingall* (1842) 11 LJ Ch 176 (a trust to provide money for the upkeep of the testator's favourite black mare) were both held to be valid, not withstanding they were clearly purpose trusts with no one capable of enforcing the trust obligation.

Similarly, in *Re Hooper* [1932] Ch 38, a testator left money to his executors on trust to use the income for the upkeep of various family graves for as long as they legally could do so. Again, a clear purpose trust which should have been void for want of a beneficiary. However, the trust was upheld.

There is no principled reason for allowing these exceptional trusts. Both have been described as 'concessions to human weakness'. Courts are not willing to extend these exceptions to new situations, and the success of subsequent trusts will be dependent on them being created in analogous circumstances. However, even then there is no guarantee of success. *Re Endacott* [1960] Ch 23 was another case involving graves and tombs; the testator's trust was to provide 'some useful memorial to myself'. This trust failed; the purpose was not specific enough to be valid, and it involved the building of something new rather than the maintenance of an existing memorial.

Although these trusts for the maintenance of animals and tombs are valid, they do not have beneficiaries; there is no legal person who derives a sufficient benefit to be regarded as a beneficiary. It is for this reason that these trusts are referred to as 'trusts of imperfect obligation'; nobody can compel the trustees to carry out the purpose. As these trusts arise in wills, if the trustees do not carry out the purpose specified in the trust, the residuary beneficiaries can go to court and claim the money as they have an entitlement to the money if it is not used for the purpose of maintaining the animal or tomb.

### 4.4.2 Purposes which benefit an identifiable group of people

There are other types of trusts which, while expressed to be for a purpose, evidence that the purpose will benefit identifiable persons who are capable of enforcing the trust. Such trusts do not offend the beneficiary principle and are called '*Denley* trusts' after the case in which they were approved and where Goff J said: 'where ... the trust, though expressed as a purpose, is directly for the benefit of an individual or individuals ... it is in general outside the mischief of the beneficiary principle'.

***Re Denley's Trust Deed* [1968] 3 All ER 65**

In *Re Denley*, a plot of land was transferred to trustees, to be held on trust to be maintained and used for the purpose of a sports and recreation ground for the benefit of employees of a particular company and for such other persons as the trustees might allow. The duration of the trust was limited to the perpetuity period.

The trust was not charitable because of the lack of public benefit (due to the personal nexus of the employees of a particular company: *Oppenheim v Tobacco Securities Trust Co Ltd* [1951] AC 297 - see **4.3.5.2(c)**).

Goff J said that, while the trust was expressed as a purpose, it was directly or indirectly for the benefit of individuals, namely, the employees. The benefit was sufficiently tangible to allow them to go to court to enforce the trust, and it did not, therefore, offend the beneficiary principle and was valid.

Goff J distinguished trusts where ascertainable individuals have a direct or indirect benefit, on the one hand, from trusts where the benefit to individuals is too intangible for them to qualify as beneficiaries with rights to enforce the trust. Trusts like the one in *Re Astor* ('to maintain good understanding between nations and to preserve the independence and integrity of newspapers') fall into the second category and are void.

(There has been some debate over the nature of each employee's benefit. Did each employee have a share in the trust property (the land)? If not, the benefit must have comprised the ability to play sport on the land, which means that *Re Denley* is authority for saying that people who can enforce trusts are not confined to those having a proprietary interest in the trust property.)

### 4.4.3 Certainty and perpetuities

The beneficiary principle is just one of the hurdles that all non-charitable purpose trusts must overcome. They must also satisfy all the usual requirements for trusts, including certainty and the rule against perpetuities.

#### 4.4.3.1 Certainty of purpose

In order to be valid, the non-charitable purpose must be stated in terms:

> which embody definite concepts, and the means by which trustees are to try to attain them must also be prescribed with a sufficient degree of certainty (per Roxburgh J in *Re Astor's Settlement Trusts* [1952] 1 All ER 1067).

Without such certainty, how can trustees be monitored to ensure compliance with the terms of the trust?

#### 4.4.3.2 Certainty of objects

*Denley*-type trusts also have 'beneficiaries' - the people who gain tangible benefit from the purpose. They too must be identified with certainty. There is no case determining which certainty of objects test applies to *Denley* trusts, but it is thought that they must satisfy the given postulant test laid down in *McPhail v Doulton* [1971] AC 424 (HL) (see **2.3.4.2**). Also, the number of people to benefit must not be so large that the trust would be administratively unworkable (as in *R v District Auditor, ex p West Yorkshire Metropolitan CC* discussed in **2.3.4.2**).

4.4.3.3 Perpetuities

The perpetuity rule relevant to non-charitable purpose trusts is the rule against inalienability. As discussed in **4.2.3**, trusts of imperfect obligation or in the *Denley* mould must either:

(a) be limited in duration to 21 years; or

(b) allow the trustees to spend all the trust capital on the purpose and thereby end the trust at any time.

***Examples***

- *'On trust to maintain my pet snake, Archie' – an example of a trust to maintain a specific animal, this particular trust is, however, invalid because it offends the rule against inalienability. The duration of the trust is not confined to 21 years. The trustees could not spend all of the trust capital and thereby end the trust at any time because this would breach their duty to maintain Archie in future years.*
- *'On trust to maintain the graves of the Waterton family for as long as the law allows' – the words 'for as long as the law allows' limit the duration of the trust to 21 years (Re Hooper). This trust of imperfect obligation (the maintenance of graves and tombs) is therefore valid.*
- *'On trust to buy sports equipment for Freshco's sports and social club' (Freshco is a supermarket; its employees have their own sports and social club.) – this is a trust in the Re Denley form; it is expressed to be for a purpose (buying equipment), but the employee members of the club have a sufficiently direct benefit from the purpose to be able to take court action to enforce it. The trust complies with the rule against inalienability because, although not limited to 21 years, it is clear that the trustees are able to spend all the trust capital on buying the equipment, whereupon the trust will end.*
- *'£200,000 on trust to repair and maintain the clubhouse at Foxtown Golf Club' – again, using the Re Denley precedent, the members of the golf club will derive a sufficiently direct benefit from the purpose to enable them to enforce the trust. However, the trust is void because it offends the rule against inalienability. The duration of the trust is not limited to 21 years, and the trustees cannot spend all the trust capital at any time on the purpose because this would leave no money for future maintenance.*

**Figure 4.2** Summary – considering the validity of purpose trusts

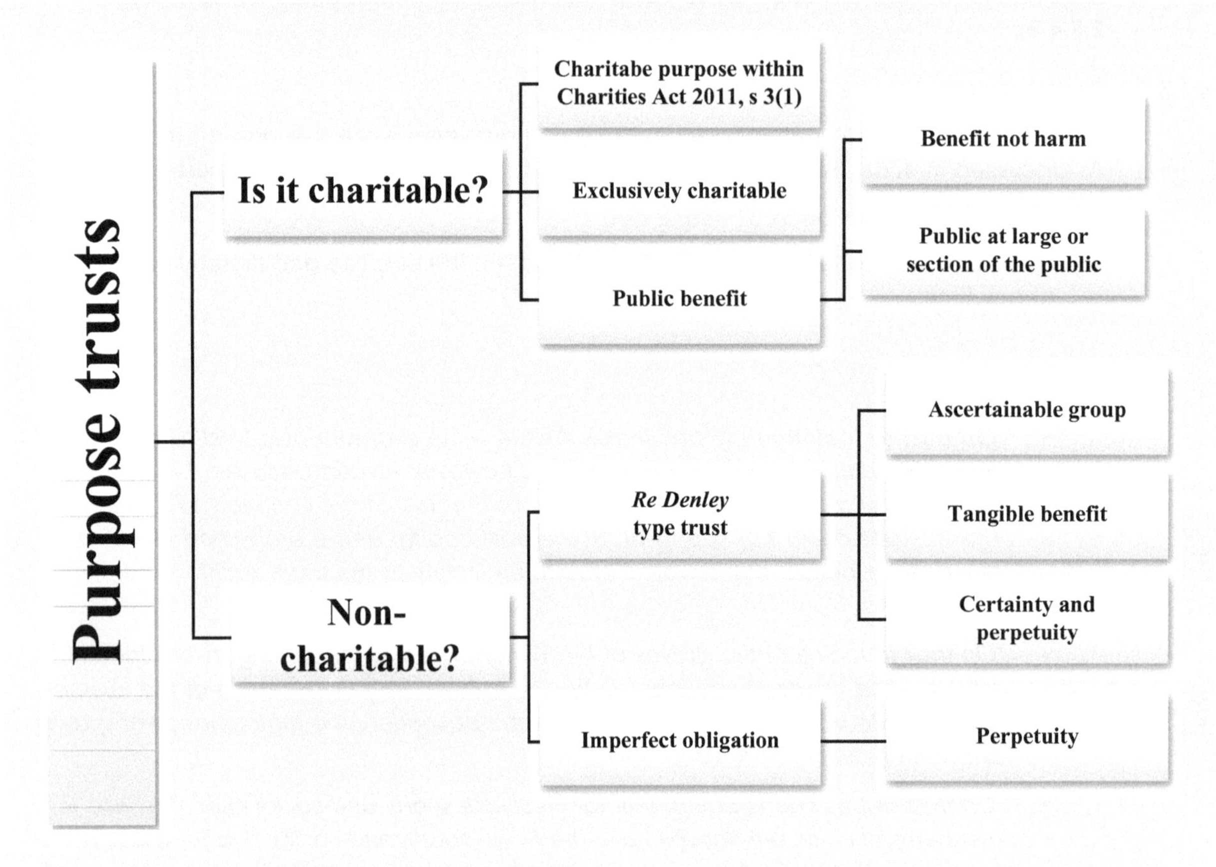


## 4.5 Non-charitable unincorporated associations

### 4.5.1 What are unincorporated associations?

'Unincorporated' means that the association is not a limited company. An unincorporated association is not a legal person (unlike a company or an individual) but rather a group of individuals joined together with common aims, usually set out in its constitution. Lawton J's definition in *Conservative and Unionist Central Office v Burrell* [1982] 1 WLR 522 is often referred to:

> Two or more persons bound together for one or more common purposes, not being business purposes, by mutual undertakings, each having mutual duties and obligations, in an organisation which has rules which identify in whom control of it and its funds rests and on what terms and which can be joined or left at will.

The 'mutual undertakings' are contained in the rules or constitution of the club. There may be rules setting out the aims of the club, regulations about joining and leaving the club, holding meetings, electing committee members, etc.

These associations are usually non-charitable on the grounds of lack of public benefit or for having non-charitable purposes.

If unincorporated associations are not legal persons capable of holding property, who owns a club's land, bank account and other assets? The answer is that this property will not be registered in the club's name; it will be held by trustees (perhaps known as the Management Committee) on a trust for the members of the association, to deal with the funds in accordance with the rules of the association.

### 4.5.2 Outright gifts to non-charitable unincorporated associations

A testator's will contains the following gift: '£10,000 to the Finchem Cricket Club'. The Club is a non-charitable unincorporated association. The Finchem Cricket Club cannot be the donee of the gift as of right because it is not a legal person and is not capable of owning property.

To avoid such gifts failing for want of a beneficiary, the courts have devised various alternative constructions. The construction which applies in a particular case depends on the wording of the gift.

In the case of *Neville Estates Ltd v Madden* [1962] Ch 832, Cross J identified three ways of approaching gifts to such associations:

(1) An outright gift to the existing individual members of the association as joint tenants - this is now considered an unlikely approach as if the donor stated a gift to the association, it is unlikely that they wanted individual members to take their share of the gift, by severing the joint tenancy.

(2) An outright gift to the existing members of the association, subject to those members' rights and duties towards one another. This prevents the property being shared by the members individually.

(3) A trust for the purposes of the association (as argued in *Leahy v AG New South Wales* [1959] AC 457) - such a trust is likely to be void as offending the rule against perpetuities.

The second interpretation from *Neville Estates* is now the most common and favoured approach - an outright gift to an association is a gift to the members of the association, as an addition to the association's funds to be dealt with in accordance with its rules. The subject-matter of the gift is to be held in the same way as the club's other property and on the same terms. An individual member cannot claim a share of the gift for their own use; it must be used for club purposes in accordance with the rules.

In *Re Recher's Will Trusts* [1972] Ch 526, the testatrix left a share of her residuary estate to a non-charitable (some of its aims were political), unincorporated society. The court had to decide whether the gift could be construed in such a way that would make it valid. Brightman J said, 'it would astonish a layman to be told that there was difficulty giving a legacy to an unincorporated non-charitable society which he had or could have supported without trouble during his lifetime.'

Accordingly, Brightman J confirmed that:

> the legacy is a gift to the members beneficially, not as joint tenants or as tenants in common so as to entitle each member to an immediate distributive share, but as an accretion to the funds which are the subject-matter of the contract which the members have made inter se.

The beneficiary principle is not offended as the gift is deemed to be to the club's members, and the subject-matter of the gift joins the club's other assets. However, it is necessary to ensure that those assets are freely alienable - the club's rules must allow the members to spend all the assets at any time. The rule against inalienability is satisfied if the rules allow the members to dissolve the association and divide the assets between themselves at any time.

***Re Grant's Will Trust* [1979] 3 All ER 359**

Here, the testator wanted to give his estate to the Chertsey and Walton Constituency Labour Party (a non-charitable unincorporated association). His will duly contained a gift to the committee in charge of property for the benefit of the Chertsey and Walton Constituency Labour Party. The court was asked to decide whether the legacy was valid.

The local Chertsey and Walton Constituency Party did not have complete autonomy; it was subject to rules laid down by the National Executive Committee of the Labour Party and the national annual party conference. The members of the local constituency party were not free to dispose of the party's property in any way they thought fit.

The gift did not offend the beneficiary principle because, in accordance with *Re Recher*, it was construed as a gift to the members as an accretion to the association's funds, to be dealt with in accordance with the rules. However, it was held that the gift was void because it offended the rule against inalienability. Under the *Recher* construction, the gift was to be added to the Constituency Party's property, but the Constituency Party's rules did not enable the members to pass a resolution to dissolve the Constituency Party and share out the property between them; such a decision needed the concurrence of the national party.

Subsequently, it has been held that if the rules allow a local branch to secede from the national organisation and dissolve itself, any gift to the local association is valid (*News Group Newspapers Ltd v SOGAT* [1986] ICR 716).

### 4.5.3 Intended for a purpose

In *Re Lipinski's Will Trusts* [1976] Ch 235, Harry Lipinski left half of his residuary estate to the 'Hull Judeans (Maccabi) Association in memory of my late wife' and added a purpose 'to be used solely in constructing the new buildings for the Association and/or improvements to the said buildings'. There is a difference between this legacy and the previous type of gift discussed in **4.5.2**; in this case, the testator gave the residue to the club for a specified purpose. Oliver J held that the legacy was valid. He stated:

> If a valid gift may be made to an unincorporated body as a simple accretion to the funds which are the subject-matter of the contract which the members have made inter se ... I do not really see why such a gift, which specifies a purpose which is within the powers of the specified body and of which the members of the body are the beneficiaries, should fail.

He went on to say that the legacy could be construed as a gift to the members as an accretion to club funds in accordance with *Re Recher* because the members would be the beneficiaries of the new buildings and, when completed, the new buildings would belong to the members beneficially just like the rest of the Association's property. The *Recher* construction is not confined to outright gifts to unincorporated associations; it also applies where the testator specifies a purpose, so long as that purpose benefits the members of the association.

As an alternative ground for his decision, Oliver J said Mr Lipinski's disposition would be valid even if one regarded it as a trust for the purpose of constructing and improving buildings. Such a trust would not offend the beneficiary principle because the members of the Maccabi Association would derive sufficient benefit from the buildings to be able to enforce the trust (as in *Re Denley*, see **4.4.2**). In short, the legacy was held to be valid following either *Re Recher* or *Re Denley*.

There was no problem with the rule against inalienability as the wording of the legacy suggested that the capital could be spent once and for all on constructing or improving the buildings. There was no ongoing purpose such as maintenance.

It is not clear whether the members of association would have been able to disregard Mr Lipinski's purpose and spend the legacy on something else. Oliver J did not have to consider this point. Under the *Recher* construction, the members could spend the money on any purpose permitted by the rules (which will include dissolving the club and sharing out the assets between the members). Thus, a testator creating a *Recher*-type legacy with a purpose attached cannot be sure that the purpose will be carried out. The purpose is regarded merely as the motive behind the gift.

If a court were to decide that the legacy was to be construed as a *Re Denley* purpose trust, then there were suggestions in *Re Lipinski* that the members could again ignore the stated purpose and treat it as a non-binding motive for making the gift.

The purpose in *Re Lipinski* benefited the members. Where the intended purpose of the gift to the association does not directly benefit its members, it could not be construed using *Recher* (a gift to the members) or *Denley* (the members gaining a tangible benefit) as there is clearly no evidence of any intention to benefit the members. The trust would be void on the ground that it offends the beneficiary principle.

**ACTIVITY Review your knowledge – purpose trusts**

Bernadette died recently. Her will, which was validly executed, contained the following legacy:

'I give £300,000 to my Trustees to hold on trust and use the income to make grants to fund university fees incurred by relatives of employees of my late father's factory at the date of my death.'

Consider whether the legacy is likely to be valid?

**COMMENT**

The legacy creates a purpose trust. Non-charitable purpose trusts are usually void because they do not have beneficiaries to enforce them (*Morice v Bishop of Durham, Re Astor*). However, a trust for a charitable purpose would be an exception to this.

To be charitable, the purpose must be charitable under s 3(1) of the Charities Act 2011, be exclusively charitable and have sufficient public benefit.

This trust is for a charitable purpose, namely the advancement of education (Charities Act 2001, s 3(1)(b)). It is also exclusively charitable because there are no non-charitable purposes.

However, the trust lacks public benefit. There is an identifiable benefit to those concerned, but the trust is not for the public at large. Those who are intended to benefit (the relatives of employees of the factory) are a section of the public connected by a personal nexus – the familial connection to employment by a common employer (*Oppenheim v Tobacco Securities Trust Co Ltd*). Therefore this trust cannot be charitable because there is insufficient public benefit.

Although the trust is not charitable, it might be valid if relatives of the employees will derive a sufficiently direct benefit from the purpose so that they will be able to go to court to enforce the trust, as in *Re Denley*. Even if the trust satisfies the beneficiary principle by virtue of *Re Denley*, the purpose and the objects of the trust must be certain. The purpose appears to be clear and, as far as the objects are concerned, there would be certainty as to whether any applicant for funds is or is not a relative of a current employee of the factory (*McPhail v Doulton* and *Re Baden's Trust No 2*).

However, the terms of the trust suggest that only the income of the trust can be used to fund the grants. There is no limitation as to how long the trust is to last. Thus, the trust breaches the rule against inalienability of capital and will not be valid.

## SUMMARY

- It is important to be able to recognise a purpose trust, a trust to do something, from one that is intended to benefit individuals specifically so as to be able to understand why, as a general rule, such purpose trusts fail.
- By applying the relevant legal tests – is the purpose for a charitable purpose, is it exclusively charitable, does it have sufficient public benefit – it is possible to advise on whether a proposed purpose trust would be classed as charitable and the benefits which would accrue if charitable status were achieved.
- Similarly, in this chapter, we have analysed when a purpose trust which is not charitable might, in certain circumstances and subject to satisfying certain requirements, be valid.
- Understanding the nature of non-charitable unincorporated associations gives rise to an appreciation of the problems surrounding gifts to such associations and how they are commonly resolved.

# 5 Creating Trusts in Commercial Settings

**LEARNING OUTCOMES**

By the end of this chapter, you should be able to:

- understand how trusts have been used to gain priority on insolvency;
- appreciate policy constraints on the use of trusts to gain priority on insolvency; and
- analyse facts and apply the requirements for a valid express trust in a variety of commercial scenarios.

## 5.1 Introduction

Although primarily concerned up to now with the creation of express trusts in private, family circumstances, there have been examples of the intervention of equity in commercial transactions where it was argued that a trust had been created. These arguments have been raised specifically in matters relating to insolvency, either the bankruptcy of an individual or the liquidation of a company. The aim of these claims is often to gain a better position against a debtor on their insolvency.

The interaction between equity and trusts with insolvency law, therefore, gives rise to policy issues which influence the court and commentators alike.

As Lord Nicholls remarked in *Royal Brunei Airlines v Tan* [1995] 2 AC 378:

> The proper role of equity in commercial transactions is a topical question. Increasingly plaintiffs have recourse to equity for an effective remedy when the person in default, typically a company, is insolvent.

## 5.2 Insolvency – a brief introduction

What follows is a brief discussion of insolvency law to put the analysis in this chapter into context.

A person is bankrupt if they have insufficient money to meet their debts as they fall due. The debtor or one of their creditors can seek a bankruptcy order. All the debtor's assets will vest in a trustee in bankruptcy (a representative of the creditors), whose job it is to distribute the bankrupt's assets among the creditors according to the statutory order of priority.

The analogous process for companies is called liquidation; in a company liquidation, the liquidator is the equivalent to the trustee in bankruptcy.

At any one time, a company (or businessperson) will usually owe money to a variety of persons – these are the company's creditors. Examples are:

(a) *Institutional lenders.* The most obvious example of a creditor is a person from whom a company has arranged to borrow money. For example, where a company wishes to fund a substantial expansion of the company and needs considerable capital to acquire new land or equipment, the company may borrow from an institutional lender (a bank or other financial institution) and will be required to pay interest on the loan until the date agreed for full repayment.

(b) *Suppliers of goods or services.* A company may operate by manufacturing raw materials into a product, which is then sold. It is not unusual for the suppliers of the raw materials to provide those raw materials 'on credit', ie they are not paid on delivery but at a later date, often after the manufactured product has been sold. In the meantime, the suppliers are owed the value of the goods provided to the company.

(c) *The Government.* A company has to pay various taxes and other compulsory payments, for example VAT and corporation tax on its business and national insurance on its employees. These are mostly paid in arrears at set times of the year.

(d) *Employees.* A company usually pays its employees in arrears.

A company may suffer financial difficulties and, eventually, become insolvent, because, for example, the company's liabilities exceed its assets, or because the company has cashflow problems and cannot pay its debts on the due date. If this happens, there are a number of procedures under the Insolvency Act 1986 which govern what happens to the company. A 'liquidator' is appointed to gather in the company's assets and use them to repay the creditors of the company. The liquidator must follow a prescribed order of payment for the distinct types of creditors. Broadly, the order of priority puts 'secured creditors' (those with a charge over some of the company's assets) and 'preferential creditors' (eg employees) above 'ordinary creditors', ie unsecured and non-preferential. The ordinary creditors may receive only a small proportion of the money owed, or even nothing at all. It is a fundamental principle of insolvency law that unsecured creditors share available assets '*pari passu*', ie in proportion to the amounts they are owed. A trustee in bankruptcy will follow the same prescribed order if an individual goes bankrupt.

### 5.2.1 Security for lenders

Those who choose to lend to a company (mainly institutional lenders, but also, to a certain extent, the suppliers of goods and services) will usually wish to protect the value of their loan against the risk of the company becoming insolvent. The most common method is for the lender to insist that the company grants a charge to the lender, thus making it a secured lender having priority if the company becomes insolvent.

The charge means that the lender will have the right, if the company defaults on the loan (for example does not pay interest or does not repay on the due date), to sell the charged assets and use the proceeds to recover the monies owed. As the charged assets will usually be worth more than the value of the loan, any surplus must be returned to the company once the lender's debt and costs have been satisfied. For this charge to be valid and effective against third parties, it has to be properly registered at Companies House in accordance with the Companies Act 2006.

A charge may be granted over specific assets, and the company is not permitted to deal with the charged assets without the lender's permission. This is a 'fixed charge', and assets such as land or fixed machinery are usually used for this purpose.

Alternatively, the charge may 'float' over a fluctuating class of assets, eg stock or even the whole company undertaking. The company may continue to deal with these assets until the charge 'crystallises' or fixes on the assets held at that time. Crystallisation may occur in various circumstances, but these include the company becoming insolvent. Where the company appears to be getting into financial difficulties, the lender may appoint an administrator to manage the company's business, and this is also an event which can trigger crystallisation.

If an asset is valuable enough, a company can grant more than one charge over the same asset, and there are various rules for establishing priority among secured creditors.

### 5.2.2 Why involve equity and trusts?

If a supplier supplies goods or raw materials to a company and gives it time to pay, there is a risk that the company will become insolvent before it pays the supplier. The supplier does not want to be an unsecured ordinary creditor, because, by the time the secured and preferential creditors have taken their entitlements, there will be precious little left for the supplier (and what little there is will have to be shared with the other unsecured creditors). If the supplier failed to take security, they may want to establish an equitable interest in money or property held by the company.

As seen in **1.4.3**, having an equitable interest in an asset brings with it proprietary rights - the right to claim the property itself. If the supplier can establish that the insolvent individual or company holds property on trust for them, the trust property is not part of the insolvent's estate available for the creditors. The supplier's beneficial interest allows them to claim the trust property in full, ahead of the creditors.

There have been three situations where potential creditors have made use of the trust to claim property ahead of other unsecured creditors.

## 5.3 Customer pre-payments

There are countless circumstances in which money is paid in advance for goods and services which are not to be delivered immediately - tickets for an arts or sporting event; a deposit on a holiday; an internet or mail-order purchase. If a supplier goes into liquidation before delivering the goods or services, the customer is a lowly unsecured creditor with little chance of recovering their money.

It might be possible for a trust to be created in these circumstances if, when the money is sent in advance to purchase an asset (or event), an accompanying letter says that the pre-payment should be held on trust by the company pending delivery. This method of creating a customer trust can be illustrated in the following diagram and is comparable to the discussions of the declaration and constitution of a trust with third party trustees (as in **Chapters 2** and **3**).

**Figure 5.1** Transfer to company as trustee to hold on trust

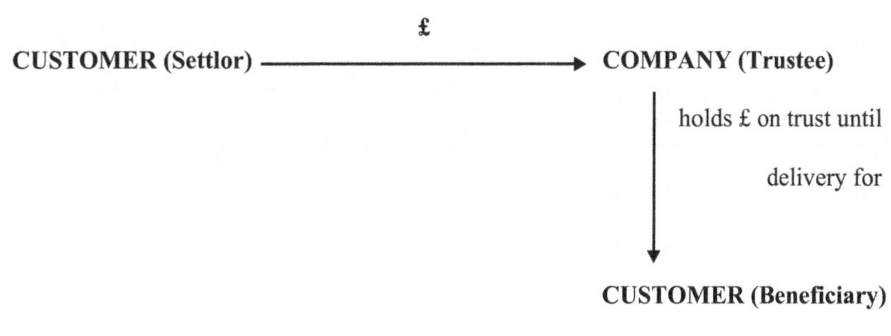


However, it would be impractical for all money received by a company to be held on trust for customers, because trust money has to be kept separate and cannot be used for the trustee's own purposes. The company would have cashflow problems because it would have no funds to pay employees, suppliers and overheads. For this reason, the terms and conditions of companies which trade on the basis of customer pre-payments often include an express statement confirming that customers' money is not being held on trust pending delivery.

Alternatively, the company itself may declare a trust over customer money pending delivery of the goods. Such a declaration would normally be in its terms and conditions of sale. The following diagram illustrates this second method of creating a customer trust.

**Figure 5.2** Declaration by company of self as trustee to hold on trust

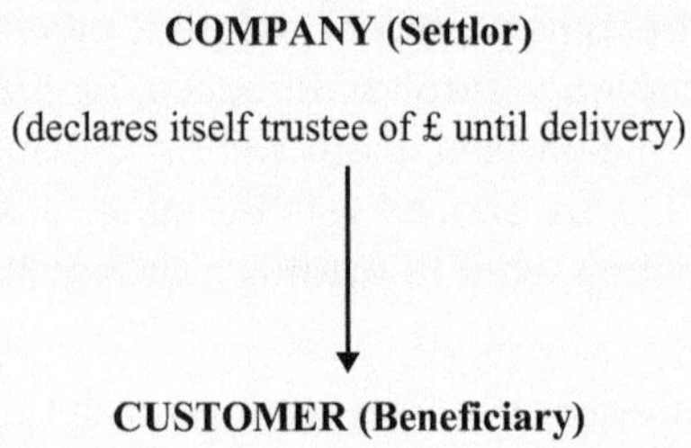


What motivates directors of companies to set up customer trusts? Directors of a failing company may create such trusts because a director who knew or ought to have concluded that there was no reasonable prospect that the company would avoid going into insolvent liquidation is required to take all possible steps to minimise the potential risk to the company's creditors (Insolvency Act 1986, s 214). If a court is satisfied that the necessary steps were not taken, it can order the errant director to contribute personally to the insolvent company's assets. Further, the Department for Business and Trade often disqualifies directors who take private customers' money in advance of delivery, if the customers' money is then lost because of a liquidation.

### 5.3.1 Does a valid trust exist?

A valid trust will be found to exist only if the usual requirements discussed in **Chapter 2** and **Chapter 3** are satisfied – a valid declaration of trust and the constitution of the trust.

When this type of customer pre-payment trust is being argued, the constitution of the trust is not generally an issue as the 'trust property' (the pre-payment) is being held by the now insolvent company and the trust is the means to recover it. The question is, therefore, whether there has been a valid declaration of trust.

**Figure 5.3** The components of a declaration of trust

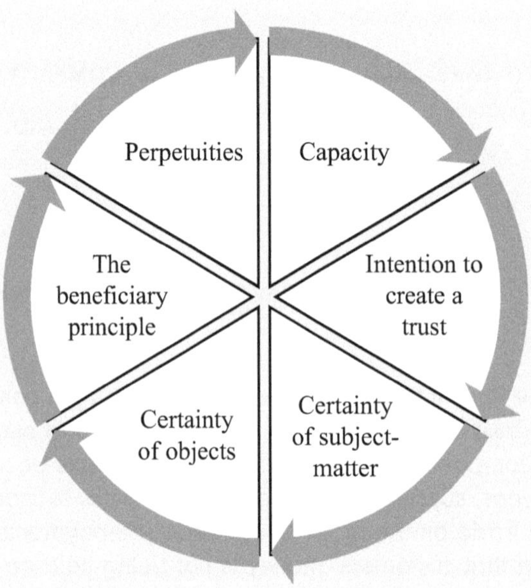

Capacity, the beneficiary principle and perpetuities are not issues here – the customer will have capacity and would be able to enforce any trust, and the arrangement between the customer and the company is short-term. Whether a valid trust for customers exists is determined by seeing if the 'three certainties' have been satisfied in the circumstances.

5.3.1.1 Certainty of intention

Given that any valid trust will be over personalty (money), intention can be determined by an analysis of words or conduct. There is no requirement for any declaration to be in writing.

***Re Kayford* [1975] 1 WLR 279**

In *Re Kayford*, the directors of a mail order company realised that the company was in financial difficulty and sought advice on how to protect customer payments for goods ordered by post. Accountants advised them to place all future customer payments in a separate account, to be called a 'Customer Trust Deposit Account'. The directors instructed the bank accordingly, and, from that point, the bank credited customer payments to a separate account; but contrary to instructions, the name of the account did not include the words 'Trust' or 'Customer'.

Megarry J held that the mail order company had declared an express trust over the customers' money. The judge inferred certainty of intention to create a trust from:

(a) the payment of customers' money into a separate bank account, which was a 'useful (though by no means conclusive) indication of an intention to create a trust'; and

(b) the fact that the company's accountants had advised that a trust bank account was the best way to protect customers' money.

The company did not have to state expressly that the bank account was held 'on trust' for the customers – 'the whole purpose of what was done was to ensure that the moneys remained in the beneficial ownership of those who sent them, and a trust was the obvious means of achieving this.'

As the company held the money on trust for the customers, they had a proprietary claim arising from their equitable interests which allowed them to recover their money ahead of the ordinary creditors.

Megarry J emphasised that different considerations may arise in relation to trade creditors. The reason is that trade creditors are more aware of the risk of insolvency and are more likely to protect themselves than commercially naïve consumers.

5.3.1.2 Certainty of subject-matter

In *Re Kayford*, the subject-matter of the trust was certain because the directors had paid the trust property (the customers' money) into a separate bank account. Uncertainty of subject-matter causes any attempted trust to fail where the trust property (be it the customers' money or goods) is not separated from other property of the same kind. For example, if a furniture company declares a trust over three of its leather sofas for customers X, Y and Z but does not separate them from its stock of identical leather sofas, the attempted trust would fail due to uncertainty of subject-matter.

In *Re London Wine Company (Shippers) Ltd*, the buyers of wine stored in a warehouse but not segregated from the general stock of wine could not establish a trust as the subject-matter was uncertain (see **2.3.3.1**).

***Re Goldcorp Exchange Ltd (in receivership)*** **[1995] 1 AC 74**

Goldcorp offered gold and precious metals for sale on the basis that it would store and insure customers' bullion. Customers each received a certificate showing how much bullion they had purchased and were told that they could expect delivery on seven days' notice. Goldcorp had not earmarked specific bullion for individual customers, and actually had insufficient stock to meet all their claims. Goldcorp went into receivership, and the Bank of New Zealand's floating charge crystallised. The issue was whether the customers had a proprietary trust interest in the purchase monies or in the bullion, so that they would not form part of the Bank's security.

The Privy Council held that Goldcorp had not declared valid trusts over the bullion in favour of individual customers, because the subject-matter was uncertain. The individual ingots had not been allocated to particular customers. The warehouse contained a stock of ingots which were not earmarked for anyone; indeed the stock was constantly changing because Goldcorp sold and replaced bullion in the course of its business. Goldcorp clearly viewed all the bullion as its stock-in-trade and freely dealt with it in the course of its business. Thus, it clearly did not intend to create a trust.

Similarly, the money sent by customers to purchase the bullion was not subject to a trust either, because there was nothing which required Goldcorp to use the payments received to purchase the requisite number of ingots for the customer. The customers' payments went into Goldcorp's general funds (unlike in *Re Kayford* where payments were segregated into a special account).

5.3.1.3 Certainty of objects

Certainty of objects was the problem in *OT Computers v First National Tricity Finance* [2004] 1 All ER (Comm) 320. OT Computers set up two bank accounts. One was held on trust for its 'customers' and was held to be valid (so the money contained in it was not available for OT Computers' creditors when the company subsequently became insolvent). The second account was held on trust for 'urgent suppliers'; this trust was held to be void because the objects were uncertain. It was not possible to draw up a complete list of every beneficiary of this fixed trust (**2.3.4.1**), and, therefore, it failed and the money in the account was part of the pool of assets to be shared among OT Computers' creditors.

### 5.3.2 An insolvency hurdle – preferences of creditors

Where a company which later becomes insolvent is found to have declared a trust in favour of its customers or trade creditors, a further consideration arises under the insolvency legislation, namely s 239 of the Insolvency Act 1986 and the potential 'preference' of creditors.

Under s 239, 'a preference occurs if a company does anything or suffers anything to be done which puts one of its creditors in a better position on the company's insolvency than it would otherwise have been'. If that preference of a creditor unconnected to the company occurs in the six-month period before the insolvency and it is clear that the company's intention was to put the creditor in that better position, the court can order that matters be returned to the position which existed before the preference took place. For a creditor connected in some way with the company, the relevant period is two years.

In *Re Kayford*, Megarry J held that the declaration of trust by the company in favour of its customers was not an unlawful preference. The declaration of trust did not put *creditors* in a better position on the subsequent insolvency. The company's action prevented the customers from becoming creditors in the first place. As soon as the customers paid their money, they were beneficiaries under a trust (of the bank account) and not ordinary creditors.

Other customers have not been so fortunate.

***Re Farepak Food and Gifts Ltd* [2006] All ER (D) 265**

Farepak operated a Christmas savings scheme under which customers could spread their Christmas savings over a year. Small contributions could be made month by month so that enough had accumulated by the beginning of November to buy a shopping voucher, or a hamper or other goods. Agents of the company collected the monthly payments (typically from customers in their circle of friends and relatives) and passed on the money to the company. In October 2006, the company went into liquidation.

In the days leading up to the liquidation, the directors sought to ringfence customers' money so that it could be returned to customers, if necessary. A deed of trust was executed indicating an account into which customers' money was to be paid and explaining that the deed was entered into to ensure the return of money in the event of insolvency.

There was a mistake as to the account identified in the deed. Customers' money actually went into the company's current account. However, Mann J was prepared to rectify the deed so that it could be regarded as referring to the current account. Customers' contributions had already been put into the bank account when the trust was declared, and contributions continued to be added after the declaration.

Farepak had tried to create the trust, and the deed of trust provided evidence of that intention. The customer payments were intended to form the subject-matter of the trust. However, customers whose money had already entered the company's bank account before the declaration of trust were creditors at the time of the declaration (entitled to their vouchers etc). Therefore, the declaration of trust constituted an unlawful preference of these customers; as a result, the declaration of trust over the money of existing customers was void.

Some customers had, however, paid their money to the company after the declaration of trust. Mann J said, 'there may not be a preference so far as those customers are concerned, because they are not creditors at the time of the creation of the trust over their money but filtering those customers out may be difficult if not impossible.' Thus, there could be no valid trust for them either, due to the lack of certainty of subject-matter – the inability to identify the beneficial interests of those customers not caught by s 239 of the Insolvency Act 1986.

## 5.4 *Quistclose* trusts

These trusts are named after *Barclays Bank v Quistclose Investments Ltd* [1970] AC 567, the case which created a new circumstance where the use of a trust was an effective safeguard against a corporate insolvency.

***Barclays Bank v Quistclose Investments Ltd* [1970] AC 567**

Quistclose lent over £200,000 to Rolls Razor Ltd ('RR'). The loan was made on condition that RR would use the money only to pay dividends to its shareholders. Time and business circumstances prevented Quistclose from taking security when the loan was made. Before the dividends were paid, RR went into liquidation. This meant that the money could not be used for the stated purpose of paying dividends. However, the loan money remained in an account at Barclays Bank. As one of RR's unsecured creditors, Barclays Bank argued that the loan money formed part of RR's assets available to pay the unsecured creditors.

Normally, if a lender lends money to a borrower, the ownership of the money passes to the borrower; the lender merely has a contractual right to repayment of the loan. If the borrower should become insolvent, the lender is a lowly unsecured creditor. However, Quistclose claimed that the money was held on trust to pay the dividends, but if that purpose could not be carried out then it was held on trust for Quistclose. As a beneficiary under a trust, Quistclose would be able to bring a proprietary action which would enable it to recover the money in full ahead of the creditors (rather like the customers in *Re Kayford*).

The House of Lords decided that a two-tier trust had been created. The settlor was Quistclose. The trustee was RR. RR held the loan money on a primary trust to pay dividends to the shareholders. Should that purpose prove to be impossible (as was the case), there was a secondary trust to return the money to the settlor/lender, Quistclose.

### 5.4.1 Certainty of intention

Quistclose, as settlor, needed to display sufficient certainty of intention to create a trust. It had not stated explicitly: 'You (RR) must hold this loan on trust to pay the dividends due to the shareholders, but if that purpose cannot be achieved, then you are to hold it on trust for Quistclose.' But a trust can be created without the settlor using the word 'trust' (as in as *Paul v Constance* [1977] 1 WLR 527 discussed in **2.3.2**).

The House of Lords (Lord Wilberforce) was satisfied that Quistclose intended to create a trust because it did not intend the loan money to be at the free disposal of the borrower:

> the essence of the bargain [between Quistclose and RR] was that the sum advanced should not become part of the assets of Rolls Razor but should be used exclusively for payment of a particular class of its creditors, namely those entitled to the dividend. A necessary consequence from this, by process simply of interpretation, must be that if, for any reason, the dividend could not be paid, the money was to be returned to the respondents: the word 'only' or 'exclusively' can have no other meaning or effect.

Lord Wilberforce went on to say that the arrangement gave rise to a recognised relationship of a fiduciary character or trust in favour, as a primary trust, of the creditors (here the shareholders) and secondarily, if the primary trust fails, of the third person (here Quistclose).

The primary trust ceases when the loan is applied for the stated purpose (here the payment of the dividends). The lender has a contractual claim to repayment of the money (ie a debt action) and will rank as an unsecured creditor on the insolvency of the borrower. Accordingly, if RR had paid the dividends before becoming insolvent, Quistclose would have lost its status as a beneficiary under a trust and would have become an ordinary unsecured creditor with only a contractual claim against RR.

In *Twinsectra v Yardley* [2002] UKHL 12, a finance company agreed to lend £1 million to a purchaser of residential land. The finance company paid the loan money to the purchaser's solicitor, but it insisted on the solicitor giving an undertaking that the money would be used 'solely for the acquisition of property on behalf of our client and for no other purpose'. Lord Millett's view was that the undertaking created a *Quistclose* trust – the lender intended to create a trust of the loan monies because the monies were not to be regarded as part of the borrower's general assets and could not be spent in any way the borrower wished.

The mere fact that a lender specifies that a loan is to be spent on a particular purpose does not create a trust. Normally, the money lent immediately becomes the borrower's property.

If the loan contract lays down how the loan is to be used and the borrower spends the money for something else, the borrower is, at most, in breach of contract. Something more is needed to establish the trust. The loan money in *Quistclose* was paid into a separate bank account and this has been used as clear evidence that the money is intended for the specified purpose only and is so subject to a trust.

In *Carreras Rothmans Ltd v Freeman Matthews Treasure Ltd* [1984] 3 WLR 1016, Rothmans paid (rather than loaned) money to its advertising agency for the sole purpose of ensuring the payment of third-party creditors with whom their adverts had been placed. The money was placed into a separate bank account, but the advertising agency became insolvent before paying the third-party creditors. Peter Gibson J held that the defendant was never free to deal the money as it pleased and that 'equity fastens on the conscience of the person who received from another property transferred for a specific purpose only'. A *Quistclose*-type trust was established.

However, the loan money being paid into a separate bank account is not essential. In *Re EVTR* [1987] BCLC 646, the claimant lent EVTR money 'for the sole purpose of buying new equipment'. The money was paid into the company's general funds. The company ordered the new equipment and paid for it but went into liquidation before it was delivered. The equipment suppliers refunded approximately 60% of the payment. It was held that the original loan had been subject to a *Quistclose* trust because it was expressly lent for a sole, exclusive purpose. The judge decided that it was not essential for the money to be paid into a separate account. It was held that the company held the refund on a *Quistclose* trust. This sum could not be used for the specified purpose of purchasing new equipment and was, thus, held on trust for the claimant lender.

A critical fact to determine if a trust exists is whether the parties intend the loan money to be at the free disposal of the borrower.

In *Re Farepak Food and Gifts Ltd*, discussed earlier, it was argued that there was a *Quistclose* trust because customers had paid their money for the purpose of receiving hampers or vouchers; this purpose became impossible and thus, it was argued, the money should be held on trust for the customers. The argument failed – there was no *Quistclose* trust because the customers' money was at the free disposal of Farepak. There was no requirement for the company to keep the customers' payments separate from its own funds pending delivery of the hampers or vouchers. It was implausible to suppose that the company had agreed to, say, keep a customer's January payment separate and intact until the hampers or vouchers were made available the following November. Everyone concerned expected the company to use customers' money for the expenses of the company (such as salaries, advertising etc). As a result, the customers were ordinary unsecured creditors.

In *Bellis v Challinor* [2015] EWCA Civ 59, investors in an airport development project sought to recover their money from the firm of solicitors which had received the investment monies into their client account. The solicitors acted on behalf of the company that had been set up to facilitate the project. The solicitors had used the funds to reduce the company's borrowings. When the project failed, the investors claimed that the solicitors had held their money on a *Quistclose*-type trust as their money had been paid to the solicitors for the specific purposes of the development project. The Court of Appeal found that the investors had not done enough to create a trust in their favour. The terms of the investment prospectus were not sufficient to indicate that, when the money was paid into the client account, it was not to be at the free disposal of the company. Therefore, the intention to create a trust was not evidenced; there was merely a reason for making the payment to the solicitor (participation in the investment project) and this did not impose any restrictions on the use of the money in the company's hands. Briggs LJ stated that 'for a *Quistclose*-style trust to be created, there must be an intention to create a trust on the part of the transferor, ascertained objectively ... by words or conduct, not innermost thoughts'.

### 5.4.2 Certainty of objects and the beneficiary principle

Another conundrum arising from the validity of *Quistclose*-type trusts concerns certainty of objects and the beneficiary principle.

As discussed in **Chapter 4**, an express trust, subject to limited exceptions, assumes the existence of a person able to enforce the trust. Without such a person, the intended express trust is void (*Morice v Bishop of Durham, Re Astor*). In *Quistclose*, Lord Wilberforce did not clearly identify the objects of the primary trust to pay the dividends (although he suggested the shareholders due to receive the dividends). As far as the secondary trust was concerned, the beneficiary was Quistclose (under the resulting trust which arose with the failure of the purpose).

In *Twinsectra v Yardley* [2002] UKHL 12, Lord Millett took the opportunity, albeit in an overall dissenting judgment, to identify the beneficiary of the *Quistclose*-type trust in depth. He suggested that there are four possible answers: (1) the lender, (2) the borrower, (3) the beneficiary of ultimate purpose, and (4) no-one, in the sense that the beneficial interest remains 'in suspense' until the purpose is or is not fulfilled.

Having analysed all these options, he dismissed three of them:

- The borrower could not be the beneficiary as the arrangement did not provide them with free use of the loan money and they had limited, restricted rights over that money.
- The beneficiary of the purpose was similarly excluded on the basis that this analysis was not able to accommodate payments made specifying an 'abstract purpose' where no one but the lender could enforce performance or guard against misuse (for instance, the purchase of property in *Twinsectra*, the purchase of new equipment in *Re EVTR*).
- The beneficial interest was not 'in suspense' as this had the effect of creating a vacuum and a resulting trust is the default which 'fills the gaps and leaves no room for any part to be in suspense'.

Lord Millett consequently determined that the beneficial interest of the primary trust remains with the lender until the purpose for which the funds are lent is fulfilled (at which time the trust comes to an end and only a contractual right to repayment remains). He said the 'money remains the property of the lender unless and until it is applied in accordance with his directions, and as far as it is not so applied it must be returned to him'. Thus, in *Quistclose*, when RR held the loan money on trust, the beneficial interest in the money rested with Quistclose who could direct how the money should be applied. Although not all commentators agreed with Lord Millett's arguments, his analysis has come to be held up as 'authoritative' and 'compelling' (Briggs LJ, *Bellis v Challoner* [2015] EWCA Civ 59).

On this basis, it has become accepted that a *Quistclose* trust will arise where money is transferred to be held on trust subject to a power for the transferee (as trustee) to apply it for a stated specific and sole purpose. The beneficial interest of the transferor (as settlor and beneficiary) continues unless and until the money is applied in accordance with that power to use for the specified purpose.

### 5.4.3 Certainty of purpose

*Quistclose*-type trusts have been upheld in cases of money lent or paid for variety of purposes – ranging from the payment of dividends, the purchase of computer equipment, the repayment of creditors, and failed investment projects. Regardless of the intended purpose attributed to the loan or payment, such purpose must be described with sufficient certainty. In *Twinsectra v Yardley* [2002] UKHL 12, the lower courts had dismissed the trust on the grounds that the stated purpose – 'to be used solely for the acquisition of property' – was too vague. However, Lord Hoffman in the House of Lords rejected this – a purpose was sufficiently certain if 'the court can say that a given application of the money does or does not fall within its terms'. In *Twinsectra*, it was held that the purpose was stated with sufficient clarity so that the court would know whether or not money had been misapplied or the purpose remained capable of being carried out.

### 5.4.4 *Quistclose* policy concerns

*Quistclose* trusts have been relied on mainly by lenders, but they have also been held to exist in respect of other payments for a specific purpose. Had the customers in *Farepak* made it clear that their money was to be used only for the purchase of hampers, and that it was not at Farepak's free disposal, they might have persuaded the court that a *Quistclose* trust existed.

*Quistclose* loans are often used where the solvency of the borrower is precarious. Various parties may have an interest in ensuring the survival of an ailing company (eg where the company is part of a group of companies and its liquidation may bring down the entire group). The aim of such a *Quistclose* loan will often be to give the borrower the appearance of financial solidity, enabling it to get credit from suppliers and other sources and continue trading, while, at the same time, ensuring the lender's priority should the borrower become insolvent. If emergency measures are necessary to save a company, there may not be time to draft a charge; a *Quistclose* loan can be created much more quickly. The policy concern is whether the courts should allow lenders to gain priority on the borrower's insolvency by using *Quistclose* trusts. Do such trusts unjustifiably interfere with the statutory order of debts on insolvency, or should they be encouraged as a means of saving businesses which might otherwise 'go under'?

Secured lenders lending money to companies are required to register their charges at the Companies House. Banks and others who are considering lending to the company can inspect the register and discover the existence of prior charges before deciding to go ahead with their transaction. At present, there is no way that prospective lenders can discover the existence of any previous *Quistclose* loans.

Unlike in *Bellis v Challinor*, contributors to failed investment projects or tax saving schemes have been successful in establishing *Quistclose*-type trusts, so recovering their funds when the projects or schemes proved unsuccessful. In *Wise v Jimenez* [2013] All ER (D) 123, former professional footballer, Denis Wise, successfully recovered £500,000 from a business associate on the basis that the money had been transferred for the specific purpose of investment in the development of a golf course. The court considered that the investment had not been fulfilled at any material time. In light of this, a *Quistclose*-type trust had been established and the £500,000 was to be repaid under the terms of the trust (see also *Brown v InnovatorOne PLC* [2010] EWHC 1321 (Comm)).

As a result, there has been recent criticism about the use of *Quistclose*-type trusts as they have provided creditors with opportunities to circumvent insolvency law in very tenuous circumstances. While there may be sound public policy considerations for allowing a trust in *Quistclose*-like circumstances, namely assisting a company in financial difficulties with access to emergency funds, there are arguably not the same public policy justifications for the decisions involving failed investment projects, or the completion of a private purchase of company car (as in *Cooper v PRG Powerhouse* [2008] EWHC 498 (Ch)).

## 5.5 Supply of goods on credit

It is normal to sell goods on credit. Usually the buyer will, according to the terms of the contract, have a given period in which to pay. In business-to-business contracts, s 18 of the Sale of Goods Act 1979 states when ownership of the goods (or 'title' to the goods) passes to the buyer, notwithstanding the fact that the buyer has not yet paid for them. The timing varies depending on the type of contract (whether, for instance, the seller has to do something to the goods before delivery to the buyer), but basically the title passes at the time the buyer gets possession. The seller no longer has a proprietary interest in the goods. The seller is simply owed a debt. If the buyer becomes bankrupt (or, if a company, insolvent), the seller ranks as an ordinary creditor in the bankruptcy or insolvency, again ranking behind all secured and preferential creditors, with the likelihood of receiving any money for the goods being low.

### 5.5.1 Retention of title clauses

If, however, the seller can somehow retain a proprietary interest (that is ownership, or 'title'), then, on the buyer's insolvency, the seller can reclaim any goods which they still own. Section 19 of the Sale of Goods Act 1979 permits the seller and buyer in business-to-business contracts to stipulate when title to the goods is to pass.

A simple version of such a term will state that title to the goods will not pass until they have been paid for in full. Thus, if the buyer becomes insolvent before title passes, the seller may reclaim their goods, ranking above others in the insolvency. These contract terms are called 'retention of title' clauses.

***Aluminum Industrie Vaassen BV v Romalpa Aluminium Ltd* [1976] 1 WLR 676**

AIV sold aluminium foil to RA for use in RA's business. The retention of title clause in their contract provided that ownership in the foil would pass to RA only when RA had paid all sums owing (for whatever reason) to AIV.

Goods were usually sold, however, on the basis that the buyer would resell them or use them in their manufacturing process before the credit period has expired. The credit period in this case was 75 days. The retention of title clause in *Romalpa*, therefore, permitted RA to resell the foil provided RA accounted for the proceeds of sale.

When becoming insolvent, RA owed AIV £122,000, but had stock of unused foil. AIV could reclaim this; the retention of title clause meant AIV was still the legal owner.

RA had also sold on some stock and had £35,000 proceeds of sale. Could AIV claim this ahead of RA's creditors as well?

The Court of Appeal held that the retention of title clause was effective. AIV was still the owner of the aluminium foil and could trace the price due to it into the proceeds of sale of the finished goods, ahead of Romalpa's unsecured and secured creditors. In the case, it was found that in selling the foil, RA acted as agent for AIV.

(Since this case, retention of title clauses have come to be known as '*Romalpa* clauses').

### 5.5.2 After *Romalpa*

In the *Romalpa* case, the retention of title clause was aimed at unused stock and the proceeds of sale of stock sold on. However, if the goods were to be mixed with other goods in the manufacturing process, there is an issue as to whether a *Romalpa* clause also gives rights to trace into the finished product, or even its proceeds of sale. Common law tracing is not possible if the property can no longer be identified. However, equity will permit tracing into a mixed fund (tracing is discussed in more detail in **Chapter 9**).

In *Borden (UK) Ltd v Scottish Timber Products* [1981] Ch 25, Borden (B) supplied resin to be used by Scottish Timber Products (STP) in the manufacture of chipboard. As part of the manufacturing process, the resin was mixed with hardeners and wax emulsion. The resin was sold on credit terms and those terms included a retention of title clause, but B had no rights in the finished chipboard or its proceeds of sale. When STP went into liquidation, B sought declarations from the court that it could trace its title to the resin under the retention of title clauses into the glue mix and the worked products. At first instance, B succeeded in its claim, but this was overturned in the Court of Appeal. STP had complete freedom to use the resin in its process, which was incompatible with the concept of beneficial ownership remaining in B, at least after STP had used the resin and destroyed its existence.

As with *Quistclose* loans, the *Romalpa* clause device permits a supplier to leapfrog other creditors in the event of the buyer's insolvency, and they can do so without public registration of their rights. A lender who requires security for the loan often creates an equitable charge, which must be registered at Companies House or is unenforceable against a liquidator. Other lenders are, therefore, unable to tell in advance of granting a loan whether the stock and its proceeds (which will be intended to be at least part of the security for the loan) will, in fact, be owned by someone other than the borrower – in the *Romalpa* case, AIV was successful against RA's bank who were seeking to exercise their floating charge.

Given that retention of title issues arise in business-to-business circumstances, there is a perceived lack of enthusiasm for *Romalpa* clauses on the part of the court given that businesses should be able to adequately protect themselves in their contractual agreements. The court is not willing for equity and trust principles to be used to compensate for deficiencies in business contracts. In *Borden*, the claimant company was chastised by the court for seeking to rely on a retention of title clause which did not offer effective security in the known circumstances of the manufacturing process. For the court in *Borden*, the conclusion was a 'simple one' – effective retention of title can only be achieved with express, well-drafted contractual provisions.

**ACTIVITY Review your understanding – trusts in commercial settings**

Consider these questions.

(1) Hightec Ltd sells computers to private individuals and businesses. Customers place an order; Hightec puts together the required package and delivers it to the customer approximately a week after the order. Hightec's terms and conditions state that customers must pay in full when they place their order and that their new computer will be held on trust for them. Hightec has gone into liquidation and is heavily insolvent.

Which one of the following statements is true?

(a) Hightec has not put aside or assembled the components of the computers ordered by customers X, Y and Z. Nevertheless, a valid trust exists for X, Y and Z.
(b) Hightec's delivery van was on its way to Customer A's premises with their new computer. There is a valid trust for Customer A.
(c) There was no certainty of intention to create a trust.

(2) When the directors of Hightec realised that it was likely to become insolvent, they placed customers' money in a separate bank account and instructed the bank that the money could be withdrawn only as and when the customer received delivery of their computer.

Which one of the following statements is true?

(a) No valid trust of the customers' money was created because nothing was put in writing.
(b) Hightec did not declare a valid trust because it did not use the word 'trust'.
(c) An intention to create a trust could be manifested by the desire to protect customers' money and determination to keep the customers' money separate from the rest of Hightec's funds.

(3) Six months ago, BEST Finance plc lent £50,000 to Greenco Ltd. A letter signed by BEST Finance's loan manager stated that the money was to be used 'solely for the payment of dividends to Greenco's shareholders and for no other purpose whatsoever'. The money was paid into Greenco's current account at the bank. The directors of Greenco then withdrew £20,000 from the account to pay insurance premiums and rent for its premises. One of the shareholders has found out and is threatening to sue the directors of Greenco.

What issues might arise for Greenco's directors?

**COMMENT**

(1) The correct answer is (b), because in that case the subject matter of A's trust (A's computer) had been segregated from Hightec's stock of computer hardware. There is no valid trust in (a) because X, Y and Z's computers have not been segregated from the rest of Hightec's stock (*Re London Wine Co*). Statement (c) is incorrect because Hightec showed an intention to create a trust in its terms and conditions.

(2) Statement (c) is correct (*Re Kayford*; *Re Goldcorp*). Statement (a) is incorrect because trusts can be declared over personalty orally. Statement (b) is incorrect because settlors can show an intention to create a trust even though they do not use technical words.

(3) *Issue 1*

Did BEST Finance plc create a trust of the loan money for the purpose of paying the dividends? The facts are similar to *Barclays Bank v Quistclose*:

- money was to be used exclusively for a particular purpose;
- money was not intended to form part of the general assets of the borrower;
- money is clearly not at the free disposal of the borrower (Millett LJ in *Twinsectra v Yardley*).

Payment of the loan into a separate bank account is strong evidence of such an intention, but it is not essential (*Re EVTR*). However, there must be other evidence to support the proposal that a trust was intended (*Bellis v Challinor*).

The trust in *Barclays Bank v Quistclose* was a two-tier trust: the primary trust was to pay the dividends, but, if that became impossible (due to the company's insolvency), a secondary trust arose in favour of the lender. Here, the borrower (Greenco) is still solvent but has used the loan money other than for the purpose. Thus we are concerned with the enforcement of the primary trust to pay the dividends.

*Issue 2*

Can the shareholders enforce the trust? Trusts are enforceable by the beneficiaries. The identity of the beneficiaries was not explored fully in *Barclays Bank v Quistclose* (there was a suggestion that the shareholders might be the beneficiaries). In *Twinsectra v Yardley*, Lord Millett rejected the argument that those benefiting from the specified purpose (ie the shareholders in this case) are the beneficiaries of *Quistclose*-type trusts. Thus, even though there may be a *Quistclose* trust in the present case, according to Lord Millett's view, the shareholders are not able to enforce the purpose.

Lord Millett decided that the equitable interest remains in the lender throughout. Therefore, the decision whether or not to enforce the trust arguably lies with BEST Finance plc. It may seek to act against the directors for the possible misapplication of the loan money.

## SUMMARY

- Parties to a commercial contract might wish to argue the existence of a trust when one of them becomes insolvent so as to benefit from the proprietary rights afforded to beneficiaries under a trust.
- The requirements for the creation of a valid trust, studied earlier in **Chapters 2** and **3**, are equally relevant to the creation of trusts in commercial circumstances.
- As well as gaining priority over unsecured creditors on an insolvency, it is important to understand that establishing a trust can also be a springboard for the claimant being able to claim all the benefits associated with having an equitable interest. This would include obtaining equitable remedies, not just against the insolvent entity, but also against third parties.
- Understanding beneficiaries' rights under a trust enhances an awareness of the policy conflicts which arise when equity and trust principles are deployed in insolvency situations.

# 6 Implied Trusts

**LEARNING OUTCOMES**

By the end of this chapter, you should be able to:

- understand the operation of resulting trusts when the beneficial interest is uncertain and who takes the beneficial interest under such a resulting trust;
- explain the circumstances in which the presumptions of resulting trust and advancement arise, and how the operation of such presumptions can be rebutted;
- discuss the use of common intention constructive trusts and proprietary estoppel in relation both to the family home and other property;
- recognise when a constructive trust might arise in a commercial setting; and
- appreciate how the use of trusts in resolving disputes between cohabiting partners is developing and controversial.

## 6.1 Introduction

Up to now, the discussion has been focused on the creation of express trusts in both private and commercial contexts. In this chapter, we move on to consider where the existence of a trust can be implied into a situation. These types of trust are the resulting trust and the constructive trust and are used as a starting point for the courts when seeking to clarify a person's intentions in the absence of clear evidence.

Implied trusts are frequently used to resolve disputes involving ownership of property. For instance, there is no concept of community of family property in English law. Spouses, and civil partners, do not automatically own half each of the family home and other assets. The courts are often asked to determine ownership of property when a relationship breaks down. When married couples and civil partners split up, the courts have the power to make property adjustment orders, ordering one party to transfer their interest to the other as it considers appropriate, assessing the parties' future needs. However, cohabiting partners are treated differently. Who owns the property, and in what proportion, is of crucial importance, because there is no power to order a transfer from one party to another if the relationship comes to an end. It is, therefore, necessary to discover who actually owns what.

If a house is in joint names, held as joint tenants, the usual inference will be that the parties own half each. If they hold as tenants in common, the proportions will be stated, and this will be conclusive in the absence of fraud or mistake. There are more issues, however, if the house is in one party's name ('Y') but the other ('X') has contributed to the purchase price. Should X be able to claim an interest in the house? What sort of contribution by X is sufficient to merit a claim? Assuming X is found to have an interest, how do you quantify it? Implied trusts play a part in providing the answers to these questions.

A person may transfer assets to another and the reason why the transfer is made may be perfectly clear, such as a sale or a gift. But if there is no evidence of the person's intention, implied trusts can help to determine the ultimate owner of the transferred asset.

Importantly, resulting and constructive trusts do not have to comply with s 53(1)(b) of the Law of Property Act 1925 even if they arise over land (discussed in **2.4.2**); implied trusts are excluded from its operation (Law of Property Act 1925, s 53(2)). They can and do arise from an analysis of conduct and words spoken rather than just documentary evidence.

## 6.2 Resulting trusts

Resulting trusts are implied where a person transfers property or money to another in circumstances where it is or becomes unclear who owns the beneficial interest. Here, the presumption is that the transferee holds the property or money on a resulting trust for the transferor.

**Figure 6.1** illustrates the position for all types of resulting trust. X transfers property to Y, but it is unclear who owns the beneficial interest. Y holds the property on resulting trust for X, who, therefore, has the equitable interest. 'Resulting' derives from the Latin word '*saltare*' meaning 'to jump'; the equitable interest jumps back to (or sometimes never leaves) the settlor.

**Figure 6.1** The operation of a resulting trust

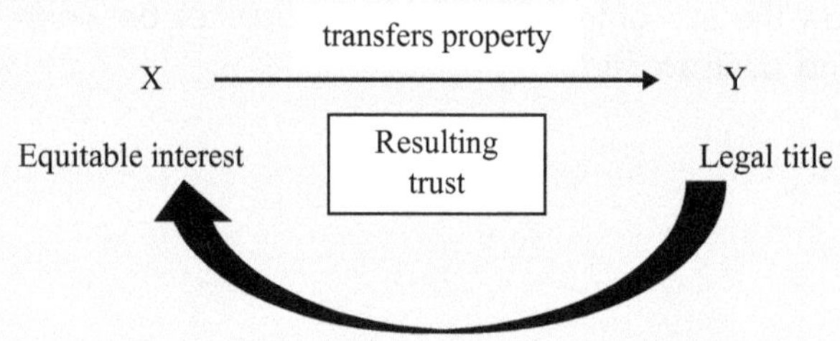


In *Westdeutsche Landesbank Girozentrale v Islington London Borough Council* [1996] AC 669, Lord Browne-Wilkinson confirmed that resulting trusts arise in two sets of circumstances.

The first is where A transfers property to B on express trusts, but the trusts declared do not exhaust the whole beneficial interest. It is the incomplete disposal of the trust's equitable interest that gives rise to the resulting trust so as to complete the disposal.

According to Lord Brown-Wilkinson in *Westdeutsche Landesbank*, a trust will also result:

> where A makes a voluntary transfer to B or pays (wholly or in part) for the purchase of property which is vested in either B alone or in the joint names of A and B.

In either circumstance, there is a presumption that A did not intend to make a gift to B: the money or property is held on trust for A (if they are the sole provider of the money) or in the case of a joint purchase by A and B in shares proportionate to their contributions. According to Lord Browne-Wilkinson, both are examples of a trust being imposed by law to give effect to a presumed intention of the parties.

However, Lord Browne-Wilkinson stressed that the presumption could be easily rebutted either by the counter-presumption of advancement or by direct evidence of A's intention to make an outright transfer.

### 6.2.1 Incomplete disposal of a trust's equitable interest

This type of resulting trust arises where the settlor:

(a) transfers property to trustees on trust; but

(b) does not dispose of all or part of their equitable interest (eg because the declared trusts are void or do not exhaust the trust fund).

The trustees will hold the property on a resulting trust for the settlor.

**Chapter 2** (at **2.5**) discussed circumstances where issues with a failed declaration of an express trust would give rise to a resulting trust:

- the attempted trust not describing the whole of the trust property with certainty;
- the attempted trust not defining the beneficial interests with sufficient certainty;
- the attempted trust lacks certainty of objects, is administratively unworkable, is capricious;
- the attempted trust offends the rules against perpetuities.

In all these circumstances, the trust property, which has been validly transferred to the trustees, will be held by those trustees on resulting trust for the settlor (or their estate) on the basis that this is what the settlor would have intended to happen when the original trust failed.

A resulting trust would also arise where there is a gap in the beneficial ownership because the trust does not name a beneficiary who attains a vested interest. For example, the beneficiary of a contingent trust does not attain the contingency and the trust instrument does not name a default beneficiary. A further example would be where the beneficiary under a trust created by will predeceases the testator (and so their interest lapses) and the will does not mention a substitute beneficiary. There will be a resulting trust for the testator's estate (either forming part of the residue of the estate or being distributed in accordance with the intestacy rules to the testator's statutory next of kin).

The case of *Vandervell v IRC* [1967] 2 AC 291 was considered in **Chapter 3** (at **3.6.1**).

***Vandervell v IRC* [1967] 2 AC 291**

Vandervell ('V'), a wealthy industrialist, wanted to donate £150,000 to the Royal College of Surgeons ('the College'). To achieve this end, he decided to transfer 100,000 shares in the family business to the College, until those shares had supplied the £150,000 by way of dividends. Thereafter, a separate company (a family trust) was given an option to purchase the shares from the College for £5,000. V's shares in the family business were held by a bank for convenience. The bank, therefore, held the legal title, and V held an absolute equitable interest under a 'bare trust'. V instructed the bank (as absolute owner he was entitled to do this) to transfer the shares to the College, which it duly validly did, and the dividends were then paid to the College.

If V still retained an interest in the shares, he would be liable for tax on the dividends. This in turn depended on whether he had transferred his equitable interest to the College.

The Revenue lost its argument that V had not disposed of his equitable interest in writing as required by s 53(1)(c) of the LPA 1925 (**3.6.1**). However, V was taxed on the dividends for another reason. V had not told the trustees whom to hold the shares for once they executed the option to purchase. Until he did so, there was an incomplete disposal of his equitable interest – the trustees must, therefore, hold the benefit of the option for him – the 'resulting trust' argument. Under the relevant tax legislation, this was a sufficient interest for V to be liable to the surtax.

### 6.2.2 Presumption of resulting trust

As Lord Brown-Wilkinson referenced in *Westdeutsche Landesbank*, a presumption of resulting trust arises when a voluntary transfer occurs between X and Y – where X transfers property, which they own, to Y for no consideration. It is presumed that X intended Y to hold the property on a resulting trust for X.

A resulting trust will also be presumed where X provides purchase money for property to be purchased in the name of Y or in the names of X and Y. Unlike the voluntary transfer scenario, where X transfers property which they already own to Y, here X buys new property, but instead of putting it in their own name, they arrange for the seller to convey the property straight to Y.

While the obvious inference to draw in these scenarios is that X intended to make an outright gift, there is a historical reason for the presumption. In the 16th century, it was extremely common for people to convey property to another (Y) to hold to the use of (on trust for) the grantor (X). Uses were so common as a means of avoiding taxation and undesirable inheritance laws that, whenever a person conveyed property without consideration, it was presumed that they intended a resulting trust (or use) for themselves.

#### 6.2.2.1 Voluntary transfers

X transfers property to Y. No consideration is supplied by Y (hence the term 'voluntary' transfers). There is no evidence as to X's intention when making the transfer. The presumption is that Y holds the property on resulting trust for X. In *Re Vinogradoff* [1935] WN 68, a woman transferred bonds into the joint name of herself and her granddaughter. When the woman died, it was held that the presumption of resulting trust applied, and the granddaughter held the bonds on resulting trust for the estate.

It is important to appreciate the limitations of the presumption:

(a) The presumption is applied only in the absence of evidence of X's actual intentions.

(b) It is only a presumption, and presumptions can be rebutted.

(c) The presumption is less likely to apply if the property in question is realty. Section 60(3) of the Law of Property Act 1925 states: 'In a voluntary conveyance a resulting trust for the grantor shall not be implied merely by reason that the property is not expressed to be conveyed for the use or benefit of the grantee.' This provision has been taken to mean that there is no presumption of a resulting trust after a voluntary transfer of land (*Lohia v Lohia* [2001] WTLR 101, *Kahan v Ali* [2002] EWCA Civ 974). However, it is still possible for there to be a resulting trust, but there must be some evidence or additional factor, such as the fact that the parties to the voluntary transfer of the land were strangers, which would point to a resulting trust.

(d) When the parties are related such that X is taken as owing a moral obligation for Y's welfare, the presumption is not one of resulting trust but of gift. This is called the 'presumption of advancement', which is considered at **6.2.3** below.

#### 6.2.2.2 Contribution to purchase

The second circumstance which Lord Brown-Wilkinson indicated gave rise to a resulting trust is where X contributes to the purchase of property in the name of Y; there is a presumption that X intended Y to hold on a resulting trust for X. The presumption applies regardless of the property purchased.

***Abrahams v Trustee in Bankruptcy of Abrahams* (1999) *The Times*, 26 July**

Mr and Mrs A were both members of a National Lottery syndicate at their local pub. There were 15 members in total. Mrs A paid £2 per week, £1 for herself and £1 for Mr A. She continued to do so even after they had separated, and so Mr A continued to be a member, even though it was Mrs A who paid 'his' contributions. It was clear that Mrs A in effect now had two shares, and the other syndicate members did not object.

Mr A was declared bankrupt, and then the syndicate won £3,632,327.

Mr A's trustee in bankruptcy claimed Mr A's one-fifteenth share, namely £242,155. It was held that Mr A held his share on resulting trust for Mrs A. There was no intention of gift to rebut the presumption of resulting trust. Thus, Mr A's share belonged in equity to Mrs A, and was not available for Mr A's creditors.

***Parrott v Parkin*** **[2007] EWHC 210 (Admlty)**

A cohabiting couple, LP and MP, purchased, first, a houseboat, then a yacht, then a replacement yacht (which they named 'UP YAWS'). It was this replacement yacht that was the subject of the dispute. The yacht was registered in MP's sole name, although LP contributed 55% of the purchase price. In the absence of evidence of an intended gift, it was held that MP held the yacht on resulting trust as to 55% for LP.

It is not uncommon for cohabitees to contribute to the purchase of a house (with the intention of living there together) but for the house to be transferred into the sole name of one cohabitee.

***Example***

*An unmarried couple buy a house for £300,000. The house is conveyed into the woman's name alone. The man provided £200,000 of the purchase money and the woman the other £100,000. Under resulting trust principles, there is a presumption that the woman holds the legal title on a resulting trust for both of them (both providers of purchase money) in equity. Under a resulting trust, each would have an equitable interest in the house proportionate to their contributions; thus, the man, who provided two-thirds of the purchase money, gains an interest equal to two-thirds of the value of the house. In a resulting trust, 'you get what you pay for'.*

In *Curley v Parkes* [2004] All ER (D) 344, the Court of Appeal considered what payments gave rise to the presumption of resulting trust. The court determined that the payment must be of part of the purchase price (not, say, for legal fees or tax associated with the transaction) and it must be made at the time of the initial purchase. Payment of the whole or part of a deposit or any other contribution to the purchase price at the time of the purchase will qualify. Many house purchases are funded by a mortgage loan which is gradually repaid in monthly instalments; payment of mortgage instalments and other outgoings *after* the date of the purchase will not give rise to a resulting trust.

The courts are moving away from using resulting trusts as a means of determining the shares of cohabitees in the home. Working out the share of a claimant under a resulting trust is a mathematical exercise based solely on the claimant's financial contribution at the time the property was originally purchased. In *Stack v Dowden* [2007] UKHL 17, Baroness Hale said:

> In law 'context is everything' and the domestic context is very different from the commercial world. Each case will turn on its own facts. Many more factors than financial contributions may be relevant to divining the parties' true intentions.

For this reason, recent cases involving cohabitants have been decided on the basis of constructive trusts, which allow more flexibility when determining the extent of the parties' respective shares in the property. Constructive trusts are dealt with later in **6.3**.

Resulting trusts still have a part to play where the parties buy the property as an investment rather than as a home for themselves as a couple (see *Laskar v Laskar* [2008] 1 WLR 2695, where a mother and daughter contributed to the purchase of a house which was then let to tenants).

However, recently, the Privy Council has suggested that where a property is bought as an investment, the parties can always have their own intention as to how the beneficial ownership is to be shared irrespective of their actual contributions. If there is evidence of that intention, 'it would be wrong to impose the resulting trust solution on the subsequent distribution of the property' (Baroness Hale in *Marr v Collie* [2017] UKPC 17).

### 6.2.3 Presumption of advancement

The presumption of resulting trust does not apply to all voluntary transfers and contribution to purchase cases. The presumption of resulting trust is displaced when the parties are closely related and a counter presumption arises. The presumption of advancement will apply where the person making the voluntary transfer or providing the purchase money is regarded as being under an obligation to provide for the other party (or, rather, was so regarded in the mid-19th century). In other words, where X is under an obligation to provide for Y, there is a presumption that X intended a gift to Y.

The presumption of advancement applies in limited situations:

(a) *Father to child* – a father makes a voluntary transfer or purchases property in the name of his child (*Bennet v Bennet* (1879) 10 Ch D 474). The child can be an infant or an adult but must have been born to parents who were married to each other.

(b) *Loco parentis* – a person *in loco parentis* makes a voluntary transfer or purchases property in the name of the child to whom they are *in loco parentis* (*Bennet v Bennet*). A person is *in loco parentis* if they have taken on a father's responsibility to provide financially for the child during their infancy.

(c) *Husband to wife* – a husband makes a voluntary transfer or purchases property in the name of his wife (*Pettitt v Pettitt* [1970] AC 777).

(d) *Fiancé to Fiancée* – a fiancé makes a voluntary transfer or purchases property in the name of his fiancée and the marriage is concluded.

The presumption of advancement is clearly outdated in that it does not apply as between mothers and children (as in *Sekhon v Alissa* [1989] 2 FLR 94), wives and husbands (as in *Abrahams v Trustee in Bankruptcy of Abrahams* discussed earlier) or between cohabitees or civil partners.

More recently, there has been some judicial comment that a mother could, in certain circumstances, be taken to be *in loco parentis* (*Re Cameron (Deceased)* [1999] Ch 386). So a widowed mother or single parent with financial responsibility for the child in infancy might be regarded as *in loco parentis*, which would give rise to the presumption of advancement.

Section 199 of the Equality Act 2010 will abolish the presumption of advancement from a date to be appointed. The abolition will apply only to transactions after that appointment date. The presumption will, therefore, still apply to transactions made before that appointment date. However, s 199 has not yet been brought into effect and there is no indication that this will happen anytime soon. At the time of writing, s 199 has no effect and the courts are free to decide cases deploying the presumption of advancement where it applies.

### 6.2.4 Evidence to rebut the presumption

It is important to remember that both the presumptions (resulting trust and advancement) are a starting point for the court. They are rules of evidence, capable of being rebutted if the transferor held a contrary intention. The presumptions prevail only in the absence of facts to the contrary.

Surrounding circumstances existing at the time of the transaction might well suggest the appropriate presumption should be rebutted. Evidence that a gift or a loan was intended would tend to rebut a presumption of resulting trust. For instance, a transfer of shares from a wife to husband at the time of his birthday would likely rebut any resulting trust.

Evidence that the transferor intended to retain some power over the property would tend to suggest a resulting trust. In *Warren v Gurney* [1944] 2 All ER 472, a father purchased a house in his daughter's name at the time of her wedding. The obvious inference would be that it was a gift. But the father retained the title deeds until his death, and there was evidence that the father intended his son-in-law to repay the cost of the house. A resulting trust was evidenced.

Evidence of statements made at the time of a purchase can be sufficient to rebut the presumption of resulting trust (as in *Loosemore v McDonnell* [2007] EWCA Civ 1531).

There is more likely to be a resulting trust if the parties to the transfer are strangers rather than family members. In *Fowkes v Pascoe* (1875) 10 Ch App 343, it was suggested *obiter* that you would expect a resulting trust rather than a gift when property is put into a solicitor's name.

Evidence of the surrounding circumstances at the time of the transaction may point to a particular intention. For instance, an explanation for the property being put into the transferee's name could exclude a presumption of advancement.

***McGrath v Wallis* [1995] 2 FLR 114**

A father (who was unemployed at the time) and son both provided some of the purchase money to buy a house. The house was conveyed into the son's name alone at the request of the mortgage provider, who did not lend to people of the father's age. When the father died, the son claimed that the father's contribution to the purchase price was a gift to him by reason of the presumption of advancement. This was rejected. The reason for the house being in the son's sole name was a technicality; it was not a gift, and so the presumption of advancement was rebutted.

The presumption between father and child is, generally, felt to be a weak presumption. In *McGrath v Wallis* it was described as a 'judicial instrument of last resort'. The presumption can be rebutted by slight evidence, especially when the child is over 18 and financially independent. It would carry the day only if there was no other evidence (as in *Kelly v Kelly* [2020] 3 WLUK 94 where, despite the son's questionable behaviour, the father was not able to rebut the presumption of advancement as the court found no viable evidence to support his argument that a loan was intended).

If there is evidence to rebut a presumption, it is necessary to consider whether it is admissible in court. Generally, the evidence presented to a court should point to intention at the time of the voluntary transfer or purchase. Subsequent acts are relevant only if they throw light on that original intention. More crucially, evidence of an act effected after the transfer or purchase may not be admissible.

Claimants attempting to rebut the relevant presumption may produce in evidence only acts done, and statements made at, or before, the time of the transactions, not subsequent self-justifying statements or acts. In *Shephard v Cartwright* [1955] AC 431, it was said:

> The acts and declarations of the parties before or at the time of the purchase, or so immediately afterward as to constitute part of the transaction, are admissible in evidence either for or against the party who did the acts or made the declaration ... But subsequent declarations are admissible only against the party who made them, and not in his favour.

What this means is that acts and declarations before the voluntary transfer/purchase or so immediately after it as to be part of the same transaction are admissible either for or against the party who did the act or made the declaration. However, evidence of acts and declarations after the voluntary transfer/purchase are admissible only against the party who did the act or made the declaration. If this were not the case, it would be easy for the parties to make up their own evidence after the event.

> ***Example***
>
> *Kirit purchased some shares in the name of his son, Anwar. Kirit informed Anwar about the purchase but gave no reason why the shares were put into Anwar's name. Six months later, Kirit executed a will leaving all the shares to his wife, Samya. Kirit recently died and Samya is claiming the shares.*
>
> *For Samya to be able to claim the shares, she (now that Kirit has died) will have the evidential burden to rebut the presumption of advancement which arose when the shares were purchased. The will suggests that Kirit intended a resulting trust as he believed he still owned them. However, the will was executed a significant time after the purchase of the shares. Thus, under Shephard v Cartwright, Kirit could not have used evidence of his will to rebut the presumption as the execution of the will was after the event and in his favour. His personal representatives and Samya are similarly barred from using this evidence. In the absence of any other evidence, the presumption of advancement would not be rebutted so Anwar retains the shares.*

**Figure 6.2** Summary of the operation of presumptions

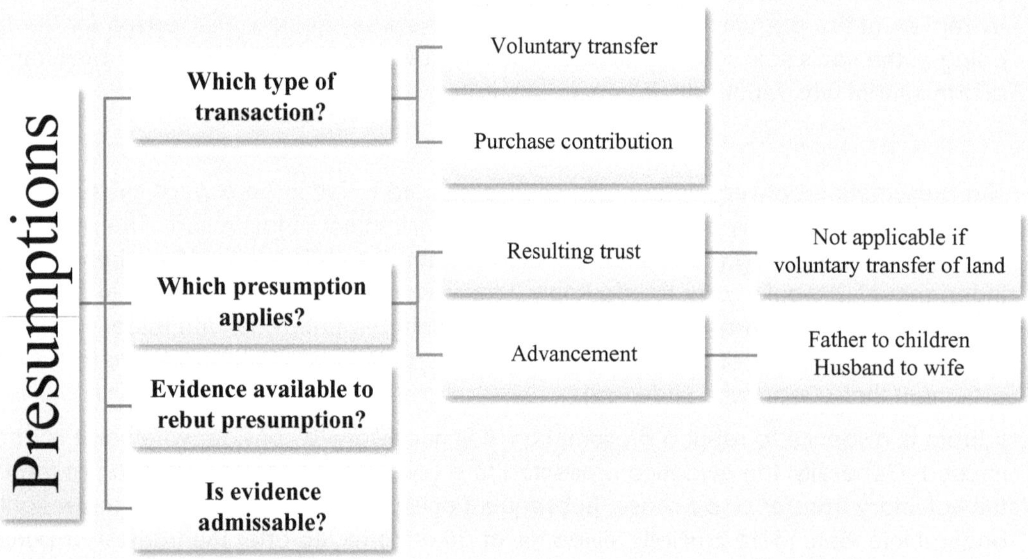


## 6.3 Constructive trusts – the family home

Constructive trusts arise by operation of law. Unlike express trusts, they do not come into being as a result of the deliberate act of a settlor and, in contrast to resulting trusts, they are not necessarily the product of implied intention. In *Paragon Finance v DB Thakerer & Co* [1999] 1 All ER 400 at 409, Lord Millett said:

> [A] constructive trust arises by operation of law whenever the circumstances are such that it would be unconscionable for the owner of property (usually but not necessarily the legal estate) to assert his beneficial interest in the property.

One of the areas where the constructive trust plays a vital role is in property disputes, in particular when determining ownership of the family home. The family home will have been purchased, usually with the assistance of a mortgage, by the parties to the relationship. There are, of course, many varied situations. The parties may be married or in a civil partnership, or not. The legal title may be invested in one or both. Only one may have contributed to the purchase of the home. If only one party contributed, was it agreed, expressly or implicitly, that the other was to own a proportion of the home by virtue of their contribution in other ways to the family?

These are questions which affect many couples at different times in their relationship. Where the parties are married or in a civil partnership, a dispute may arise when the marriage or civil partnership breaks up. Here, the court has wide powers to make property adjustment orders under the divorce/annulment/dissolution legislation. However, when non-married or unregistered cohabitees split up, the court must decide the ownership by reference to the law of trusts.

Alternatively, in both circumstances, sometimes there is a lender who has a charge over the property vested in one party as sole legal title holder, and a spouse/civil partner/cohabitee is arguing that they have an equitable interest unaffected by the charge, by virtue of these same trust law principles.

### 6.3.1 Legal ownership in both names

Here, the parties have purchased the home in their joint names. The legal title must be held as joint tenants. What of the beneficial (equitable) interests? There may be an express declaration of trust which, to be enforceable, must be evidenced in writing to satisfy s 53(1)(b) of the Law of Property Act 1925. If the parties hold as tenants in common, their respective proportions will inevitably be stated. This is conclusive in the absence of fraud or mistake. If the equitable interests are expressed to be held as joint tenants, again, in the absence of fraud or mistake, this is conclusive; the parties will have equal shares in the sale proceeds if the property is sold.

In *Stack v Dowden* [2007] 2 AC 432, the House of Lords considered the position where the trusts were not expressly stated. The majority held as follows:

> Where a domestic property was conveyed into the joint names of cohabitants without any declaration of trust there was a prima facie case that both the legal and beneficial interests in the property were joint and equal; that the onus of proof lay upon any party seeking to establish that equity should not follow the law; that such a party had to prove that the parties had held a common intention that their beneficial interests be different from their legal interests.

In order to determine the parties' common intention, the court said that there needed to be consideration of the parties' 'whole course of conduct in relation to the property'; many more factors may be relevant here beyond respective financial contributions. The court considered that cases where the joint legal owners would be found to have intended that their beneficial interests should be different from their legal interests would be very unusual.

In this particular case, there were unusual circumstances. The parties had kept their respective finances separate over a period of 20 years. There was no indication that they had intended any pooling of their resources. It was held that the defendant was able to show that there was a common intention that the parties should not own the family home equally.

The approach taken by the House of Lords in *Stack v Dowden* was affirmed by the Supreme Court in another joint legal ownership case, *Jones v Kernott* [2011] UKSC 53. It was also held that, coupled with a common intention that the beneficial interests were to be other than equal, there must also have been detrimental reliance by the claimant on that intention of different beneficial interests. Recently the Court of Appeal has confirmed that in joint name cases, 'detrimental reliance remains a key component' to the unconscionability necessary to establish a constructive trust giving rise to something other than equal shares (*Hudson v Hathway* [2022] EWCA Civ 1648).

### 6.3.2 Legal estate in the name of one party only

In the absence of written evidence of an express declaration of trust as to beneficial ownership, there is a presumption that a sole legal owner of a property also owns the entire equitable interest (*Stack v Dowden*). A claimant who asserts that they have an equitable interest has various options as set out below.

Where the claimant has made direct contributions to the purchase of the property registered in the name of a sole legal owner, the claimant acquires an equitable interest under a resulting trust (assuming that the presumption of advancement does not apply). The size of the equitable interest reflects the proportion of purchase price contributed (**6.2.2.2**).

Because of the perceived rigidity of determining the size of any equitable interest under resulting trust principles, in *Stack v Dowden* and *Jones v Kernott* [2012] 1 AC 776, it was held that constructive trusts are more appropriate to determine the equitable interests of cohabitees in a property purchased as their home, in particular a *common intention constructive trust.*

However, it was accepted, in both *Stack* and *Kernott*, that the claimant in sole legal name cases has a difficult task. In joint name cases, the trust has already arisen; the court is merely being asked to quantify the beneficial interest. In sole name cases, the first issue for the court is to consider whether the claimant has an equitable interest at all.

Early considerations of the common intention constructive trust (such as in the pre- Matrimonial Causes Act 1973 divorce cases, *Pettit v Pettit* [1970] AC 777 and *Gissing v Gissing* [1971] AC 886) indicated that to establish a beneficial interest under such a trust, the claimant needed to evidence that:

(a) there was a common intention between the parties that both were to have an interest (ie that the sole legal owner holds on trust for them both); and

(b) the claimant acted to their detriment relying on that common intention.

In both *Pettit* and *Gissing* the claimants failed to establish the trust (*Pettit* because of a lack of evidence of a common intention, *Gissing* because of lack of detrimental reliance). Questions arose about how a claimant might be able to evidence a common intention and what actions amounted to detriment.

The House of Lords case of *Lloyds Bank v Rosset* [1991] 1 AC 107 subsequently provided answers to these questions. The case itself was not a divorce matter. Rather, the family home was in the husband's sole name, and he had charged the house to the bank as security for an overdraft to fund renovations. When the husband defaulted on the loan, his wife claimed the existence of a constructive trust and her beneficial interest to prevent the bank's sale. She failed because she could not show a common intention between the two of them that both should have an interest. Her actions (supervision of builders during the renovations and some decorating) were not sufficient to infer an intention that she was to have an interest in the property.

However, in his judgment in *Rosset*, Lord Bridge fully outlined the requirements to evidence the common intention constructive trust. There were suggestions in *Stack v Dowden* that Lord Bridge's approach in 1990 may be outdated (Lord Walker said that 'the law has moved on', a comment approved by Baroness Hale in the Privy Council case of *Abbott v Abbott* [2007] UKPC 53). However, Lord Walker's observations were *obiter* as *Stack v Dowden* was not a case of a sole legal owner and *Abbott* is not binding as it is a Privy Council case. Numerous, subsequent Court of Appeal cases (for instance, *Morris v Morris* [2008] EWCA 257 and *James v Thomas* [2007] EWCA Civ 1212) suggest that Lord Bridge's approach is still to be used in cases where the legal title is in the sole name of one party.

In *Rosset*, Lord Bridge confirmed that two criteria must be present to establish a common intention constructive trust where the legal title is held by one party:

(1) the common intention of the parties to share ownership of the land; and

(2) the party claiming an equitable interest by way of constructive trust showing that they acted to their detriment in reliance on the common intention.

Lord Bridge also outlined that there were two ways in which the trust could arise.

#### 6.3.2.1 Express common intention constructive trust

This trust will exist where an agreement, arrangement or understanding was reached between the parties at the time the property was purchased (or exceptionally later) that the property was to be shared between them. Lord Bridge gave examples of cases where such an arrangement had been evidenced – *Eves v Eves* [1975] 1 WLR 1338, where discussions as to the claimant's age preventing her from having a share in the property were evidence of a common intention, and *Grant v Edwards* [1986] Ch 638, where the Court of Appeal decided that there was an express common intention as the legal owner had told the claimant that her name would have been on the legal title but for the fact that it might prejudice her divorce proceedings.

In *Curran v Collins* [2015] EWCA Civ 404, the Court of Appeal observed that the giving of a specious excuse why the claimant's name is not on the title does not necessarily constitute an express common intention that the claimant has an equitable interest. Curran lost her claim as it was held that his 'excuse' (joint names would require expensive life assurance policies) did not indicate a common intention that Curran had an equitable interest.

In addition to establishing the common intention, the claimant would have to evidence that they acted to their detriment in reliance on the common intention. Lord Bridge said this meant that the claimant had to show that they had 'significantly altered [their] position in reliance on the agreement'. In *Grant v Edwards*, the claimant's substantial contribution to household expenses (other than the mortgage) and bringing up the children were held to amount to sufficient detriment. Nourse LJ said detriment comprised 'conduct on which the woman could not reasonably be expected to embark unless she was to have an interest in the house'. Browne-Wilkinson VC took a more liberal view saying, 'any act done by her to her detriment relating to the joint lives of the parties is, in my judgment, sufficient detriment to qualify. The acts do not have to be referable to the house.' However, it is important that any act of detriment is in reliance on the common intention, and not something that would have been undertaken regardless of any intention about shared ownership.

As with cases involving disputes between joint legal owners, in a claim against the sole legal owner it has been stressed that:

> detrimental reliance remains an essential ingredient of a successful claim to a beneficial interest in a residential property under a common intention constructive trust.

Henderson LJ in *O'Neill v Holland* [2020] EWCA Civ 1583 went on to indicate that what constitutes detriment is to be objectively determined.

#### 6.3.2.2 Inferred common intention constructive trust

If there is no evidence of express common intention, the court will infer a common intention from direct monetary contributions to the purchase, such as contributions to the purchase price or deposit at the time of the acquisition or subsequently to mortgage repayments. Lord Bridge controversially said that 'it is extremely doubtful whether anything less will do'. Consequently, it was thought that subsequent monetary contributions other than to the mortgage, such as the payment of household expenses, would not lead the court to infer a common intention to share ownership of the house.

However, payment of household expenses might be regarded as an indirect contribution to the purchase price if the payments are substantial and are made pursuant to an agreement that the parties will share the mortgage and expenses equally, with one paying the mortgage and the other paying the general household expenses. In another claim by a wife against a lender (and her husband in divorce proceedings), *Le Foe v Le Foe and Woolwich plc* [2001] 2 FLR 970, there was an express agreement between the parties that one should pay the mortgage and certain outgoings, and the other should meet all the other (substantial) household expenses to enable the mortgage to be paid. It was 'an arbitrary allocation of responsibility' that the husband paid the mortgage and the wife the domestic expenditure. Accordingly Nicholas Mostyn QC as deputy High Court judge felt able to infer a common intention trust. He drew support from previous cases which were not cited in *Rosset*. This view was supported (*obiter*) by the House of Lords in *Stack v Dowden* and the Privy Council in *Abbott v Abbott*.

It is accepted that non-financial acts such as looking after the family or actions having no connection to the acquisition of the land will not lead to the inference of a common intention to share ownership.

As far as detrimental reliance is concerned, the financial contributions to the purchase are likely to suffice.

#### 6.3.2.3 Quantification of the beneficial interest

If the equitable interest under a constructive trust is established (whether expressly or by inference), the court then has to consider how to quantify that interest.

A leading earlier case on quantification of the equitable interest under a constructive trust is *Midland Bank v Cooke* [1995] 4 All ER 562. The Court of Appeal held that a mathematical calculation, based on the proportion of the purchase price contributed (as used in determining the size of an equitable interest under a resulting trust), is not the correct approach. Once the claimant has established a constructive trust, the court will then look at the whole course of dealing between the parties to ascertain what shares were intended. It will consider all factors, including indirect contributions.

In *Stack v Dowden* [2007] 2 AC 432, the House of Lords considered this issue further. As discussed earlier, the starting presumption will be that the beneficial interest will reflect the legal position – joint legal owners will be entitled to a 50% share. However, the presumption can be displaced, and the size of each party's share will be what was said or agreed at the time the property was acquired. If there is no evidence of any such agreement or discussion, each will be entitled to that share which the court considers the parties intended each to own, having regard to the whole course of dealing between them in relation to the property. In considering that course of dealing, the court will consider advice and discussions at the time of the purchase, the purpose for which the house was acquired and the nature of the relationship, the presence of children, whether resources were pooled, contributions to mortgage payments, payment of outgoings such as council tax and utilities, repairs, insurance and payment for improvements. Looking at the 'whole course of dealing' in the circumstances of the *Stack v Dowden* case, it was decided that the equitable ownership should be 60:40 in Stack's favour.

In *Jones v Kernott* [2011] UKSC 53, the Supreme Court considered the correct approach to quantification further. The majority held that if it was not possible to ascertain what shares the parties intended by direct evidence or by inference, then each party would be entitled to the share which the court considered to be fair having regard to the whole course of dealing. The 'whole course of dealing' encompassed not only financial contributions but also the other factors considered to be relevant evidence in *Stack v Dowden*. It was also accepted that an initial agreement as to the shares in which the beneficial interest was held could change over time.

***Gallarotti v Sebastianelli* [2012] EWCA Civ 865**

Two friends decided to buy a flat together. The flat was purchased in the sole name of S. Both parties made cash contributions to the initial purchase price (with S providing the largest contribution) and the rest of the purchase price was raised by a mortgage in S's name. They agreed that they would each have a 50% share in the flat, but when they realised that their contributions were unequal, they agreed that G would pay a larger share of the mortgage repayments. In fact, G did not pay a larger share of the mortgage.

The Court of Appeal inferred that the original 50:50 sharing agreement ended and was replaced by an inferred agreement that their beneficial ownership should reflect their financial contributions. It was implausible to suggest that S would have wanted to make a substantial gift to G when they were two flat sharers who were not a family unit but for convenience lived together until they established their own homes.

## 6.4 Constructive trusts - commercial setting

The term 'constructive trust' has been used to describe a diverse range of situations. It is difficult to find a single unifying concept to connect these circumstances, other than to prevent unconscionable behaviour. Consequently, the concept of the constructive trust has been used with great flexibility by the courts. Until now the constructive trust has been considered in a private context of family property. By way of comparison, it will now be considered in an alternative, commercial setting.

What is known as a *Pallant v Morgan* equity (from the case of the same name, [1953] Ch 43) will be invoked where the defendant has acquired property in circumstances where it would be inequitable to allow them to treat it as their own. For the equity to arise:

(1) There has to be a pre-acquisition arrangement or understanding that one party (Y) will try to buy property and that if they succeed, the other party (X) will obtain some interest in it. When the property is acquired, X believes that the arrangement still holds good. It is this pre-acquisition arrangement which impacts the subsequent acquisition by the defendant (Y) and leads to them being treated as a trustee if they seek to act in conflict with it.

(2) It is not necessary for the arrangement or understanding to be contractually enforceable (an enforceable contract would render the equity redundant as the aggrieved party could obtain remedy elsewhere).

(3) Further, it is necessary that (whatever private reservations Y may have) they have not informed X before the acquisition (or, perhaps more accurately, before it is too late for the parties to be restored to a position of no advantage/no detriment) that they no longer intend to honour the arrangement or understanding.

(4) The claimant (X) should have done something or refrained from doing something in reliance on the agreement and that act or omission confers a benefit on Y or is detrimental to X's ability to acquire the property. It is the existence of the advantage to the one, or the detriment to the other, gained or suffered as a consequence of the arrangement or understanding, which leads to the conclusion that it would be inequitable or unconscionable to allow Y to retain the property for themselves, in a manner inconsistent with the arrangement or understanding which enabled them to acquire it.

***Banner Homes Group v Luff Developments Ltd* [2000] Ch 372**

Two development companies ('L' and 'B') agreed in principle that they would form a joint venture to develop a site by means of a jointly owned company. There was no contract between the parties. A company (Stowhelm Ltd) was bought off the shelf and was wholly owned by L. L had reservations about proceeding with the joint venture but did not inform B about these reservations. B stayed out of the market to purchase the site, relying on the understanding that the development would be a joint enterprise. L then bought the site alone and told B it no longer wished to continue jointly. B claimed a constructive trust in its favour. The Court of Appeal agreed that the requirements for the *Pallant v Morgan* type of equity were present. First, there was a clear arrangement that L should acquire a property and that B should have an interest in it. Secondly, B had acted in reliance on that arrangement to its detriment because B had kept out of the market and had not bid for the property. At the same time, this decision not to compete for the purchase of the site conferred an advantage on L because it thereby acquired the site more cheaply. (However, it was held that it was not necessary to prove both detriment to one party and advantage to the other; one or other will suffice.)

In cases involving family homes, the parties are less likely to express their intentions and protect their rights formally. In commercial ventures, however, the parties often do not intend to be bound unless they enter into a formal contract. Until this point is reached, the parties want to be free to withdraw. There was no contract between Banner and Luff; this is why the question of a constructive trust arose. Yet Luff was bound by the parties' informal arrangement. Unlike a contract, it is unclear at what point in their dealings the parties will be bound by a constructive trust. Arguably this introduces another potential level of uncertainty into the world of commerce.

## 6.5 Proprietary estoppel

An equitable interest can be created without the usual formalities by means of a constructive or resulting trust. The doctrine of proprietary estoppel is another method by which a person may become entitled to an equitable interest in property in the absence of appropriate formalities. Despite its name, proprietary estoppel applies to personalty as well as land.

For example, in *Pascoe v Turner* [1979] 1 WLR 431, the legal owner of a house had repeatedly told his unmarried partner that the house was hers. He was estopped from denying her an interest in the house after she had made improvements, repairs and decoration in reliance on his assurances. The legal owner had stood by and acquiesced in her doing the work and spending what amounted to a few hundred pounds. Contrary to s 53(1)(b) of the Law of Property Act 1925, there was no written evidence of a declaration of trust in her favour; nevertheless equity would not allow him to deny his assurances when he had allowed the claimant to act to her detriment.

The doctrine of estoppel is generally used as a shield not a sword. In other words, it can be used only as a defence to a claim brought by another. Proprietary estoppel is the exception; it can be used as a cause of action. However, it is not a remedy in itself. It raises an 'estoppel equity'; the court then decides which remedy will satisfy that equity. In other words, there are two stages: first, consider whether the proprietary estoppel equity has been established; and, secondly, decide which remedy will satisfy the equity.

### 6.5.1 Establishing the equity

The legal owner must have behaved in such a way that the claimant believes they have, or will get at some point in the future, some rights in relation to the property (the 'expectation'), and the claimant has acted to their detriment in consequence of this belief, such that it would be unconscionable for the legal owner to insist on their strict legal ownership.

The behaviour may take the form of an active or a passive assurance. An example of an active assurance would be *Pascoe v Turner*, referred to above. In *Inwards v Baker* [1965] 2 QB 29, a father persuaded his son to build a bungalow on the father's land. It was then unconscionable for the father to claim that as the bungalow was on his land, it belonged to him.

A passive assurance occurs where the legal owner stands back and lets the claimant act to their detriment in the belief that they are entitled to an interest in the property.

The assurance might relate to future rights in property. In *Gillett v Holt* [2001] Ch 210, G worked for H, a gentleman farmer for nearly 40 years. G worked for little pay. He incurred expenditure on the farmhouse. As Robert Walker LJ stated: 'Mr G and his wife devoted the best years of their lives working for Mr H.' They went far beyond the usual extent of an employee's duties and G refused offers of alternative employment. Why? Because H repeatedly assured G that he would leave his entire estate to him.

*Thorner v Major* [2009] 3 All ER 945 was another case of a claimant who worked for many years for a farmer, this time for no pay. Various oblique remarks were made by the farmer which led the claimant at first to hope and later to expect that he would inherit the farm on the farmer's death. Unlike in *Gillett v Holt*, however, the farmer was a man of few words who never stated that he intended the claimant to inherit the farm. The House of Lords, however, did find there was sufficient evidence for such an assurance to be established with sufficient clarity.

Lord Neuberger formulated the test as follows:

> [T]he authorities ... support the proposition that, at least normally, it is sufficient for the person invoking the estoppel to establish that he reasonably understood the statement or action to be an assurance on which he could rely.

The claimant must act to their detriment in reliance on the assurance. There must be a causal connection between the assurance and the detriment. The promises relied on do not have to be the sole reason for the claimant acting to their detriment but must be a reason. The onus is on the claimant to show the causal connection as a matter of fact.

Detriment can take many forms. Financial and personal detriment was evidenced in *Gillett v Holt*, improving the legal owner's land in *Inwards v Baker*. In *Greasley v Cooke* [1980] 1 WLR 1306, the claimant established sufficient detriment with evidence that she had looked after the family including a mentally ill member. In *Gillett v Holt*, Robert Walker LJ said that detriment did not have to be financial so long as it is something substantial. The proper approach was to treat detriment as part of a broad inquiry as to whether repudiation of the assurance was unconscionable.

However, the detriment must be undertaken in reliance on the assurance.

***Re Basham* [1986] 1 WLR 1498**

The claimant looked after the deceased, her stepfather, in reliance on his assurance that she would inherit the house he lived in, paid for by the claimant's mother. In the case, the judge detailed the claimant's acts which she 'might not have done but for [the] expectation of inheriting the deceased's property':

- refraining from selling her own land;
- not taking a job elsewhere in the country which would have made it impossible to continue the care of the deceased;

- instructing solicitors at her own expense in connection with the boundary dispute between the deceased and his neighbour;
- expenditure of time and money on the house and garden and on carpeting the house, when the deceased had ample means of his own to pay for such matters.

It was the cumulative effect of these acts which supported the judge's view that the claimant had gone well beyond normal family moral duties, well beyond 'what was called for by natural love and affection' for someone to whom the claimant had no blood relationship.

Once it is shown that the defendant intended the claimant to act on any assurance, there is a presumption of reliance. The burden would lie with the defendant (or their personal representatives) to show that the claimant would have carried out the detrimental acts anyway (*Greasley v Cooke*).

In *Gillett v Holt,* Robert Walker LJ said that the doctrine of proprietary estoppel cannot be neatly subdivided into three or four watertight compartments. The assurance or encouragement, reliance and detriment are all intertwined. *Thorner v Major* confirmed that the court should ask the broader question of whether it is unconscionable to deny the claimant what was promised or understood. If assurance or encouragement, reliance and detriment are present, then it is usually unconscionable to deny the claimant what was promised.

Many claims for proprietary estoppel are made after the death of the legal owner, when it becomes clear that a promise to leave property by will has not been kept. Wills are by their nature revocable. The courts will not issue injunctions to prevent testators changing their wills. However, a number of recent claims have been made seeking to establish the estoppel while a testator is still alive - for instance in *Gillet v Holt,* Mr Gillett brought a claim to establish his interest in the farm only after Holt sought to change his will disinheriting him. More recently, *Davies v Davies* [2016] EWCA Civ 463 and *Guest v Guest* [2022] UKSC 27 involved children challenging the decisions of their parents to disinherit them after family and business disagreements. The effect of being able to establish an estoppel might be seen as a powerful means of allowing a claimant to override the long-held principle of testamentary freedom as to the disposal of assets on death.

### 6.5.2 Satisfying the equity

The essence of the doctrine of proprietary estoppel is to do what is necessary to avoid an unconscionable result. What this means depends on the facts of each case.

***Jennings v Rice*** **[2003] 1 FCR 501**

Here the estoppel was established; the issue was the extent of the relief to be awarded.

Robert Walker LJ considered there would be cases where the claimant and defendant have reached a 'mutual bargain'; the expectation was clear and was roughly equivalent to the detriment. Here the court would fulfil the expectation. However, he went on to say that in cases where the claimant's expectations are uncertain, or are not focused on specific property, or do not reflect the defendant's assurances, or bear no relation to the amount of detriment. the 'court may take the claimant's expectations as a starting point but will also take account of other factors'. These other factors included:

(i) the extent of the detrimental reliance;

(ii) any unconscionability, including misconduct by the claimant as well as by the defendant;

(iii) any alteration in the defendant's finances;

(iv) financial obligations owed by the defendant to others;

(v) the effect of taxation;

(vi) any benefits the claimant has derived from the situation, such as rent-free accommodation;

(vii) whether the proposed remedy is practical (for instance, the court will not try to compel people to live together when this is the last thing they would want to do);

(viii) proportionality - the remedy to the detriment suffered.

The remedy should be the 'minimum to satisfy the equity', that is, to award the appropriate minimum remedy to do justice.

In this case, the expectation was a generous legacy - all or part of an estate which was valued at more than £1.2 million. At first instance (and upheld by the Court of Appeal) the expectation was found to be out of all proportion to the detriment suffered (work and care provided for no payment). The court, therefore, awarded compensation equivalent to the cost of full-time nursing care for the time the claimant had looked after the deceased.

In *Joyce v Epsom and Ewell BC* [2012] EWCA Civ 1398, Davies LJ modified the approach. He said that 'the overall focus has to be on what is fair and proportionate as between the parties'.

It is, therefore, for the court to determine the appropriate remedy to award to satisfy the equity. In *Gillett v Holt*, the court ordered Holt's estate to transfer the farm to Gillett to fulfil the assurance. A similar order was made in *Thorner v Major*. However, the court has also awarded other types of interest in property. For example, in cases where the expectation is a home for life, the court has awarded a long lease terminable on the claimant's death, or a life interest. In other cases the courts have given claimants an equitable interest in property under a constructive trust.

However, the court has also awarded monetary compensation rather than a proprietary interest to satisfy the estoppel. In *Southwell v Blackburn* [2014] EWCA Civ 1347, the claimant was awarded a monetary sum to reflect the investment lost in giving up her secured tenancy and her relocation costs when moving in with the defendant (but received nothing to reflect her mortgage and household expense contributions during her 10-year occupancy).

The claimant in *Davies v Davies* [2016] EWCA Civ 463 (widely reported in the press as the so-called 'Cowshed Cinderella') had an initial expectation that she would inherit her parents' farming business in return for her work on the farm for no wages (but receiving board and lodging and money for clothes and leisure). On appeal, she was awarded £500,000 reflecting compensation for what she had failed to receive when not a partner or shareholder in the farm business rather than a share of the farming business outright.

There have been differing academic and judicial opinions as to whether what is a 'fair and proportionate' remedy means giving effect to the claimant's expectations in light of the assurances given or whether it is to compensate the claimant's detrimental reliance. In *Davies v Davies*, Lewison LJ commented, albeit *obiter*, that if the detriment could be compensated by a monetary award, this would remove the basis of the claim. However, he agreed with the argument that 'the [claimant's] expectation is likely to be the starting point and that there might be a sliding scale - the clearer the expectation, the greater the detriment, and the longer the passage of time during which the expectation was reasonably held, the greater weight would be given to the expectation'.

More recently, the Supreme Court was asked to visit the debate (*Guest v Guest* [2022] UKSC 27). In another case involving a dispute about the inheritance of the family farm, as it had been accepted that the estoppel had been established, the court was merely addressing what would be a fair remedy for the son in view of the fact that both his parents were still living, and the son was in effect receiving what he had been promised (an inheritance) early. The Court of Appeal had awarded the son monetary compensation which the parents could only settle by selling the farm.

The Supreme Court's majority conclusion, given by Lord Briggs, was that if the estoppel has been established, the starting point for the remedy would be to enforce the promise, giving effect to the expectation rather than compensating the detriment. However, there may be instances which would justify departing from this starting premise, awarding something other than full performance - for instance practical issues which would arise from performance of the promise (for instance, forced cohabitation between disputing parties), the nature of the promise not being clearly defined, or the remedy being out of all proportion to the detriment suffered. It was necessary to identify the remedy which satisfactorily addressed the unconscionability suffered by the claimant but with the least prejudice to the defendant and any third parties and taking account of any early receipt.

## 6.6 Comparing constructive trusts and proprietary estoppel

There is considerable overlap between constructive trusts and proprietary estoppel. The similarities were recognised in *Lloyds Bank v Rosset* [1991] 1 AC 107. In *Yaxley v Gotts* [2000] 1 All ER 711, a builder had refurbished and converted a house into flats on the basis of an oral agreement with the owner that he would acquire the ground floor flat for himself. The Court of Appeal decided that the builder was entitled to an interest by proprietary estoppel but that the facts would alternatively create an interest under a common intention constructive trust.

That being said there are differences between the two and they remain separate claims which can be made to achieve an interest in property.

Constructive trusts are based on the common intention of both parties to share ownership, whereas proprietary estoppel stems from reliance on an assurance given by the legal owner as to some kind of property interest (either now or in the future).

Detriment is an essential element of constructive trusts as well as proprietary estoppel. However, the detriment required is different; in the context of proprietary estoppel, there is a much greater willingness to accept non-financial acts such as caring for an elderly person, giving up a secure tenancy or giving up job opportunities (provided they were done in reliance on the assurance and were not acts which the claimant would have done anyway).

With proprietary estoppel, the courts have a discretion over the remedy to award. This may be a trust interest, but it could also be monetary compensation or a right to occupy. However, if a constructive trust is established, the only remedy is a beneficial interest under that trust.

Also, as proprietary estoppel is an equitable remedy, claimants may be impacted by two of the equitable maxims discussed in **Chapter 1**. A party who fails to claim their estoppel rights within a reasonable time may find themselves without any remedy on the basis of 'delay defeats equity' (**1.3.4**). Similarly, a claimant who has acted in some way unconscionably (ie with dishonesty or fraud) will be denied equitable relief on the basis of 'whoever comes to equity must come with clean hands' (**1.3.2**).

**Figure 6.3** Summary – considering implied trusts and the family home

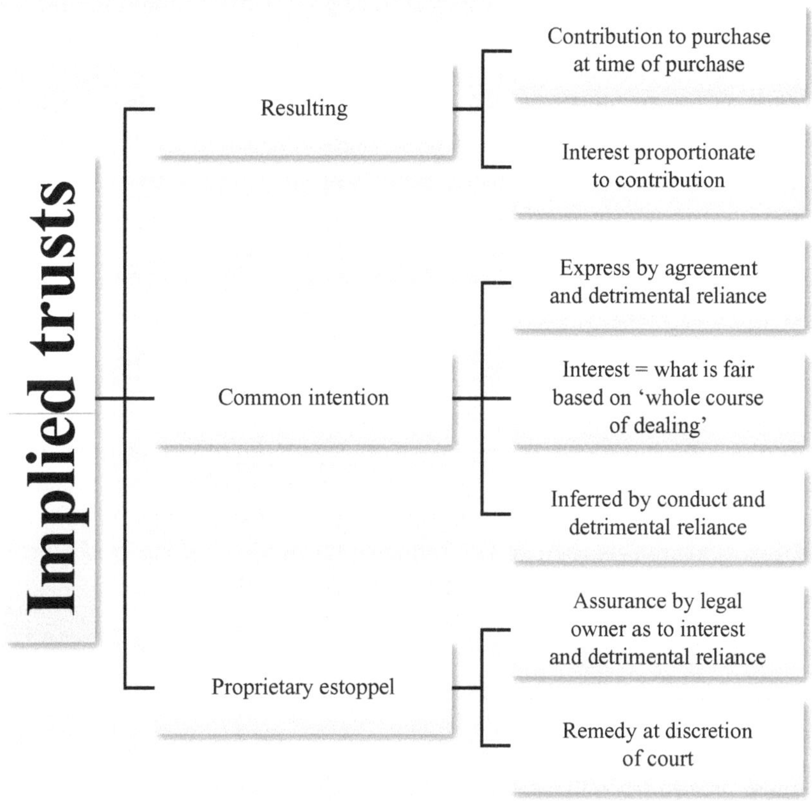


## 6.7 Using implied trusts

Lawyers tend to like structure and certainty. They want to give clients clear, reasoned legal advice and arrive at obvious and unmistakable solutions. Unfortunately, things are never that simple and the use of implied trusts is an area of law that has been criticised for not being as clear, certain or obvious as many would like it to be.

As discussed in **6.4**, there is disquiet about the use of constructive trusts in commercial contexts given the uncertainty they potentially bring to business contracts. There are also many arguments made about the use of implied trusts to resolve property disputes between cohabiting couples.

There is an argument that making cohabitants rely on the 'patchwork of legal rules' that are implied trusts and proprietary estoppel, which may or may not provide them with an interest in their partner's property, is unsatisfactory (see Law Commission, 'Executive Summary to Cohabitation: The Financial Consequences of Relationship Breakdown' (2015)). Claimants may have arguable claims to a constructive trust or to the estoppel. However, where litigation arises, so costs are incurred. Coupled with this, for many applications there is considerable uncertainty as to whether the claim will succeed – people often do not think it necessary to document formally their agreements or understandings, and the passage of time impacts on recollections and results in a lack of a paper trail evidencing monetary contributions. Even if successful, there is uncertainty as to what the remedy will be. Similarly, the failure to recognise the interdependence of cohabitants' contributions (financial and non-financial) to their relationship and the entanglement of their lives together does potentially give rise to substantial unfairness.

There is legislation in Scotland providing statutory financial remedy for separating cohabitants (Family Law (Scotland) Act 2006). However, in the absence of legislation providing similar property rights to couples going through divorce or dissolution (as the Matrimonial Causes Act 1973 or the Civil Partnership Act 2004), separating cohabitants in England and Wales are forced to rely on equity and trusts to resolve dispute on relationship breakdown.

There have been numerous calls for the situation to be changed – a 2007 report from the Law Commission proposed a new scheme specifically for cohabitants, a 2017 Early Day Motion tabled by Caroline Lucas MP proposed 'legal rights for cohabitees who separate', and various private members' bills raised in the House of Lords since 2008 sought to provide protective legislation for cohabitees. There have also been frequent campaigns from charities and professional bodies. However, the proposed reforms and campaigns have lacked sufficient support. They are often seen as undermining marriage and civil partnerships – one leading opponent of proposed reform suggested that cohabitants 'dissatisfied with their legal lot' should marry to obtain marital rights (Baroness Deech in 2009 delivering a Gresham College lecture, 'Cohabitation and the law'), and there is concern about the difficulty in coming up with a definition of 'cohabitant' to determine eligibility for any new scheme. November 2022 saw the latest government rejection of requests for reform (on the basis that proposed reforms of the law of marriage and divorce had to be addressed first).

**ACTIVITY Review your understanding – implied trusts**

Review the facts below:

Lizzie has just broken up with her long-term boyfriend, Bill. For the last eight years, Lizzie has been living in 'Oak View' (registered in Bill's sole name). Bill is now selling the house for £600,000. Lizzie feels that, in view of all her contributions to Oak View and to the family and the relationship, she should be entitled to a share in the sale proceeds.

Consider how Lizzie could establish an equitable interest in Oak View through:

(a) an express trust;

(b) a resulting trust;

(c) a constructive trust; and

(d) proprietary estoppel.

**COMMENT**

Registration in Bill's sole name indicates that he is the only owner of the legal title. To obtain a share in the sale proceeds, Lizzie is going to have to establish that Bill holds on trust for her or that he is estopped from denying her an interest.

(a) An express declaration of trust over land would have to be evidenced in signed writing to be enforceable (Law of Property Act 1925, s 53(1)(b)). A declaration of trust in the transfer deed would be conclusive evidence of Lizzie's share in the house.

(b) If Lizzie has made direct contributions to the purchase price (eg the deposit) then it will be presumed that Bill holds on resulting trust for her. Only payments at the time of acquisition give rise to a resulting trust (*Curley v Parkes* [2004] All ER (D) 344).

A resulting trust would reflect the proportion her contribution bore to the purchase money. Thus, if she contributed one-tenth of the purchase money, a resulting trust would produce an equitable interest of one-tenth of the value of the house. However, resulting trusts are unlikely to be used in these circumstances (*Stack v Dowden*).

(c) To establish a constructive trust over a family home, Lizzie would have to bring herself within one of the two categories referred to in *Lloyds Bank v Rosset*, namely:

- express common intention constructive trust; or
- inferred common intention constructive trust.

    (i) An express common intention trust would exist if Bill gave assurances or there was some agreement that ownership of the property was shared (perhaps as in *Grant v Edwards*). Further information is needed about any discussions Lizzie and Bill may have had when the property was purchased. In addition, Lizzie would have to prove that she acted to her detriment in reliance on the common intention (*Neill v Holland*). Has she 'significantly altered her position in reliance on the agreement' (*Lloyds Bank v Rosset*). Has she made any contributions to the mortgage or a substantial contribution to household expenses (enabling Bill to pay the mortgage). On a narrow view, it is doubtful whether any care Lizzie provided to the family would be a significant alteration of her position pursuant to the agreement; she would look after the family anyway regardless of the existence of an agreement to share ownership of the property.

    (ii) The court will infer a common intention from direct contributions to the purchase price, such as contributions to the purchase price or deposit or mortgage (*Lloyds Bank v Rosset*). Non-financial acts such as looking after the family will not lead to the inference. The indirect contribution by way of any payment of household expenses might be sufficient if substantial and made pursuant to an agreement that the parties will share the mortgage and expenses equally with one paying the mortgage and the other paying the general household expenses (Le *Foe v Le Foe and Woolwich plc*). Assuming that any such payments were substantial, they would also suffice for detriment.

If Lizzie establishes an equitable interest under a constructive trust, the court will quantify her interest by considering what she and Bill may have agreed or in the absence of any agreement but considering 'the whole course of dealing' between them (*Stack v Dowden, Jones v Kernott*) to determine what they intended, or what is fair. This will involve consideration not only of monetary contributions but other factors such as advice they may have received, their relationship, the purpose behind the purchase of Oak View, any children they share, and their financial arrangements.

(d) To establish proprietary estoppel, Lizzie with need to provide evidence of an active or passive assurance from Bill that she was to have to interest in Oak View (perhaps comparable to any evidence available to establishing an express common intention) and that she acted to her detriment in reliance on that assurance. It is unlikely that caring for any children would constitute a detriment (she would have done this anyway) but financial contributions or substantial non-financial contributions might. If the estoppel is established, the remedy will be linked to the expectation arising from Bill's assurance. As the property is to be sold in any event, the monetary amount Lizzie might receive could reflect a beneficial share in the property under a trust or could reflect compensation for her detriment. However, the rights of any lender would also be considered.

## SUMMARY

- Implied trusts, as opposed to the express trusts dealt with in the previous chapters, are an area of trusts law which attempt to solve questions of the ownership of the property.
- Resulting trusts are used to clarify ownership when a settlor or testator has failed to deal fully with the beneficial interest under a trust.
- The presumptions of resulting trust and advancement can have an influence on the determination of ownership in specific circumstances.
- Understanding that there is no concept of community of family property enhances an awareness of how equity and trusts play a key role in determining the outcome of disputes in the event of relationship breakdown.
- Recognising the circumstances which could give rise to a common intention constructive trust or to proprietary estoppel is important in appreciating the effect that both can have on property ownership issues.
- Similar facts may give rise to a claim for a common intention constructive trust or support a claim in proprietary estoppel. However, the two actions are not the same and give rise to different considerations by the court.
- There are current issues with the use of the law of implied trusts as applied to the ownership of the family home of unmarried cohabitees on relationship breakdown, and this is an area of law that might develop in the future.
- Implied trusts can and do operate in commercial situations. There is some disquiet as to this use, given the lack of certainty as to when such trusts arise and the issues that could consequently result in business dealings.

# 7 Running a Trust - Trustee Duties and Powers

**LEARNING OUTCOMES**

By the end of this chapter, you should be able to:

- explain when and how trustees are appointed, retire, or can be removed;
- understand the duties imposed on trustees when they are involved in the running of the trust;
- discuss trustees' duties in relation to investment of trust funds, and how trustees may appoint an investment manager to administer the investments;
- explain in what circumstances trustees may make trust income or capital available to beneficiaries during the running of a trust;
- outline the degree of control beneficiaries and the court have over trustees; and
- appreciate the ways in which beneficial interests may be varied.

## 7.1 Introduction

The creation of express private trusts, whether by a settlor in their lifetime or a testator by their will, was discussed in **Chapters 2** and **3**. With express trusts, trustees are appointed in a variety of circumstances. It is important to know how trustees are appointed, originally at the outset of the trust and later by replacement. Equally important is understanding when and how they can retire, or if they can be removed against their will.

Once appointed, trustees of an express trust, whether professionals or lay persons, need to know the legal tools available to them to enable them to manage and administer a trust correctly and effectively. This involves considering the trustees' duties and powers in relation to the administration of the trust for the benefit of the beneficiaries.

Trustees' duties to beneficiaries are what they should or should not be doing in the administration of the trust. Their powers are what the trustees can do to manage the trust effectively.

Understanding how these duties and powers operate is an important consideration for both trustees and beneficiaries regardless of whether the trust is created by a settlor in their lifetime or by a testator under their will. If the trustees breach any of their duties, this would constitute a breach of trust. A trustee could be personally liable to compensate the beneficiaries for this breach. However, if a beneficiary is not happy with how the trustees have exercised their powers, there may be little that the beneficiary can do. Having a power to do something does not mean that you actually have to exercise it; you merely have to think about exercising it. Trustees generally cannot be made liable if they exercise a power in a way that a beneficiary does not like.

These duties and powers will govern a variety of administrative matters trustees might have to address. Initially, they will come from the trust instrument itself - to a certain extent, a settlor or testator is free to impose such duties on and give whatever powers to their trustees as they wish. These express instructions from the settlor/testator will take precedence. However, in the absence of guidance from the settlor or testator, there are a variety of statutory provisions that will be read into the trust to enable the trustees to administer the trust effectively. Additionally, the courts have also given guidance on trust administration matters.

## 7.2 Appointment, retirement and removal of trustees

### 7.2.1 Types and numbers of trustees

Any person with legal capacity has the capacity to be a trustee. A trustee may be a private individual, a professional person or a trust corporation - a company whose purpose is to act as trustee.

A private trust of pure personalty may have any number of trustees (although for ease of administration, numbers are generally limited).

For trusts involving land, the maximum number of trustees is four (as only four can be registered as the legal owners). If land is to be sold by trustees, there must be a least two trustees or a trust corporation to give a receipt for the proceeds of sale.

The Charity Commission usually requires at least three trustees for a registered charity.

### 7.2.2 Original appointment of trustees

The settlor/testator normally appoints the original trustees. Thereafter, the settlor has no further power to appoint new trustees unless they expressly reserve such a power in the trust instrument.

A trustee cannot be compelled to accept office and can disclaim their appointment provided they do so before they have done any act showing acceptance. A trustee who has accepted office but who then wishes to give it up must retire in the appropriate way.

If a trust is validly set up and for any reason there are no trustees, 'equity never wants for a trustee'. The court has various powers to appoint someone to act as trustee.

### 7.2.3 Subsequent appointment, retirement and removal of trustees

The power to appoint (select) trustees is crucial. Trustees are potentially managing large values of assets which requires honesty and judgement. It is, therefore, vital to know who is entitled to appoint the trustees after the trust has been created by the settlor/testator. Any appointment of money from the trust is invalid if not made by people validly appointed trustees. The case of *Yudt & Others v Leonard Ross and Craig* [1998] 1 All ER (D) 375 is a good illustration of just how vital this is.

Statutory provisions apply to the extent that they are not modified or excluded by the settlor/testator in the trust instrument. The main provisions are contained in the Trustee Act 1925. They seek to address the various circumstances which could arise in the lifetime of a trust and if relevant they apply to all trusts regardless of when and how created.

#### 7.2.3.1 Appointing new trustees to replace

Section 36(1) of the Trustee Act 1925 anticipates that there may be circumstances when a trustee needs to be or must be replaced - for instance they die, they remain out of the UK for more than 12 months, they want to retire, they are refusing to, become incapable of or are unfit to act (the Act also provides for replacement if a trustee is an infant, but this rarely occurs now in practice as the age of majority is 18, rather than 21 as it was in 1925). In the absence of anyone being expressly named in the trust itself, s 36(1) provides the other, continuing trustee or trustees with the power to bring about the replacement.

Should the replacement be needed for the last surviving trustee, the power to appoint the replacement(s) passes to the personal representatives of the last surviving trustee.

7.2.3.2 Appointing additional trustees

Current trustees have a power to appoint a new, additional trustee, provided there are not currently more than three trustees at the time of the appointment (Trustee Act 1925, s 36(6)). This is something the trustees might wish to consider in order to acquire the expertise of a professional (a solicitor or accountant) to assist in the management of the trust.

7.2.3.3 Retirement without replacement

A trustee could chose to retire, and, in certain circumstances, there would be no requirement for them to be replaced (Trustee Act 1925, s 39). After the retirement there must be either a trust corporation or at least two persons remaining as trustees. Additionally, the retirement must be evidenced by deed (see **7.2.3.4** about the effect of the retirement by deed) and the co-trustees must (in the same deed) consent to the trustee being discharged from their role.

7.2.3.4 Evidencing a change of trustee

To be effective under s 39, the retirement and discharge from the trusteeship must be contained in a deed so as to provide for the automatic vesting of the trust assets in the remaining trustees.

Other appointments are also generally undertaken by deed so as to benefit from a similar automatic vesting provision contained in s 40 of the Trustee Act 1925.

As regards some trust assets, this deed supports the formal requirements for the transfer of the legal title of the assets to the new trustees. Stocks and shares title does not fully vest until the names of the new trustees (or the remaining trustees after a resignation) are on the company register (stock transfer forms in favour of new/continuing trustees will have to be executed). Similarly, any change of trustees must also be registered at the Land Registry where the trust contains land.

**Figure 7.1** Summary - trustees' powers to appoint, replace, retire

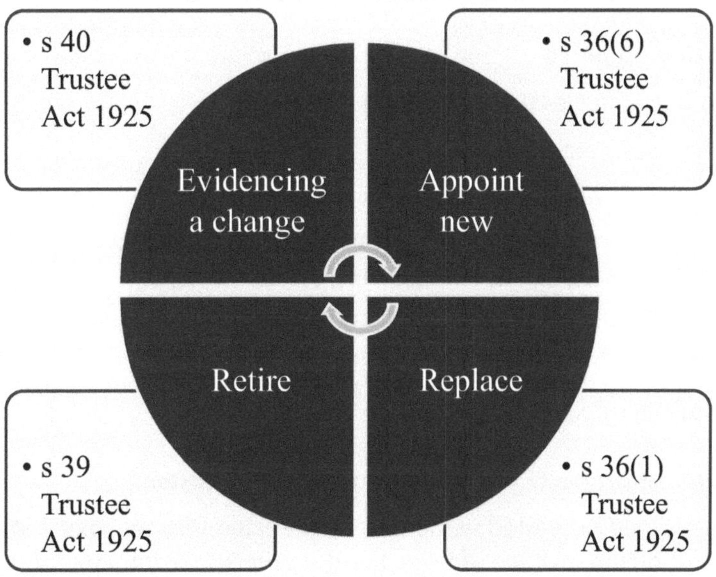

7.2.3.5 Power of court to appoint new trustees

Section 41(1) of the Trustee Act 1925 provides the court with the power to make an order appointing new trustees where such an appointment is needed. The court could entertain an application to effect such a change from either the beneficiaries or trustees.

However, as the court will only consider removing a trustee or appointing additional or substitutional trustees where it is 'inexpedient, difficult, or impracticable for the appointment to be made without the court's assistance' (Trustee Act 1925, s 41(1)), an application to the court would have to be a last resort. For instance, if the appointed trustees were refusing or unable to work together, the court might step in to appoint new trustees to facilitate the administration of the trust (*Mohammed v Khan* [2005] EWHC 599 (Ch)); if a sole trustee becomes incapable of acting as a trustee due to incapacity, the court may order the appointment of a new trustee (Trustee Act 1925, s 41(1)).

There are circumstances when the beneficiaries might also be able to insist upon a change of trustee which are considered in **7.6.3**.

## 7.3 Duties of trustees

Duties are obligations. The beneficiaries can force trustees to perform their duties, if necessary, by court action. Beneficiaries can sue the trustees for compensation if the trustees have breached a duty and this has caused loss to the trust. Trustees' duties are laid down by statute and the general law. The duties can be modified by the trust instrument (which can always prescribe rules for running the particular trust).

At a basic level, the trustees have duties to observe the terms of the trust and distribute to the correct beneficiaries. If there is doubt as to whom the beneficiaries are because of ambiguous wording in the trust instrument, trustees should seek directions from the court.

### 7.3.1 Standard of care

In fulfilling their duties, the trustees must exercise the appropriate standard of care. Traditionally, this meant using such care as would a prudent person of business in the conduct of their own affairs (*Speight v Gaunt* (1883) 9 App Cas 1). This standard of care remains relevant to trustees today, although a higher standard of care is expected of professional trustees, and there is now also a statutory standard of care in relation to the exercise of duties in the Trustee Act 2000 involving investment and associated matters.

### 7.3.2 Duties on taking up office

On taking up office, trustees owe duties to:

(a) ensure they are properly appointed;

(b) become familiar with terms of the trust;

(c) inquire into the past business of the trust to discover previous breaches of trust and to take appropriate action to remedy any past breaches.

A new trustee will be liable to the beneficiaries for any loss caused to the trust by a failure to undertake these initial obligations. New trustees appointed in *Yudt v Ross & Craig*, mentioned above at **7.2.3**, failed to ensure the validity of their appointment, resulting in a liability in excess of £400,000 to the beneficiaries.

### 7.3.3 Duty to keep trust property in the joint names of all trustees

Trust property should be vested in the names of all the trustees jointly. Vesting the property in the names of all the trustees reduces the risk of misappropriation of the property by one of them.

### 7.3.4 Duty to provide information

Trustees must keep trust accounts showing how the trust fund is invested and the money coming in and going out of the trust. They must allow the beneficiaries to inspect these accounts together with documents creating the trust. This issue will be discussed further in **7.6.2**.

### 7.3.5 Duty to act impartially between beneficiaries

The trustees must act in the best interests of all beneficiaries, and they consequently must balance the interests of the beneficiaries when making decisions. This is especially an issue when the trust contains beneficiaries with differing interests, for instance a life tenant entitled to income and any remaindermen interested in capital growth.

### 7.3.6 Duty to be active in the running of the trust

Trustees are under a duty to play an active role in the administration of the trust. Decisions to exercise powers should be taken unanimously.

The trustees may be able to delegate to co-trustees (or other agents) on a formal basis under the Trustee Act 2000 (discussed in **7.4.1**). Similarly, an individual trustee can appoint an attorney to act on their behalf for a short period of time should the need arise (see **7.4.2**). In the absence of such delegation, passive trustees can be liable for the defaults of the active trustees (*Bahin v Hughes* [1886] 31 Ch D).

This active involvement in the running of the trust also includes a duty to watch over their co-trustees (*Styles v Guy* (1849) 19 LT Ch 185). In the same way that newly appointed trustees must remedy the breaches of previous trustees, so current trustees must monitor the conduct of their co-trustees and correct any breaches they have brought about.

### 7.3.7 Duty to invest the trust fund

There is a fundamental duty imposed on trustees to protect and enhance the value of the trust fund over which they have administrative control.

#### 7.3.7.1 Background information on investments

Before considering the statutory and equitable rules relating to trustee investments, it will be useful to have some background knowledge on investment generally. This will help to explain why some of the rules on trustee investments exist.

A person may invest money in order to produce income and/or capital growth. 'Income' consists of regular receipts such as interest from a bank account, dividends from shares or rent from property. Income has the quality of recurrence. 'Capital growth' refers to the profit investors see when they sell the investment for more than they paid for it. Some investments concentrate on capital growth. Some only yield income and no capital growth. Others aim to achieve both. It is important to be able to identify which types of receipt are capital and which ones are income.

From a trustee's point of view, the distinction is important because different beneficiaries may be entitled to capital and/or income. For example, in a trust for X for life remainder to Y, X is entitled to income and Y is entitled to capital when X dies. To fulfil the trustees' duty to act impartially and strike a balance between life tenant and remainderman, the trustees must ensure that the trust investments produce both capital growth and income.

When trustees are choosing investments, they owe a duty to choose suitable investments and should be heavily influenced by the nature of the beneficial interests.

However, there are other elements to consider when trustees are planning an investment strategy.

(1) *Size of investment fund available.* Strategic investing with a small fund is difficult. It is hard to diversify profitably because there will be insufficient money to buy worthwhile amounts of a variety of different investments.

(2) *Type of yield required.* Is the investment need mainly capital or income profit or a combination of the two? Investments which yield income only include bank and building society accounts; capital only returns come from investment in antiques, land (unless leased which would produce income in the form of rent) and units and investment products which focus on capital growth. Company shares (often referred to as 'equities') yield both income (dividends) and, hopefully, capital profit when they are sold. Similarly, government stocks (also known as 'gilts', 'government bonds') yield a fixed rate of interest and may show a modest capital gain on redemption or earlier sale. More generalised unit and investment trusts may also provide both income distributions and capital growth.

(3) *Timescale of investment commitment.* In principle, investment should always be considered a long-term strategy But sometimes, for instance when a trustee is holding a fund for a 15-year-old until they reach 18, the investment commitment is a short-term one.

(4) *Required rate of return.* To avoid the trust value of the capital invested being diminished, the return should be at the rate of inflation at least.

(5) *Degree of risk.* Every investor must decide how risk averse they are as no investment is totally safe. Risk may involve a diminution in the capital value of the investment or in some cases complete loss of the capital invested. Consequently, trustees cannot afford to be as adventurous as ordinary investors. They are under constraints which do not apply to individuals as trustees are investing 'for the benefit of other people for whom [they] are morally obliged to provide' (*Re Whiteley* (1886) 33 Ch D 347). Where safety is a big investment factor, investing in high-risk companies, sectors or asset types may not be appropriate. Trustees invariably have to (and should) balance their portfolio.

(6) *Diversification.* The danger of investing all your money in one company is that you put 'all your eggs in one basket'. At worst, the company may fail and go into liquidation resulting in the loss of all your money. Alternatively, the company may not be successful and, so, the value of the shares declines. Investors should diversify or spread their money between a number of different companies. Some of these companies may not flourish, but this should be compensated by gains made on shares in other companies that are successful.

#### 7.3.7.2 Investments under the Trustee Act 2000

Trustees have a duty to invest trust money. If the document creating the trust is silent, then statute governs the trustees' approach to this investment.

Before the Trustee Act 2000, the law adopted an ultra-cautious approach to protect beneficiaries against trustees selecting unsuitable investments. Statute provided that trustees could only select investments from a restricted list. Trustees were not even allowed to invest any trust money in company shares because of the risk that the capital invested might be lost. Eventually, it was recognised that the ban on investment in shares meant that trust funds were losing out on capital growth. A further problem arose because trustees could not delegate all of their investment functions to investment experts. The ultimate decision on selection of investments and which ones to sell or buy had to remain with the trustees. Consequently, on the recommendation of the Law Commission, the Trustee Act 2000 was passed to reform the law (coming into force on 1 February 2001).

The Trustee Act 2000 applies to all trusts whether created before or after the Act came into force (s 10). Existing trusts will, therefore, benefit from the widening of investment powers and the Act's other provisions.

The aim of the Trustee Act 2000 was to maximise trust assets. It set out to achieve this aim by giving trustees:

- unfettered powers to invest; and
- powers to employ experts to manage the trust investments.

These wide powers would, it was hoped, result in a profit for most trust funds. However, the expanded powers brought with them an enhanced element of risk; this is counterbalanced by the trustees' ancillary duties when undertaking any investment (highlighted in **Figure 7.2**).

**Figure 7.2** Trustee investment duties under the Trustee Act 2000

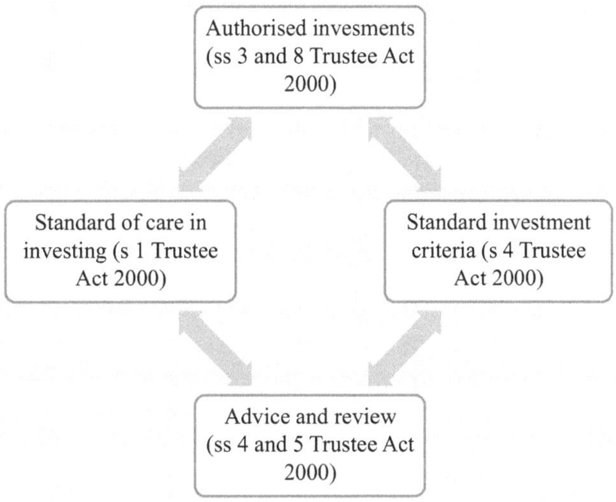


### (a) Authorised investments

Section 3 of the Trustee Act 2000 provides that trustees can make any investment that they could make as if they were 'absolutely entitled' to the assets of the trust. In other words, the trustees can choose to invest in anything at all.

While s 3 appears to confer an unrestricted power to invest in anything, it is necessary to consider the meaning of the word 'investment' before drawing this conclusion. Traditionally, something which does not generate income was not regarded as an investment. It is now possible to purchase unit trusts which pay out no income with the intention of achieving capital growth. The Law Commission took the view that something is an investment if it is expected to produce income or capital growth, citing *Harries v Church of England Commissioners* [1992] 1 WLR 1241 as its authority. *Cook v Medway Housing Authority* [1997] STC 90 also supports this definition. A depreciating asset, such as a private car, is not an investment because it will not yield an income or capital return; it is, therefore, not permitted by s 3.

Trustees can lend money as an investment, provided they obtain a mortgage over the borrower's land (Trustee Act 2000, s 3(4)). Thus, it is possible to use trust funds to lend a beneficiary money to buy a house provided the loan is secured by a mortgage on that house. In *Khoo Tek Keong v Ch'ng Joo Tuan Neoh* [1934] AC 529, the Privy Council held that an unsecured loan was not an investment.

Additionally, s 8 of the Trustee Act 2000 permits trustees to purchase freehold or leasehold land in the UK as 'an investment, for occupation by a beneficiary or for any other reason'.

Sections 3 and 8 seem to give trustees considerable scope in their investment choices. In order to safeguard against speculative investment putting the trust fund at risk, the 2000 Act lays down duties that the trustees must comply with when making investment decisions.

### (b) Complying with ss 4 and 5 of the Trustee Act 2000

Section 4 of the Trustee Act 2000 provides that when exercising a power of investment, trustees must have regard to the 'standard investment criteria'. These criteria involve consideration of suitability and diversification:

- *Suitability.* The trustees must consider the suitability of the investment on two levels. First, they need to decide whether it is appropriate for the trust to invest in the particular asset type (ie should we invest in public company - 'plc' - shares?). Secondly, they must be satisfied that the particular investment proposed is a suitable example of its type (ie should we invest in the shares of Bigco plc?). They should consider suitability in relation to the interests of all beneficiaries.
- *Diversification.* Trustees must consider the need for diversification of investments as far as is appropriate to that trust. The 2000 Act recognises that diversification is not always possible. Investors need a considerable sum of money to diversify effectively because they should invest reasonable amounts in a wide range of different companies and institutions. There may also be assets contained within the trust that have a connection to the beneficiaries (for instance, shares in a privately owned family company).

Additionally, under s 5 of the Trustee Act 2000, trustees must obtain and consider proper advice about the way they should exercise their power of investment having regard to the standard investment criteria. This duty can be excluded if the trustees reasonably conclude that in the circumstances it is unnecessary or inappropriate to obtain such advice. For example, it would be inappropriate to seek advice if trustees just wanted to place trust money temporarily in a bank or building society pending re-investment. The re-investment would benefit from professional advice, but there is no point wasting trust money on advice regarding the temporary stopgap. Similarly, a professional trustee may be sufficiently qualified so that further advice is reasonably not required.

Trustees must obtain the advice from a person whom they reasonably believe is qualified to give such advice. Trustees are not obliged to follow the advice they receive, but they must give that advice proper consideration. If they decide not to follow the advice, they must be clear in their decision-making process and reasoning.

Under both s 4 and s 5, trustees must from time to time review trust investments and consider whether they should be varied. On such review, the trustees owe the same duties as apply to the selection of investments (ie they should consider the standard investment criteria and seek advice unless they reasonably conclude that it is unnecessary or inappropriate) (ss 4(2) and 5(2)). The 2000 Act does not prescribe a timeframe for when the reviews must be undertaken. The trustees need to determine this for themselves given the circumstances of the trust they are managing.

As duties, a failure to consider suitability or diversification, or to obtain advice, or to keep investments under review would be a breach of trust. If this causes loss to the trust, the trustees must compensate the beneficiaries.

### (c) The statutory duty of care under the 2000 Act

The Trustee Act 2000 also lays down the statutory standard of care trustees must adopt in relation to investment. This duty of care is laid down by s 1 of and Sch 1 to the Act. Unless excluded by the trust instrument, it applies to investment and the purchase of land under the 2000 Act and also any investment powers conferred by a trust instrument.

Under s 1 of the Trustee Act 2000, trustees must exercise such care and skill as is reasonable in the circumstances. Although taken from pre-2000 Act law (the House of Lords in *Learoyd v Whitely* (1886) 33 ChD, approving the Court of Appeal in *Re Whiteley* (1886) 33 ChD 347), the s 1 standard of care is the same standard of care as a reasonable businessperson would take when investing for someone for whom they felt morally bound to provide.

It is not true to say that there is a common standard applying to all trustees. The standard demanded of each trustee varies according to the circumstances. The size of the trust fund may well be relevant here. Also, the standard expected depends on the special knowledge or skill the trustee has or professes to have. A higher standard is expected of a professional trustee acting in the course of their business or profession.

The trustees' investment duties do not require them to obtain a certain return, just act with reasonable care and skill.

***Nestle v National Westminster Bank*** **[1993] 1 WLR 1260**

The trust forming the basis of the dispute was established in 1922. At that time, the fund's value was £54,000. When the claimant became absolutely entitled to the trust over 60 years later, it was valued at approximately £270,000. The claimant argued that with proper investment (so rising in line with inflation or stock exchange indices) the fund should have been valued at in excess of £1 million and the trustees' actions (or lack of them) were a breach of trust.

It was established that the trustees had failed to understand the express investment powers they had been given in the trust instrument and had not taken legal advice. The bank had also not undertaken regular views of the investments they held.

Although, the bank was admonished by the Court of Appeal for its failures, there was, however, no remedy for the claimant. The actions of the bank 'were symptoms of incompetence or idleness ... they were not, without more, breaches of trust' (Staughton LJ). There was no evidence to show that the trustees' failures actually caused the loss of value to the trust; the trustees had done no worse than other investors in the then investment climate. A trustee was not expected to achieve a higher return than an ordinary prudent investor.

Similarly, trustees' performance is not to be judged with hindsight. Their decisions are to be assessed according to investment policies applying at the time the decisions were made. Trustees cannot be held liable for losses caused by the restrictions the law (or the trust instrument) imposed on trustee investments at the time.

The trustees may legitimately pursue other goals apart from capital growth such as tax exemptions for the beneficiaries and income for a life tenant. Both these aims may mean the capital of the trust fund may not appreciate as quickly as it might otherwise do. Further, trustees are encouraged to choose safe investments, and these will not show the same rate of growth as precarious investments that turn out to be successful.

In *Wight v Olswang (No 2)* [2000] WTLR 783 it was said that a trustee is not liable for an investment decision unless it is one which no reasonable trustee (with similar knowledge and skill) would make.

Trustees are also not liable just because one investment in the trust's portfolio has shown a loss. The court will look at the performance of the whole trust fund (or portfolio of investments).

7.3.7.3 Investment duties under the general law

The trustees' decisions on how to invest the trust fund are of a fiduciary nature. Because of this, in addition to the duties laid down by the 2000 Act, case law has established that certain other duties are still relevant.

Trustees must act impartially between beneficiaries. For example, in a trust for X for life remainder to Y, the trustees cannot choose a preponderance of investments that produce only income and no capital growth as this will prejudice the remainderman, Y.

Trustees are subject to fiduciary duties not to place themselves in a position where their personal interest conflicts with their duty to the trust and not to make an unauthorised profit. For example, if the trustee is the principal shareholder and director of a private company that requires funds to expand, the trustee may be tempted to invest trust money in the purchase of new shares in the company. This would be in breach of the trustee's fiduciary duty not to allow a conflict of interest. The impact of fiduciary duties owed by trustees will be considered further in **Chapter 8**.

Trustees must act in the best interests of all the beneficiaries. The purpose of trusts set up for the benefit of individuals is, in the main, to generate money. The purposes of the trust will usually be best served by the trustees seeking to obtain the maximum return, whether by income or capital growth, subject to the overriding duty of prudence and care. It is expected that the trustees' choice of investments should, therefore, be based on well-established investment criteria rather than individual choice. Thus, in *Cowan v Scargill* [1985] Ch 270, it was held that trustees of the NUM pension fund had to put aside their own social, moral and political views when deciding how to invest. The duty to act in the best interests of the beneficiaries meant their best financial interests. The trustees were not justified in avoiding overseas investments and those connected with the oil industry on the basis that these competed with coal mining.

However, there are four circumstances when trustees may take ethical considerations into account when they are choosing investments:

(a) In *Cowan v Scargill*, it was recognised that if investment in Company A (an ethical concern) yielded as good a return as investment in Company B (a company concerned with armaments, tobacco, or a repressive foreign regime), the trustees could invest in Company A.

(b) If the beneficiaries are all adults with very strong views against say, tobacco, it may not be in their best interests for trustees to invest in a tobacco company. Similarly, if the sui juris beneficiaries have strong views in favour of investments in companies which evidence sound environmental, social and/or corporate governance credentials, these views might be a relevant consideration in trustees' investment decisions.

(c) It may not be appropriate for charitable trustees to invest in a company whose objects are directly opposed to the purposes of the charity. In *Harries v Church of England Commissioners* [1992] 1 WLR 1241, it was held that trustees of the Church of England's funds would be acting properly if they refused to invest in companies manufacturing armaments and those concerned with tobacco, gambling, etc. Thirty years later, *Butler-Sloss v The Charity Commission for England and Wales* [2022] EWHC 974 (Ch) confirmed the relevance of the Trustee Act 2000 to charity trustees, stressing that charity trustees must exercise their power of investment in a way that furthered the charity's purposes. Consequently, where the trustees reasonably took the view that a particular investment class or type conflicted with those purposes (which would be a charity-by-charity determination), the trustees could decide to exclude such investments. The trustees could take into account the impact of the investment on the reputation of the charity, and the alienation of donors and supporters when making their decision. However, the judgment stressed that any investment decision had to be made in good faith and linked to the charity's purposes rather than purely on moral grounds. As a result of the decision, in the summer of 2023, the Charity Commission issued a new draft of its investment guidance to charity trustees.

(d) The settlor or testator can expressly provide in the trust instrument that trustees are not to invest in certain sectors.

## 7.4 Delegation

Historically, equity would not allow trustees to delegate their powers to an agent. As Lord Langdale MR observed in *Turner v Corney* (1841) 5 Beav 515, 'trustees who take on themselves the management of property for the benefit of others have no right to shift their duty on other persons'.

However, trusts often need the specialist services of professional advisers and so the law adapted to allow trustees to use agents. According to Lord Radcliffe in *Pilkington v IRC* [1964] AC 612, '[T]he law is not that trustees cannot delegate; it is that trustees cannot delegate unless they have authority to do so.' The law allows for authorised delegations in two ways.

### 7.4.1 Collective delegation

Trustees are unlikely to carry out all the tasks their office entails personally, especially if they are unpaid. The trustees may need to employ experts to give advice and do work for the trust. This is the situation where the trustees together want to delegate some of their functions. Such collective delegation is now covered by the Trustee Act 2000.

Before the Trustee Act 2000 was passed, the ability of trustees to delegate was severely restricted; there were many problems, particularly in the field of trust investments.

(a) Trustees could not delegate discretions. Trustees could ask agents for advice, and they could employ agents to execute a sale or purchase, but the actual decision on whether to sell and what to buy had to be taken by the trustees. The choice of trust investments was a discretion and discretions could not be delegated. This approach was clearly out of step with modern investment practices. Investors often give their adviser wider powers, including the ability to decide to sell the investor's shares and buy others without the need to consult the investor.

(b) Trust property could only be vested in the names of all the trustees. However, it is quite common for substantial investors to transfer their investments to discretionary portfolio managers as nominees, to hold on a bare trust for the investors. The bare trust ensures that the investor can demand the shares back at any time. The purpose of the arrangement is to enable transactions to be carried out quickly so that valuable investment opportunities are not lost. Transactions can be undertaken rapidly because the manager can deal with the shares without having to bother the investor at all; the manager can even sign the transfer form because they have legal title. Many investment advisers will only agree to act on this basis. Thus, it was felt that the old rule preventing trustees from entering into this arrangement deprived some trusts of good investment advice.

There is another reason investors may want to put their shares in the name of their investment adviser. For most private investors, it is possible to use CREST (the electronic method of selling and buying shares) only if the shares are vested in the name of a CREST user as nominee for the investor. CREST users are usually stockbrokers. The rule forbidding anyone other than trustees to hold trust investments denied trusts access to CREST.

The Trustee Act 2000 widened the powers of collective delegation considerably in response to the problems discussed above. The 2000 Act's provisions apply to trusts whether created before or after the commencement of the Act (s 27(1)). The provisions can be excluded by a clause in the trust instrument.

While expanding the trustees' powers of collection delegation, the 2000 Act does, however, limit the functions that are capable of delegation and contains safeguards in an attempt to minimise the risk to the trust from the poor performance of any agent.

#### 7.4.1.1 Delegable functions

Under s 11 of the Trustee Act 2000, trustees 'may authorise any person to exercise any or all of their delegable functions as their agent'. If they wish, the trustees can authorise one of their own to act as their agent (Trustee Act 2000, s 12(1)), but they are not permitted to appoint a beneficiary to act as their agent (s 12(3)).

Section 11(2) details what is meant by 'delegable' functions. Generally, it means that trustees can now delegate most functions that relate to the general administration of the trust. What they cannot delegate are their 'dispositive' powers or discretions, their decisions as to the distribution of trust capital or income among beneficiaries (for instance, in a discretionary trust exercising a discretion in favour of one beneficiary over another) (s 11(2)(a)) or deciding whether the trust is to pay its fees out of income or capital (s 11(2)(b)).

Also, it was considered inappropriate to allow a non-trustee to choose new trustees, so the trustees cannot delegate their power to appoint new trustees (s 11(2)(c)).

Where delegation is permitted, trustees can pay the agent reasonable remuneration out of trust funds (Trustee Act 2000, s 32).

#### 7.4.1.2 Protection for the trust

Trustees owe the duty of care set out in s 1 of the Trustee Act 2000 when they appoint the agent and settle the terms on which the agent is to act (Sch 1, para 3). Trustees would need to check that any proposed appointee is reputable and possesses the necessary skill and expertise to perform the delegated tasks.

Section 13 of the Trustee Act 2000 makes it clear that any agent must comply with any conditions attached to the specific function they have been asked for undertake, for instance if exercising the trustees' power of investment, complying with the requirements of s 4 (the standard investment criteria). The agent would, however, not have to seek advice if they were sufficiently qualified.

For general administrative matters, the trustees can employ the agent on such terms as to remuneration etc as the trustees may decide (s 14). However, if the agent is to carry out asset management functions, for example making investment decisions, managing trust assets and acquiring property, s 15 requires the trustees take certain steps to protect the trust when they undertake such delegation, namely:

(a) The trustees must enter into a written agreement with the agent (s 15(1)).

(b) They must provide the agent with a written policy statement to ensure that the agent does not adopt an inappropriate investment strategy (s 15(2) and (4)). The statement must set out the investment objectives of the trust and how the agent is to exercise the delegated functions. It should ensure that the functions are exercised in the best interests of the trust (s 15(3)). In this case it should include the following information:

   (i) the fact that the client is a trust and the consequent fiduciary obligations;

   (ii) the nature of the beneficial interests and whether the priority is capital growth, income generation or both;

   (iii) any provisions in the trust instrument dealing with investment;

   (iv) when the trustees will need to sell or realise the investment (eg when the beneficiaries reach 25).

   The trustees must exercise the s 1 duty of care when they prepare this statement (Sch 1, para 3). In the written agreement, the agent should agree to observe the terms of the policy statement (s 15(2)(b)).

Under ss 21 and 22, trustees must keep under review the arrangements under which their agents act and how they are being put into effect. This means they must consider whether the agent is a suitable person to act for the trust and whether the terms of engagement and any policy statement are still appropriate. If it is not, the trustees must have the ability to revoke the appointment of the agent.

The 2000 Act does not state how often trustees should conduct these reviews, nor how they should be done. It depends on what is reasonable in the circumstances.

#### 7.4.1.3 Liability of trustees for defaults of an agent

Where an agent is incompetent or dishonest and this causes loss to the trust, the trustees may be able to sue the agent for negligence or breach of contract and hold any damages on trust for the beneficiaries. However, the agent may not be worth suing – they may have disappeared or become bankrupt. In this situation, the beneficiaries may seek to sue the trustees for compensation.

Trustees are not vicariously liable for the defaults of their agents. They are not automatically liable if their chosen agent causes loss to the trust. The beneficiaries have to show that the trustees have breached their duty of care as regards the initial appointment or review (s 23) and this has caused loss to the trust. In these cases, the beneficiaries can sue the trustees for compensation for breach of trust.

### 7.4.2 Individual delegation

If a trustee is going abroad for a time or about to go into hospital for a prolonged period, decisions and transactions concerning the trust could be delayed. If the trustee does not wish to retire, they should appoint an agent or attorney to take over their duties for the requisite period that they are unable to act as trustee.

Section 25 of the Trustee Act 1925 (as substituted by the Trustee Delegation Act 1999) confers a wide power of 'individual' delegation on trustees by way of a power of attorney (here, the term 'attorney' does not bear the American meaning of a lawyer). Effectively, they can appoint an attorney to function as their alter ego. As all trustees are under a duty to play an active role in trust (**7.3.6**), they should always consider taking this step when they will be unavailable for longer than a couple of weeks.

#### 7.4.2.1 Delegable functions

Under a s 25 power of attorney, an individual trustee can delegate 'any of their powers, discretions, and duties'. The trustee can delegate their entire office or selected functions. Unlike under s 11 of Trustee Act 2000 (which does not permit delegation of 'any function relating to whether or in what way any assets of the trust should be distributed'), delegation under s 25(1) of the Trustee Act 1925 would include decisions as to the distribution of capital and/or income to beneficiaries.

#### 7.4.2.2 Protection for the trust

Under s 25(2)(b), the delegation by the trustee can only be for any period up to a maximum of 12 months. If nothing is stated, the power will expire after 12 months (s 25(2)(b)).

The trustee appointing an attorney must give written notices of the power of attorney to their co-trustee and anyone to whom the trust instrument gives power to appoint new trustees before or within seven days of the date of the power (s 25(4)).

#### 7.4.2.3 Liability of the trustee for defaults of an attorney

A trustee appointing an attorney will be vicariously (automatically) liable for the attorney's acts just as if they were their own acts. Therefore, if the appointed attorney commits a breach of trust and this causes loss to the trust, the donor trustee will have to make good the loss (s 25(7)).

## 7.5 Powers of trustees

Statutory powers are implied into a trust only if there is no contrary provision in the trust. When deciding whether trustees have power to do something, it is advisable to look at the trust instrument, as it might modify, extend or exclude the statutory powers.

Two important statutory powers given to trustees are their powers of advancement and maintenance. A beneficiary may not be entitled to the capital of the trust until some future time. Where trustees are holding property 'for Yasmin if and when she attains 25', Yasmin will not receive the capital of the trust as of right unless and until she satisfies the contingency of reaching 25. However, Yasmin may need money in the meantime to pay for her maintenance and education. She may need a capital sum to buy a house or set herself up in business before reaching 25. The settlor probably imposed the contingency to prevent Yasmin receiving a large amount of money at an early age when she would be too immature to handle it sensibly. Nevertheless, the settlor would not want her to be short of money before attaining the contingency age.

To overcome these difficulties, the law gives the trustees powers that enable them to apply trust money for the benefit of beneficiaries before they have become entitled to possession of their share of the trust fund. The power of maintenance allows them to apply the income of the trust fund for minor beneficiaries. The power of advancement allows trustees to apply part of a beneficiary's share of trust capital before that beneficiary is strictly entitled to receive it.

The trust instrument can exclude these powers if the settlor wishes, but this is unusual. It is also possible for the settlor to grant express powers of advancement and maintenance in the trust instrument, or to extend the statutory powers.

### 7.5.1 Power of maintenance

A trust fund will usually comprise income-producing assets (company shares produce income by way of dividends; bank and building society accounts yield income in the form of interest; land can generate rental income). The terms of the trust often determine what the trustees should do with such income. If there is an adult life tenant, the trustees must pay the income to the life tenant. Alternatively, the trust may direct that the income must not be spent but should be accumulated (invested by the trustees like the trust capital).

In the absence of express provisions in the trust document, s 31 of the Trustee Act 1925 and the power of maintenance are concerned with how that trust income could (or should) be dealt with, and it applies to vested and most contingent trusts for minor children.

#### 7.5.1.1 Section 31 of the Trustee Act 1925 and vested interests

Where a beneficiary with a vested interest is under 18 (eg '£100,000 on trust to my grandson' and the grandson is currently 12), the trustees must hold the trust capital on trust for the beneficiary until they reach 18. Only at 18 will the beneficiary be able to give the trustees a good receipt for the money.

Under s 31(1) of the Trustee Act 1925, while the beneficiary is under 18, the trustees have a power to apply trust income 'towards the beneficiary's maintenance, education or benefit'. If the trust arose on or before 1 October 2014, under s 31(1(i), the trustees could apply a reasonable part of the income (what is reasonable depending on the beneficiary's age, needs and the general circumstances). For trusts created after 1 October 2014, the trustees can apply the whole or any part of the income (Inheritance and Trustees' Powers Act 2014). Will trusts are deemed to be created when the testator dies.

Because of the beneficiary's inability to give a good receipt while under 18, the income will be applied for them - to the provider of the benefit direct (eg to a school to pay fees). Any income not used must be accumulated (Trustee Act 1925, s 31(2)).

The trustees cannot be compelled to exercise their power of maintenance; their only duty is to consider from time to time whether to exercise it.

At 18, the beneficiary will be paid the trust capital and any income accumulated during their infancy. If the beneficiary were to die before 18, the trust capital and accumulated income would be paid to their estate.

The power of maintenance in s 31(1) is expressly subject to prior interests. Accordingly, s 31 will not apply while there is a life tenant still alive. The life tenant has the right to all the trust income, and none can be applied for the benefit of any other beneficiary.

#### 7.5.1.2 Application of s 31 to contingent interests

Section 31 of the Trustee Act 1925 (as amended) operates differently when considering its application to beneficiaries with a contingent interest in both the capital and the income of the trust fund (ie 'on trust for my granddaughter if she attains 21' and the granddaughter is currently 10).

While the contingent beneficiary is under 18, the trustees have a discretion to apply trust income for their maintenance, education or benefit. They are under a duty to accumulate any not so applied. This is the same as if the beneficiary had a vested interest (**7.5.1.1**).

However, from the age of 18 onwards, the situation changes because of the effect of s 31(1)(ii) of the Trustee Act 1925:

> if such person on attaining the age of eighteen years has not a vested interest in such income, the trustees shall thenceforth pay the income of that property and of any accretion thereto under subsection (2) of this section to him, until he either attains a vested interest therein or dies, or until failure of his interest:

Despite the fact that the contingent beneficiary may not have become entitled to the capital (the contingency not being satisfied), s 31(i)(ii) provides that the beneficiary, at 18, now has the right to receive all the trust income as and when it arises. The trustees must pay it to them. Any discretion to apply the income for the beneficiary's maintenance, education or benefit ceases. When the contingency is satisfied, the beneficiary will receive the trust capital and the income accumulated during their minority.

If the contingent beneficiary were to die before satisfying the contingency, their estate would not have to repay any income paid to them, but the estate would not receive any trust capital or income accumulated during the minority because the beneficiary would not have satisfied the contingency. These items would pass according to the provisions of the trust instrument or on resulting trust back to the settlor or testator's estate.

The statutory power is sufficient in most cases and there is no need to create an express power of maintenance in the trust instrument. However, the settlor or testator may wish to amend the statutory power. For example, having imposed a contingency on a beneficiary in their will, the testator might not wish that beneficiary to have a statutory right to income at 18. In this circumstance, the testator could expressly postpone the right to income to an age greater than 18 and allow the power of maintenance/duty to accumulate to continue for longer.

### 7.5.2 Power of advancement

This power is useful when beneficiaries need trust capital earlier than they are strictly entitled to it under the trust. The term 'advancement' does not mean a loan. It is a way of releasing part of the beneficiary's entitlement to trust capital early.

#### 7.5.2.1 Section 32 of the Trustee Act 1925

The statutory power of advancement is contained in s 32 of the Trustee Act 1925. Section 32 was amended by the Inheritance and Trustees' Powers Act 2014 but is still applicable in its previous form to trusts created on or before 1 October 2014.

The power does not apply to all beneficiaries and there are restrictions on the power. The trust instrument may also modify the power (for instance, by removing some of the restrictions).

Under s 32(1):

> Trustees may at any time or times pay or apply any capital money subject to a trust, for the advancement or benefit, in such manner as they may, in their absolute discretion, think fit, of any person entitled to the capital of the trust property or of any share thereof, whether absolutely or contingently on his attaining any specified age or on the occurrence of any other event ...

Section 32 only applies to beneficiaries who have an entitlement to trust capital. It applies to remainder beneficiaries as they are interested in capital, albeit their entitlement to that capital is postponed until the life tenant's death. Similarly, it applies to beneficiaries with an interest in capital, even if that interest is contingent and they have not yet satisfied the contingency (ie 'to my children at 25' and the children are currently aged 20 and 15).

Section 32 does not, however, apply to life tenants as they only have an interest in trust income, not the trust capital. Nor does it apply to the objects of a discretionary trust as an object has no interest at all unless and until the trustees exercise their discretion in their favour. (However, if an object needed capital, the trustees could exercise their discretion.)

Under s 32(1), the release of the capital must be 'for the advancement and benefit' of the beneficiary entitled to capital.

***Pilkington v IRC* [1964] AC 612**

The advancement under discussion (half the entitlement of Penelope, a 2-year-old girl, under Trust A) was into a new trust (Trust B) for her. The advancement effectively meant that her interest in the capital money advanced was postponed from 21 to 30. The purpose behind the transaction was to save tax (hence the challenge by the IRC) and this was the only benefit to Penelope.

Viscount Radcliffe defined 'advancement or benefit' as meaning 'any use of the money which will improve the material situation of the beneficiary'. It was held to be a valid advancement from Trust A as the saving of the tax was a sufficient benefit to her. However, there was a perpetuity issue with Trust B, so the transaction was struck down.

Examples of 'advancement or benefit' would include the purchase of a house and furniture, the purchase of an apprenticeship, the maintenance and education of the beneficiary, and the discharge of a beneficiary's debts. It has also been held to include making a charitable donation on behalf of the beneficiary to discharge a moral obligation the beneficiary believed they owed to the charity (*Re Clore Settlement Trusts* [1966] 1 WLR 955).

As with income under s 31, capital advancements under s 32 should not be made to minor beneficiaries direct. In the case of infant beneficiaries, advancements can follow requests from the beneficiary's parents. In *Re Pauling's Settlement Trust* [1964] Ch 303, trustees purported to make advancements for young adult beneficiaries at the request of their father. The money, however, was used to pay off the parents' debts, buy a house and maintain a high standard of living for the family. The court described the arrangements as 'systematic looting' of the beneficiaries' interests. It was held that these purported advancements were improper and that trustees must be cautious when they are approached by the parents of young beneficiaries. They must ensure that any advance will be for the benefit of the beneficiary. If there is reason to suppose that the beneficiaries are unlikely to use the money for the purpose for which it was advanced, the trustees should apply the money direct for the purpose, eg directly to the school to pay the beneficiary's school fees.

#### 7.5.2.2 Limitations on the application of s 32

Section 32 authorises trustees to pay capital to beneficiaries with an interest in capital if the payment is for the beneficiary's advancement or benefit. The section authorises payment; it does not compel it. Thus, a beneficiary has no 'right' to an advancement. It is up to the trustees whether or not to advance in their favour.

There are further restrictions on the trustees' use of s 32.

(a) *How much the trustees can advance*. For trusts created on or before 1 October 2014, the maximum that can be advanced is one-half of the beneficiary's presumptive entitlement. However, s 9 of the Inheritance and Trustees' Powers Act 2014 amended s 32 by removing the one-half restriction; it allows trustees to advance the full amount of the beneficiary's share. This amendment applies only to trusts created or arising after the Act's commencement date of 1 October 2014. In *Re Marquess of Abergavenny's Estate Act Trusts* [1981] 2 All ER 643, it was held that once beneficiaries have received an advancement of one-half of their share, the trustees cannot give them a further advancement if the trust fund increases in value.

(b) *Any payment must be brought into account.* The beneficiary must bring any advancement they receive into account on becoming absolutely entitled. When the beneficiary becomes entitled to their share of the trust capital, any advancements previously made to them will be deducted (unless the trust instrument dispenses with the need to account for advancements). However, if a beneficiary with a contingent interest receives an advancement but then dies before satisfying the contingency, the beneficiary's estate does not have to repay the advancement received.

(c) *Any advancement must not prejudice a beneficiary with a prior interest.* If there is a beneficiary with a prior interest, that beneficiary must consent in writing to the advancement (and must be over 18 to be able to do so). A person with a prior interest would be a life tenant (entitled to income before the remainder beneficiaries). Such a life tenant would see a decrease in the income they would receive due to the reduction in the capital available for investment as a result of any s 32 advancement.

**Figure 7.3** Summary – trustees' powers in relation to early release of income and/or capital

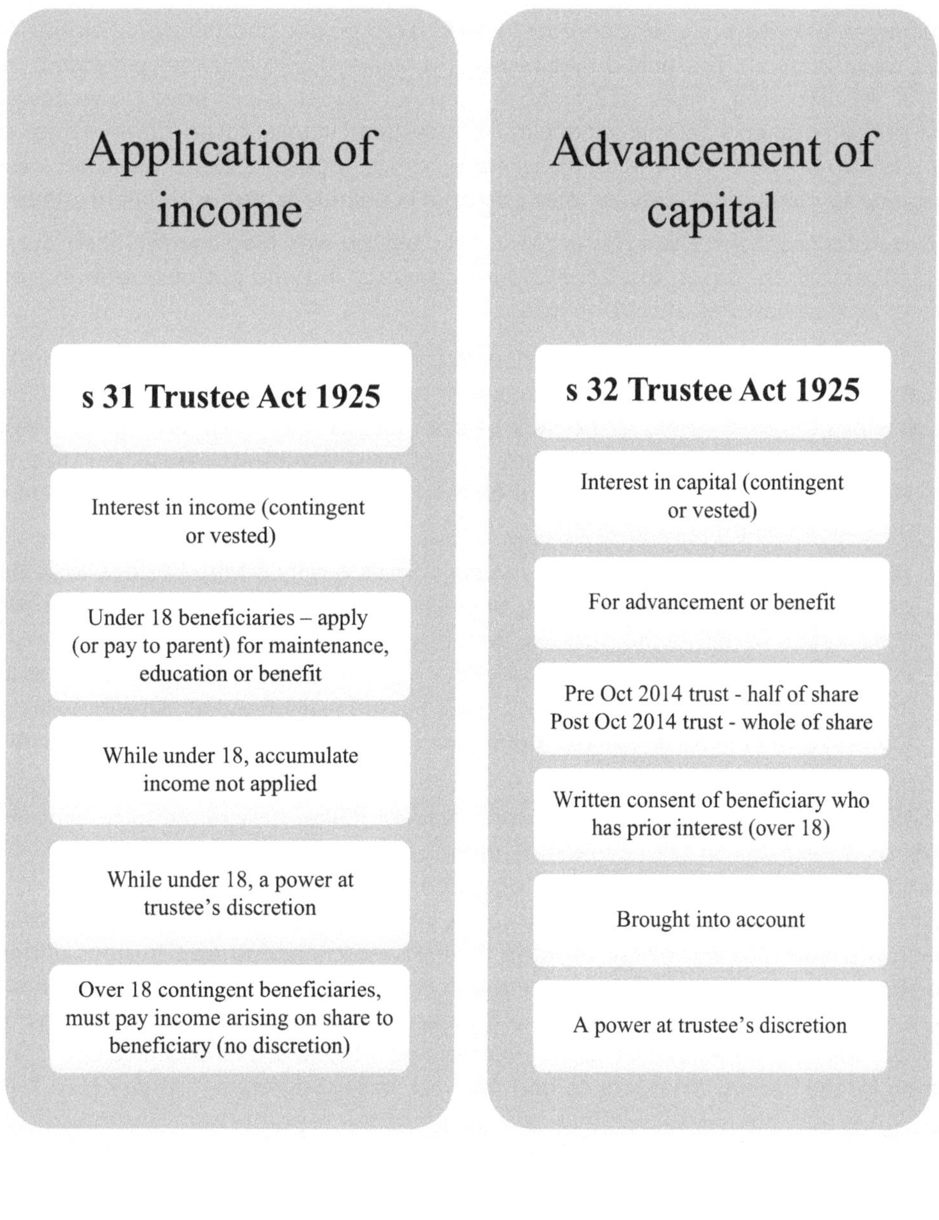

## 7.6 Beneficiaries' control of the trustees

Once the trust is set up, the settlor has no further say in its affairs (unless the trust instrument provides to the contrary or the settlor is one of the trustees). The prime responsibility for supervising the activities of the trustees lies with the beneficiaries. The degree of control vested in the beneficiaries depends on such questions as whether they can force trustees to perform certain acts, whether they can dispute the trustees' decisions, whether the trustees are obliged to follow the wishes of the beneficiaries, how much information the beneficiaries can demand, and whether they can bring the trust to an end.

### 7.6.1 The exercise of duties and powers

Whether beneficiaries can compel trustees to carry out an act in the administration of the trust largely depends on whether the beneficiaries are complaining about the non-exercise of a power or a duty. The distinction is apparent from the terms themselves. Duties must be discharged, whereas trustees need not exercise powers.

The beneficiaries can compel the trustees to perform their duties, if necessary by court action. For example, trustees are under a duty to distribute trust property, at the appropriate time, to the correct beneficiaries. Should the trustees refuse to do so, the beneficiaries can enforce the duty by obtaining a court order.

In contrast, trustees are under no duty to exercise a power and the beneficiaries cannot force them to do so. The only duty owed by the trustees is to consider whether to exercise the power. As discussed, under s 32 of the Trustee Act 1925, trustees have powers to distribute trust property among certain beneficiaries in certain circumstances. Beneficiaries cannot complain to the court if the trustees do not advance capital to them. The court will not intervene to compel the exercise of a power; it is entirely a matter for the trustees.

In two instances the trustees are under a duty, but the way they exercise their duty is in their discretion. In these cases, the beneficiaries can insist that the trustees perform their duty but cannot dictate how this should be done.

(a) *Investment.* Trustees are under a duty to invest trust funds in authorised investments, but the choice of authorised investments is in their discretion. Beneficiaries can force the trustees to invest as this is a duty. However, they cannot insist that trustees exercise their discretion in a particular way – they cannot insist that the trustees invest in a particular investment type (ie shares rather than land) nor can they insist on the investment in a particular company or property.

(b) *Discretionary trust.* A discretionary trust imposes a duty on the trustees to select an object or objects, but the question of whether they should select A as opposed to B is a discretion vested in the trustees. Beneficiaries can take action if the trustees fail to undertake their discretion in any way (the court will ensure that the duty is exercised in some way). However, the beneficiaries cannot insist that the trustees exercise their discretion in favour of one beneficiary over another The trustees only have to consider them.

Beneficiaries can force trustees to perform duties whether they relate to administrative matters (such as investment and the day-to-day management of the trust) or to dispositive matters (such as the distribution of trust funds among beneficiaries). However, they cannot compel trustees to exercise powers. In *Re Brockbank* [1948] Ch 206, the beneficiaries (who were all over 18) wanted the trustees to exercise their power to appoint new trustees under s 36 of the Trustee Act 1925 in accordance with the beneficiaries' wishes. It was held that the trustees could not be compelled to do what the beneficiaries wanted, because s 36 gave the trustees a discretion and beneficiaries cannot interfere with the exercise of a discretion. The only option for the beneficiaries was to end the trust under *Saunders v Vautier* (see **7.7**).

Trustees may exercise a discretion or power, and beneficiaries make seek to challenge this exercise in court if they do not like the outcome. In *Tempest v Lord Camoys* (1882) 21 ChD 571, it was said that the court will intervene in the exercise of a power or discretion if it is 'improper'. What is considered 'improper'? The court will intervene:

- to prevent the exercise of the discretion in favour of a non-object;
- if there is a capricious exercise of the trustees' discretion, ie an exercise 'irrational, perverse or irrelevant to any sensible expectation of the settlor' (*Re Manisty's Settlement* [1974] 1 Ch 17);
- to set aside actions where the trustees had failed in their duty to properly consider whether to exercise the power. In *Turner v Turner* [1983] 2 All ER 745, the court declared the trustees' appointments to be invalid because they had blindly followed the orders of the settlor without even appreciating that they had a discretion to exercise the power;
- if the exercise of the power is wholly unreasonable - the trustees considered the wrong question or did not apply their minds to the right question or shut their eyes to the right question or 'did not act honestly or in good faith' (*Dundee General Hospitals Board of Management v Walker* [1952] 1 All ER 896).
- if the trustees exercise a power outside the intention and purpose for which it had been given and where the exercise of the power did not further the interests of the beneficiaries (*Grand View Private Trust Co Ltd v Wen-Young Wong* [2002] UKPC 47).

The general law gives the beneficiaries only limited rights; however, it is possible for the settlor or testator to provide for the beneficiaries to play an active role in the trust by inserting an appropriate provision in the trust instrument.

### 7.6.2 Access to reasons and information

To mount an effective legal challenge to the trustees' decisions, the beneficiaries will need evidence to prove their case, and, in particular, they will need to know how the trustees reached their decision; only then can they assess whether the trustees have breached their duties.

However, trustees are not obliged to provide the beneficiaries with reasons explaining why they exercised a power or discretion in the way that they did (*Re Beloved Wilkes Charity* (1851) 3 Mac & G 440). If the trustees do state reasons, the court can enquire into their adequacy. This was illustrated in *Klug v Klug* [1918] 2 Ch 67, where a trustee refused to exercise a discretion to give trust capital to a beneficiary and revealed that she had reached this decision because the beneficiary, her daughter, had married without her consent. The court held that the decision was irrational and therefore void.

It is accepted that the beneficiaries (or objects of a discretionary trust) are entitled to see 'trust documents' and trustees have a duty to provide them (**7.3.4**). In *Schmidt v Rosewood Trust* [2003] 3 All ER 76, it was held that beneficiaries are allowed to see trust documents (subject to confidentiality) because beneficiaries and potential beneficiaries are entitled to protection from the court, which might result in disclosure of the documents. 'Trust documents' include the trust deed itself (and any associated deeds relating to appointments of new trustees, appointment to beneficiaries), trust accounts, certificates, deeds and building society books showing how the trust capital is invested.

According to *Re Londonderry's Settlement* [1965] Ch 918, beneficiaries are not allowed to demand documents that contain trustees' deliberations on a discretion or power, as trustees are not bound to disclose their reasons. The confidentiality of the trustees' reasons was justified on two grounds. First, disclosure of the reasons would cause bad feeling within families. Secondly, it was said that no trustees would accept office if they thought that their decisions on discretionary matters would be open to challenge. It is unlikely that professional trustees would be discouraged but their fees might increase if they were forced to justify all decisions.

However, in *Schmidt v Rosewood Trust*, the Privy Council said that the courts have a discretion to order disclosure, even of confidential documents. When deciding whether to exercise this discretion, the court will consider all interests (eg of beneficiaries, trustees and settlor). So, while beneficiaries are not entitled to see a minute book which reveals the trustees' reasons as to why they exercised a power or discretion in any way or correspondence between trustees discussing which objects should be chosen under a discretionary trust, they could ask the court to exercise its discretion under *Schmidt* to disclose them.

Occasionally, when creating a discretionary trust, the settlor or testator may leave a letter of wishes to the trustees providing an indication of how their discretion might be exercised. Such a letter is not binding, but trustees often consider them. Such a letter of wishes from the settlor/testator to the trustees is felt to be 'closely connected to the trustees' decision making process'. It is, therefore, protected by confidentiality (*Breakspear v Ackland* [2008] EWHC 220 (Ch)).

In *Scott v National Trust* [1998] 2 All ER 705, Walker J suggested that where beneficiaries have a legitimate expectation that a discretion will be exercised in their favour, they are entitled to be warned if trustees decide to change their policy. An example might be where an object of a discretionary trust has received a particular amount from the trust every year for the last 10 years. No reasonable trustee would discontinue these payments without warning the object and without giving them an opportunity to persuade the trustees to continue with the payments.

### 7.6.3 Replacing trustees

In certain circumstances, the beneficiaries might be able to direct who should be appointed as trustee:

(a) The trust instrument might give beneficiaries a power of appointment of new trustees.

(b) As discussed in **7.2.3.5**, in exceptional circumstances, by application to court under s 41 of the Trustee Act 1925.

(c) Under s 19 of the Trusts of Land and Appointment of Trustees Act (TLATA) 1996.

Section 19 of the TLATA 1996 allows beneficiaries to give a written direction to a trustee or trustees to retire. Alternatively, or in addition, they can serve a written direction demanding the appointment of new trustees(s) of their choice.

Despite the name of the Act, s 19 applies to trusts of personalty as well as land. However, s 19 will only be available to the beneficiaries in certain circumstances. For the beneficiaries to be able to rely on s 19, the trust instrument must not nominate anyone to appoint new trustees and all the beneficiaries must agree, be sui juris (ie 18 years or more and of sound mind) and together be absolutely entitled to the property in the trust.

### 7.6.4 Ending the trust

Even where the beneficiaries are all sui juris and between them absolutely entitled to the trust property, they cannot dictate how trustees should exercise powers and discretions. They must generally accept the decision of the trustees. However, if beneficiaries remain dissatisfied and all else fails, provided they are all sui juris and absolutely entitled to the trust fund, they can consider closing down the trust, perhaps setting up a new one, and insisting that the old trustees transfer the trust property to new trustees chosen by the beneficiaries (*Saunders v Vautier* (1841) 4 Beav 115).

## 7.7 Variation of beneficial interests

As discussed in **Chapter 1** (at **1.7.4**), regardless of a settlor's or testator's intentions in setting up the trust in the way that they did, the rule from *Saunders v Vautier* (1841) 4 Beav 115 provides that a legally competent sole beneficiary with a vested interest or a group of sui juris beneficiaries (ascertainable, in existent and absolutely entitled to the trust fund) can require the trustees to transfer the trust property to them or to other trustees, and thereby end the trust.

The need to vary administrative or beneficial provisions can rise after the trust was created - for instance changes in the tax laws or the circumstances of beneficiaries. Rather than bringing a trust to an end, the *Saunders v Vautier* rule could be applied to bring about such changes. However, *Saunders v Vautier* applies only if all the beneficiaries are sui juris and ascertained. Thus, in most cases the rule cannot be used; many trusts include beneficiaries who are infants, or possible beneficiaries who are to be born or ascertained in the future. In these cases, the adult ascertained beneficiaries may want to vary the trust, and indeed such a variation may be for the benefit of infant or unascertained beneficiaries - for example it may save tax. Arguably, it is discriminatory to permit a variation of the terms of the trust where the trust consists of adult beneficiaries, but not to permit it where there are under-age (or unborn) beneficiaries.

### 7.7.1 The Variation of Trusts Act 1958

If it is not possible for the beneficiaries to agree on a variation of trust under *Saunders v Vautier*, it is possible for an application to be made to the court for their agreement to any proposed change. While they are able to consider a proposed change to a trust whether of real or personal property and regardless of when or how it was created, the court's jurisdiction to vary trusts is limited.

#### 7.7.1.1 Persons for whom the court can give consent

The court only has the ability to agree to a variation on behalf of a select group of people (Variation of Trusts Act 1958, s 1(1)). The group includes:

(a) a person with an interest in the trust who cannot consent because they are a minor or lack mental capacity;

(b) a person with a hope or expectation of obtaining an interest in the trust in future (examples would include a prospective or presumptive next of kin, a potential future spouse (*Re Moncrieff's Settlement Trust* [1962] 1 WLR 1344));

(c) a person who has not been born;

(d) a person who is a discretionary beneficiary under a protective trust.

The court has no ability to agree to a variation on behalf of any person who does not fall within s 1(1). The court has no power to agree on behalf of an adult ascertained beneficiary who is capable of consenting for themselves (*Knocker v Youle* [1986] 2 All ER 914).

#### 7.7.1.2 Agreement to a variation

The court will approve only a variation and not a resettlement on whole different terms. The requirement is for any proposed arrangement to leave the 'whole substratum of the trust' and merely effect the purpose of the original trust by other means (Megarry J in *Re Ball's Settlement* [1968] 1 WLR 899).

Despite the comments in *Re Ball's Settlement,* the courts have not been deterred from approving arrangements involving a radical reshaping of trusts. Even if an arrangement provides for the existing trusts to be revoked and replaced by new trusts, the arrangement can be approved under the Variation of Trusts Act 1958 (*Re Holt's Settlement* [1960] 1 Ch 100).

In *Ridgewell v Ridgewell* [2007] EWHC 2666 (Ch), the original trust was to H for life, remainder to children. The proposed arrangement was the addition of a new successive interest after the death of H (ie H for life, then W for life, remainder to children). The addition of a totally new beneficiary was not considered to be an example of a change to the 'whole substratum of the trust'. The court looks to substance, not form, and agreed the variation.

7.7.2.3 Variation must be of benefit

The court will 'not approve an arrangement on behalf of any person unless the carrying out thereof would be for the benefit of that person ...' (Variation of Trusts Act, s 1(1)).

Case law has established what can constitute 'benefit' in this context:

- Benefit can be financial (particularly the avoidance of tax, as in *Ridgewell v Ridgewell*), but other forms of benefit, such as educational or social benefit, may also be sufficient. The postponement of vesting beyond the age of majority has been considered a benefit as there is a likelihood of the beneficiaries being more responsible with money (*Re T* [1964] Ch158; *Wright v Gater* [2011] EWHC 2881 (Ch)).
- Financial benefit may be outweighed by other disadvantages, such as the undesirability of uprooting minors merely for tax advantages (*Re Weston's Settlement* [1969] 1 Ch 224).

7.7.2.4 Considerations

When exercising its discretion, the court will generally take the trustees' view into account. The trustees will be asked for their view on the proposed arrangement, although it is not a conclusive indication of the court's likely decision (Upjohn LJ in *Re Steed's Will Trust* [1960] Ch 407).

However, the court does not consider the wishes of the settlor to be relevant to the exercise of its jurisdiction. According to *Goulding v James* [1997] 2 All ER 239, it does not matter if the proposed variation is contrary to the settlor's wishes.

**ACTIVITY Review your understanding – trustees' duties and powers**

Review the facts below and then consider the questions that follow.

Pavati, who died eight years ago, left her large estate to Arum and Deepa to hold on trust for her son, Krishnan, for life, remainder to her grandchildren, Mahika and Rohan, in equal shares. The will contained no provision relating to the powers of the trustees. The two grandchildren, Mahika (aged 20) and Rohan (aged 12), are the children of Pavati's deceased son, Nihal. Krishnan is still alive.

Krishnan and Mahika are both unhappy with the investment of the trust fund. Krishnan has complained that he has received little income in the last two years, and Mahika has concerns about the trustees' investment strategy. Two years ago, Arum and Deepa approached Wizzo Finance Ltd for investment advice. They ignored the poor online reviews that Wizzo had received because Arum was a friend of one the company's directors. Arum and Deepka handed over to Wizzo full responsibility for the trust investments. Arum and Deepa have found out that Wizzo devised an investment strategy to focus on capital growth rather than income generation and invested 85% of the fund in peach.com plc. The value of the peach.com plc shares has fallen dramatically, and Arum and Deepa have been advised that Wizzo has been put into liquidation.

Mahika has approached the trustees asking them to provide money from the trust fund to help her buy a house. Rohan's mother has also asked for some income or capital from the trust fund to pay for Rohan's school fees. The trustees refused both requests. When Mahika asked for some trust accounts and the reasons for the trustees' decision, Arum and Deepa told her it was none of her business.

(a) Will Arum and Deepa be liable for the poor performance of the trust investments in the hands of Wizzo Finance Ltd?

(b) Do Arum and Deepa have power to help Mahika and Rohan as requested? Can they be compelled to do so?

(c) Can Mahika force Arum and Deepa to provide more information?

(d) Can the beneficiaries remove Arum and Deepa from office?

**COMMENT**

(a) Wizzo Finance Ltd

- Trustees have power to delegate their 'delegable functions', which includes investment decision-making (Trustee Act 2000, s 11).
- Such delegation relates to 'asset management'; s 15 of the Trustee Act 2000 requires the delegation to be in (or be evidenced in) writing and to be accompanied by a written policy statement giving guidance on how the investment is to be exercised in the best interests of the trust. Here, the policy statement ought to have made it clear that:
    - o the money was subject to a trust;
    - o there was a need for income return on the investments to provide for Krishnan;
    - o hazardous investments were to be avoided and there was a need to diversify (Trustee Act 2000, s 4).

  It is not clear whether such a policy statement was produced.
- Even if the delegation itself complied with the above requirements, the trustees may still be personally liable for the loss if they failed to comply with the statutory standard of care. The statutory standard of care (Trustee Act 2000, s 1) requires them to have acted with 'such skill and care as is reasonable in the circumstances' (there is no indication that Arum and Deepa are professional trustees so warranting a higher standard). It would appear that Arum and Deepa may have breached this standard in a number of areas:
    - o when selecting Wizzo. They may have had reason to doubt Wizzo's competency, but did not investigate further, perhaps due to Arum's friendship.
    - o reviewing the delegation to Wizzo (Trustee Act 2000, ss 22 and 23). During the two-year period of Wizzo's employment, they should have demanded regular reports as to the value of the trust fund and how it was invested. Allowing the agents to devise an inappropriate strategy and then invest most of the trust fund in a single dot.com company is likely to be a breach (blatant disregard of need for diversification and a lack of monitoring).

Given that Wizzo Finance Ltd is in liquidation, the beneficiaries may choose to sue Arum and Deepa to recover the loss to the trust fund caused by the delegation and poor investment choices.

(b) Requests for money

*Rohan*

Section 31 of the TA 1925 does not apply to Rohan because he is not entitled to income until the life tenant, Krishnan, dies. As a remainderman, Rohan has an interest in capital. Accordingly, s 32 advancement of capital may be a possibility as Rohan has an interest in the trust capital. As the trust was created after October 2014, the entirety of Rohan's prospective share of the capital could be advanced for his advancement or benefit. This advancement should be paid directly to the relevant third-party provider of that benefit (as Rohan is a minor). Any advance would have to be brought into account on final distribution to Rohan. However, any advance would require the life tenant to give his written consent. (Is this likely in the circumstances?)

*Mahika*

Like Rohan, Mahika has an interest in the capital, so an advancement under s 32 would be possible but subject to the same conditions as to amount, bringing into account and need for consent. Another possibility is a loan secured by a mortgage of the house (Trustee Act 2000, s 3). It is also possible to consider the purchase of land under s 8 of the TA 2000, but would the trustees fail in their duty to balance the interests of all the beneficiaries if they bought the house and allowed Mahika to live in it?

All the above are in the discretion of the trustees. They cannot be forced to exercise a discretion even if all the beneficiaries agree (*Re Brockbank*). However, they are under a duty to consider whether or not to exercise the discretion.

If beneficiaries were in a position to end the trust under *Saunders v Vautier*, they could compel the trustees to share out the capital between them. However, this will not currently work because Rohan is only 12 years old.

(c) Documents

Krishnan, Mahika and Rohan, as beneficiaries, can demand trust documents, eg accounts and information on how the trust fund is invested (*Re Londonderry's Settlement*), but not the reasons for the non-exercise of discretion. Under *Schmidt v Rosewood*, the court has a discretion to order disclosure as part of its jurisdiction to monitor the way trustees run their trusts. In the circumstances here, the court might entertain such an application.

(d) Removal

Section 19 of the TLATA 1996 allows the beneficiaries to remove and appoint trustees. It could apply where all the beneficiaries are of full age and capacity, are together the only persons entitled to the trust property and are all in agreement. In this case, 'all the beneficiaries' includes Krishnan, Mahika and Rohan. However, use of s 19 is not possible here because Rohan is under 18.

Under s 41 of the TA 1925, the court will only remove a trustee if it is expedient to do so. In view of the disastrous investment delegation, it may not be in the best interests of the trust for Arum and Deepa to continue so the court might entertain an application from the beneficiaries to remove them.

## SUMMARY

- It is essential to be aware of the legal rules and principles governing the practical running of trusts and to understand the various sources for these rules and principles – the trust deed itself, statute and case law.
- Knowing how trustees are appointed and how an individual's trusteeship might end is critical to ensuring the effective and efficient administration of a trust.
- Although trustees have a duty to be actively involved in the administration of the trusts, there may be times when the trustees, either collectively or individually, wish or need to appoint an agent to act on their behalf. It is important to ensure that such delegation is undertaken correctly.
- It is a fundamental duty for trustees to safeguard the trust. There are many elements to appreciate in relation to the duty to invest trust funds – the considerations for trustees in devising their investment strategies, the extensive impact of the Trustee Act 2000 and the consequences of issues with investment performance.

- Trustees have statutory powers of maintenance and advancement over the income and capital of a trust. Being able to identify when these statutory powers might be available could enable trustees to help beneficiaries before they are strictly entitled to trust assets.
- Appreciating the difference between duties and powers gives rise to understanding what control, if any, beneficiaries have over the actions of trustees.
- Regardless of the initial wishes of the person creating a trust, in certain circumstances, it is possible to vary the interests of the beneficiaries under that trust, either by the actions of the beneficiaries themselves of by application to the court.

# 8 Fiduciary Duties

**LEARNING OUTCOMES**

By the end of this chapter, you should be able to:

- recognise circumstances in which a fiduciary relationship can arise;
- identify the core duties underpinning the fiduciary relationship;
- understand the circumstances in which fiduciary duties affect trustees in the administration of a trust;
- appreciate the concept of strict liability and its impact on breaches of fiduciary duty;
- explain the steps which can be taken by trustees and other fiduciaries to avoid liability for breach of fiduciary duty; and
- outline the remedies available where trustees and other fiduciaries have made an unauthorised profit.

## 8.1 Introduction

There is no formal definition of when a fiduciary relationship arises. However, in *Bristol and West Building Society v Mothew* [1998] Ch 1, Millett LJ explained that:

> a fiduciary is someone who has undertaken to act for or on behalf of another in a particular manner in circumstances which give rise to a relationship of trust and confidence. The distinguishing obligation of the fiduciary is the obligation of loyalty.

There are a number of relationships which give rise to this 'obligation of loyalty', and to ensure that loyalty, various fiduciary duties arise. These fiduciary duties are negative in nature; they aim to prevent a fiduciary from placing themselves in a situation where their duties to their principal may conflict with their own personal interests. If fiduciaries flout this rule, they must surrender any personal gain they make.

## 8.2 Who are fiduciaries?

### 8.2.1 Status-based fiduciaries

Trustees are the obvious example of fiduciaries. Trustees have control of the trust property, and they are under a duty to manage it in such a way as to promote the best interests of the beneficiaries. However, the fact that the trustees have this degree of control provides the opportunity for them to abuse their position for their own advantage. As is to be expected, self-preferment by the trustees undertaking their role is not permitted; their fiduciary obligations to the beneficiaries prevent this.

However, trustees are not the only people who are regarded as fiduciaries because of the role that they play in a specific relationship. Other examples include personal representatives (as regards beneficiaries under the will or on intestacy), agents (vis-à-vis their principals), partners in a business (who owe fiduciary duties to each other), directors (who owe fiduciary duties to their company), and senior employees with access to confidential information (who owe fiduciary duties to their employers). They are called 'status-based' fiduciaries because the fiduciary label attaches to their office regardless of the facts of the particular case.

### 8.2.2 Fact-based fiduciaries

The courts have long accepted that 'a fiduciary relationship can arise outside the archetypal circumstances' (*Kelly v Baker & Braid* [2022] EWHC 2879 (Comm)). These fiduciary relationships are said to be 'fact-based' as it is the courts who have decided that a fiduciary relationship exists in the circumstances of the case.

***Examples***

*English v Dedham Vale Properties Ltd [1978] 1 All ER 382 – here purchasers negotiating to buy land and purporting to act on behalf of the sellers sought and obtained planning permission. It was held that as 'self-appointed agents' the purchasers had put themselves in a fiduciary position, and they had to account to the sellers for the profit arising from the grant of planning permission.*

*LAC Minerals Ltd v International Corona Resources Ltd (1989) 61 DLR (4th) 14 – in this Canadian case a fiduciary relationship was held to exist because of the disclosure of confidential information by the claimant in the course of contract negotiations for a possible joint venture with the defendant. The defendant had used the information for its sole benefit rather than for the benefit of the joint venture and was required to account to the claimant.*

*Murad and another v Al Saraj and another [2004] EWHC 1235 (Ch) – here the first instance judge decided that there was a fiduciary relationship where the claimants were totally reliant on the defendant to disclose all relevant information and to negotiate with the seller and instruct professionals for the all parties in connection with their joint venture to buy a hotel. According to the judge it was a 'classic [case] in which the claimants reposed trust and confidence in the [defendant] by virtue of their relative and respective positions'. The decision was upheld on appeal.*

*Cobbetts v Hodge [2009] EWHC 786 (Ch) – a solicitor was found to be in a fiduciary relationship with his employer because he was paid commission for introducing clients to the firm. He had misused his fiduciary position by purchasing shares in a company who was a client of his employers, an opportunity he had acquired only because of his employment. He had to account to the firm for the shares.*

## 8.3 Fundamental fiduciary duty

A fiduciary owes their principal duties of honesty, loyalty and good faith. Underpinning these duties is the fundamental duty for the fiduciary to avoid conflicts of interest. In the words of Lord Herschel in *Bray v Ford* [1896] AC 44, at 51:

> It is an inflexible rule of a Court of Equity that a person in a fiduciary position ... is not, unless otherwise expressly provided, entitled to make a profit; he is not allowed to put himself in a position where his interest and duty conflict. It does not appear to me that this rule is, as has been said, founded on principles of morality. I regard it rather as based on the consideration that, human nature being what it is, there is a danger, in

> such circumstances, of the person holding a fiduciary position being swayed by interest rather than duty, and thus prejudicing those whom he was bound to protect.

The duty to avoid conflict of interest as outlined by Lord Herschel in *Bray v Ford* applies to all fiduciaries (whether status- or fact-based) and is applied against the fiduciaries regardless of the circumstances.

***Regal (Hastings) Ltd v Gulliver* [1942] 1 All ER 378**

Regal Hastings owned one cinema and formed a subsidiary company to obtain leases of two other cinemas (with a view to creating a more valuable sales package). The landlord would grant the leases to the subsidiary only if its share capital was fully paid up. However, Regal could afford to pay for only some of the shares in the subsidiary. Regal directors personally paid for and then held the other shares. The directors eventually sold these shares at a profit. Shareholders brought a claim against the directors, on the basis that this profit was in breach of their fiduciary duty to the company and the shareholders' consent had not been obtained for the share arrangement.

The House of Lords (reversing the decisions of High Court and the Court of Appeal) held that the defendants had made their profits 'by reason of the fact that they were directors of Regal and in the course of the execution of that office'. The directors had to account to Regal for the profit.

The fact that the directors were honest, that Regal could not have purchased the shares themselves and that Regal benefited from the arrangement was irrelevant,

Lord Russell said that the duty to account for the profit did not depend on:

> fraud, or absence of bona fides or upon questions or considerations as whether the property would or should otherwise have gone to the plaintiff, or whether he took a risk or acted as he did for the benefit of the plaintiff, or whether the plaintiff has in fact been damaged or benefited by his action. The liability arises from the mere fact of a profit having, in the stated circumstances, been made.

The recent landmark decision of *Rukhadze v Recovery Partners GP Ltd* [2025] UKSC 10 on fiduciary liability to account for unauthorised profit restated the core fiduciary obligation of loyalty as the basis of the no conflict and no profit rules. This case considered causation, and it was held that whilst a sufficient link between the fiduciary duty and the profit is required, the 'but for' test does not apply to a breach of fiduciary duty.

## 8.4 Fiduciary duties and trustees

For trustees there are a number of specific circumstances which could impact on them in the administration of the trust. In these circumstances, they could find themselves in a position where their personal interest could conflict with their duty to the beneficiaries.

### 8.4.1 Trustee as a purchaser of trust property

A trustee may decide that they wish to buy some of the trust property for themselves personally.

The rule governing this situation is called the *self-dealing rule*, because trustees are effectively selling trust property to themselves, acting on both sides of the transaction as both seller and buyer. There is a clear conflict between the trustee's duty to get the best price for the trust asset being sold in the interests of the trust and their personal interest in buying for a low price.

The self-dealing rule does not, however, mean that any sale of trust property to a trustee is automatically void and not permitted. A sale of trust property to a trustee is voidable by the beneficiaries within a reasonable time. It is for the beneficiaries to decide whether to overturn the sale and there is no obligation on them to do so. The sale to the trustee may be a good deal as far as the beneficiaries are concerned and they may not want to upset it. The only requirement of beneficiaries is that they must make their decision to object to the sale within a reasonable time. If the beneficiaries decide to avoid any sale, they must refund the price paid by the trustee and any expenses incurred in return for the purchased asset.

The self-dealing rule has been applied strictly where a transaction has been challenged. The courts are unwilling to consider whether the trustee has gained an unfair advantage (*Ex p Lacey* (1802) 6 Ves 625). It also makes no difference whether the trustee buys from themselves alone or from themselves and their co-trustees. Nor will a sale by auction circumvent the rule's application. Even with an auction there is a possibility that a trustee could still promote their own interests by, for example, choosing to sell trust property at a time when market prices are low. Similarly, a trustee cannot retire and then purchase the trust property (unless a significant period of time has lapsed between the retirement and the purchase, for instance 12 years as in *Re Boles* [1902] 1 Ch 244).

The court did allow a sale to a trustee by auction in the case of *Holder v Holder* [1968] Ch 353. However, this was very specific to the circumstances – the 'trustee' had played no part in arranging the sale as he believed that he had formerly disclaimed his position as trustee.

Nonetheless, there are ways to circumvent the application of the self-dealing rule:

- If all the sui juris beneficiaries have agreed to a sale, the court will uphold it (unless all the beneficiaries were not fully informed about relevant details).
- The trust instrument can provide express permission from the settlor/testator to the purchase of trust property.
- The trustee could seek a court order authorising the sale, although this would be a costly and time-consuming course of action for the individual trustee.

### 8.4.2 Trustee as purchaser of a beneficial interest

Rather than considering the purchasing of the legal interest in a trust asset, these circumstances relate to the purchase by the trustee of a vested beneficial interest in the trust itself, for example a life interest or a remainder interest.

***Example***

*Gordon and Harry are holding property on trust for Ian. Ian has a vested equitable interest that can be sold. Gordon buys the equitable interest from Ian. If the transaction is allowed to stand, Gordon and Harry will hold on trust for Gordon.*

In this example, there is a danger that Gordon, as trustee, may use his position of trust to gain an unfair advantage. The beneficiary may be in the habit of relying on the trustee's professional skill or superior knowledge and blindly accept the trustee's advice. There is, therefore, a presumption of undue influence. Consequently, a beneficiary can set aside such a transaction, unless the trustee can show that it was fair and there was no undue influence. This is called the *fair-dealing rule*.

To prevent a beneficiary setting aside the trustee's purchase of the beneficial interest at some point in the future, trustees need to ensure that:

(a) they disclose all material facts to the beneficiary before the purchase;

(b) the transaction is fair and honest; and

(c) they can show that they took no advantage, and that the beneficiary exercised an independent judgement and was not the subject of undue influence.

The fair-dealing rule is more relaxed than the self-dealing rule because the transfer of an equitable interest will be upheld if it was fair and not the result of undue influence. In contrast, fairness and good faith are irrelevant to the application of the self-dealing rule. This may be because beneficiaries negotiate sales of their beneficial interests themselves and are aware of the key facts. A sale of trust property by trustees may proceed without the beneficiary's involvement, so it is impossible for anyone (other than the trustees) to know whether it was fair or not; the problem is overcome by making the sale voidable without regard to fairness.

### 8.4.3 Trustee in competition with the trust

Where the trust includes a business and a trustee sets up their own business in competition, the trustee is accountable for any profits made out of the competing business. A further remedy is an injunction to prevent the trustee carrying on the competing business. In *Re Thomson* [1930] 1 Ch 203, it was held that a trustee could be restrained by injunction from setting up as a yacht-broker in the same town as the yacht-broker business carried on by the trust. Setting up a competing business put the trustee in a position where their personal interest conflicted with their duty to the trust. In the case, competition would have been inevitable because the business in question was so specialised.

### 8.4.4 Trustee being paid by the trust

Trustees can recover out-of-pocket expenses from the trust fund, such as the cost of travelling to trustees' meetings (Trustee Act 2000, s 31(1)(a)).

However, the basic rule of equity is that trustees cannot demand payment (remuneration) for their services (their time and expertise) unless authorised in the ways set out below. If there were no restrictions, trustees would be able to charge as much as they liked, which would obviously produce a conflict of interest. Remuneration may be authorised in a number of ways.

#### 8.4.4.1 Charging clause in the trust instrument

Trustees can charge fees if there is a clause authorising remuneration in the trust instrument. It is common for wills and trust documents to contain these clauses. They are called 'charging clauses'.

#### 8.4.4.2 Beneficiaries' consent

If the beneficiaries are all legally competent, they can agree to pay the trustees remuneration (so such an agreement is not possible if one beneficiary is under 18). It is presumed that, in negotiating such an agreement, the beneficiaries are subject to the undue influence of the trustees. Unless the agreement is fair and the trustee makes full disclosure of all relevant facts, the beneficiaries can set it aside later.

#### 8.4.4.3 Court order

The court has inherent jurisdiction to authorise remuneration. This power used to be exercised sparingly. However, in light of *Re Duke of Norfolk's Settlement Trusts* [1981] 3 All ER 220, the courts can now be more generous to trustees. Fox LJ said the courts must balance the need to protect the beneficiaries from trustees' claims against the effective administration of the trust. The court should order remuneration if it is in the interests of the beneficiaries because, for example, the trust needs the skill of the trustee in question and their fees are not excessive compared with those of other professionals.

#### 8.4.4.4 Under the Trustee Act 2000

The rule prohibiting remuneration was considered to be out of date, and, in 1999, the Law Commission recommended that the law should permit professional trustees to charge fees. Relevant provisions were included in the Trustee Act 2000.

Under s 29 of the Trustee Act 2000, certain trustees are entitled to recover remuneration. To claim the benefit of s 29, it is necessary for the trustee to act in a professional capacity (s 29(2)(a)). Section 28(5) provides that trustees act 'in a professional capacity' where they 'act in the course of a profession or business which consists of or includes the administration of trusts'. Section 29(2) provides that a trustee who is not a trust corporation can charge fees only if all the other trustees agree in writing.

The s 29(2) requirement to obtain the consent of other trustees means that sole professional trustees (unless a trust corporation) are not able to charge for their services under the Trustee Act 2000. They must rely on the pre-Trustee Act 2000 possibilities detailed above.

A trustee can charge 'reasonable' remuneration for any services provided on behalf of the trust (including work a layperson could have done). When determining what is reasonable, s 29(3) requires consideration of the nature of the services being provided (by reference to the size of the trust, the specialist nature of the services provided and the trustee providing them).

Section 29 cannot be used 'if any provision about [trustees'] entitlement to remuneration has been made by ... the trust instrument' (s 29(5)). This could be a provision for or against remuneration. Thus, s 29 will not apply if there is a charging clause in the trust instrument or an express prohibition on remuneration.

### 8.4.5 Trustee being paid by third parties

As the legal owners of trust property, trustees are uniquely placed to gain the opportunity to obtain payments from third parties by virtue of being trustees of the trust. Consequently, trustees must account to the trust for any personal profit they gain from third parties.

#### 8.4.5.1 Commission

A trustee might receive commission from a company for providing the company with trust business, for example an insurance company paying a trustee commission for taking out a trust insurance policy, a stockbroker for the trust's investment business.

The conflict of interest is between the trustee's duty to give impartial advice on the choice of company providing the service and the trustee's personal interest in recommending the firm to gain commission for themselves. The profit will have been out of and by reason of their trusteeship, and they have to account to the beneficiaries (*Williams v Barton* [1927] 2 Ch 9) unless the trust instrument authorises trustees to keep it.

An example of the same principle applying in a commercial setting arose in *Imageview Management Ltd v Jack* [2009] 2 All ER 66. Here, Jack was an international goalkeeper from Trinidad and Tobago who wanted to play professionally in the UK. Imageview acted as Jack's agent and secured a two-year contract with a club. Jack paid Imageview its fee. Unknown to Jack, the club paid Imageview £3,000 (an inflated sum) to obtain a work permit for Jack. It was held that the £3,000 was a secret profit; football agents are fiduciaries just like any other agent and Imageview had to account to Jack for the sum.

#### 8.4.5.2 Directors' salaries

If a trust holds a substantial shareholding in a company, it may be necessary for the trustees to become actively engaged in the company's affairs so as to safeguard the trust's interest (*Bartlett v Barclays Bank Trust Co Ltd (No 2)* [1980] 1 Ch 515). The trust's shares will give the trustees (as legal owner) the right to vote at shareholders' meetings; the number of votes will correspond to the number of shares held. The trustees will attend a shareholders' meeting called to appoint new directors of the company. For the appointment of a director, the resolution must be supported by more than 50% of the shareholders who are eligible to vote. The trustees can use the votes attached to the trust shares to get themselves appointed as directors. Companies generally pay their directors a fee for undertaking their role. The issue for a trustee who has been appointed as a company director is whether they are able to keep that fee or whether they have to surrender these fees to the trust.

The basic principle is that where the trustee has had to rely on the trust's shareholding to become a director, the trustee cannot retain any fees paid to them as director; they must account for the fees to the trust (*Re Macadam* [1946] Ch 73). If the trustee was already a director of the company before becoming a trustee, the trustee can keep the fees because they did not become a director by virtue of the trust (*Re Dover Coalfield Extension* [1908] 1 Ch 65). Similarly, if the trustee has been appointed as a director without reference to the trust's shares, they will be able to keep the fees notwithstanding they are a director as a result of the trust's shareholding (*Re Gee* [1948] Ch 284).

***Examples***

*A trust holds 45% of all the shares in a company. One of the trustees was voted onto the board of directors by a vote of 100% of the shareholders. Here, even if the votes attached to the trust shares had been used against the trustee, they would still have secured the position; they are able to keep any director's fee paid.*

*A trust holds 45% of all the shares in a company. One of the trustees was voted onto the board of directors by a 60% majority comprising the votes attached to the trust share. In this case had the votes attached to the trust shareholding been used against the trustee's appointment, they would not have become a director. They became a director and will receive any fees by virtue of being a trustee and using trust property. Therefore, they are in breach of their duty not to profit from the trust, and they will have to account to the trust for the fees they receive.*

The principle from *Re Macadam* will not apply if the trust instrument expressly allows trustees to retain any directors' remuneration. In exceptional cases it might be possible to get authorisation from the court. The court has to be satisfied that it was in the interests of the trust for the trustee to become a director, and that the trustee has put in more time and effort than is needed just to protect the trust's shareholding.

### 8.4.6 Trustee renewing trust property

It is possible that the trust property includes a lease of premises. The trustees may rent the premises to accommodate a business which forms part of the trust, or they may hold a lease of residential premises. Such leases may last for a fixed term, eg four years or 21 years. When the lease is approaching its expiry date, there may be the opportunity to renew it, getting the landlord to agree to grant a new lease for a new fixed term. Another possibility is that the landlord offers to sell their freehold estate to the tenant-trustees. If the trustees arrange to take the new lease or buy the freehold on their own account and not as part of the trust property, this will be a breach of their fiduciary duty.

***Keech v Sandford* (1726) 2 Eq Cas Abr 741**

Here, the trustee held a lease on trust for an infant. When the lease expired, the landlord refused to renew the lease in favour of the trust. However, he indicated that he would be willing to renew the lease to the trustee personally. The new lease was granted to the trustee, and this was challenged on behalf of the beneficiary. It was held that the trustee had to transfer the lease to the trust and account for the profits they had made. The trustee was strictly liable for a breach of fiduciary duty. The honesty of the trustee and the fact that the trust could not have obtained the new lease made no difference.

*Keech v Sandford* is a good example of how strictly fiduciary duties are applied. The court justified the use of this strict liability by saying that it would act as a deterrent to other trustees who might be tempted to obtain renewals for themselves.

The principle from *Keech v Sandford* was applied in a modern commercial circumstance in *Don King Productions Inc v Warren and Others* [2000] Ch 291. Here two boxing promoters, King and Warren, had been in a partnership agreement which provided that they each held the benefit of any management or promotion agreement concluded previously, on trust for the partnership. In any event, as partners they would have owed each other fiduciary duties with regard to partnership. The partnership subsequently came to an end and was dissolved but was not fully wound up when Warren personally renewed what had been partnership agreements. Lightman J held that the principle established in *Keech v Sandford* would extend beyond the renewal of trust leases to cover the case. He decided that the renewals were also held on trust for the partnership. Warren had placed himself in a position of conflict of interest; his duty was to renew such contracts for the benefit of the partnership in order to maximise the assets available on the winding up.

## 8.5 Use of information and opportunities

By virtue of their position, fiduciaries are often uniquely placed to gain valuable information or opportunities which they could turn to their own advantage instead of using them for the benefit of their principal.

In *Industrial Development Consultants v Cooley* [1972] 2 All ER 162, Cooley, the managing director of IDC, was in negotiation with a company to obtain a contract for IDC. The negotiations were unsuccessful; Cooley was told that IDC would not get the work. However, Cooley was informed that he would stand a good chance of getting the work if he were to tender for it personally. Cooley resigned from IDC (claiming ill-health) and entered into the contract with the company. It was held that Cooley had to account to IDC for the profit he made, even though IDC had little chance of getting the contract. His duty was to pass on the information about the contract to IDC and to do his best to get the company to change its policy and award the contract to IDC.

*IDC v Cooley* was another example of the application of strict liability, although possibly coupled with Cooley's bad faith in leaving IDC. However, strict liability in relation to a fiduciary's use of information for personal gain has been applied even when the fiduciary acted in good faith at all times.

***Boardman v Phipps*** **[1967] 2 AC 46**

This case involved a trust (for a testator's widow and children) but did not involve a claim against a trustee. Instead, the defendants were the trust's solicitor, Boardman, and an associate, T (who was also one of the beneficiaries of the trust).

The trust held a large shareholding in a private company. The shares in the company were not publicly available and there were only a handful of shareholders. Boardman and one of the trustee's (an accountant) were dissatisfied with the financial position of the company. Boardman and T attended a shareholders' meeting as proxies of the trustees and gained valuable information about the company. Consequently, Boardman and T decided to make a takeover bid to obtain control of the company.

The trustees had no power to purchase more shares in the company for the trust, and while they could have applied to the court for authorisation, the accountant trustee said he would not have considered doing so. However, Boardman continued to negotiate with the company, purporting to act on behalf of the trust, and gained further information about the value of the company's assets.

Three trustees has been appointed in the trust document - the testator's widow (who lacked mental capacity and took no part in trust affairs) and daughter as well as the accountant. The accountant and daughter were asked if they objected to Boardman and T purchasing the shares in their own names out of their own funds. They did not object. Boardman and T proceeded with the purchase in their own names out of their own funds.

By skillful management, they were able to turn the fortunes of the company around and make a large distribution of capital to the trust and to themselves personally. One of the other beneficiaries complained and demanded that the defendants account to the trust for their shares and profit.

Boardman and T were found to be self-appointed agents of the trustees and as such they were found to be in breach of their fiduciary duties (having not obtained the fully informed consent of all the trustees to their actions).

Breach 1 - Use of information: Boardman and T had received the information about the company which would not have otherwise been publicly available. As the company's shares were not traded on the open market, the opportunity to bid for the shares only came about because Boardman and T had purported to represent the trust. They had been able to make a profit from their use of the information they had obtained and their position.

Breach 2 - Conflict of interest: there was the possibility that the trustees might have asked Boardman whether the trust should apply to the court for power to buy the shares for the trust; he could not have given impartial advice. The fact that it was unlikely that this advice would be sought was immaterial as, according to Hodson LJ, 'whenever the possibility of conflict is present between personal interest and the fiduciary position the rule of equity must be applied'.

Boardman and T had to account to the trust for their shares and profit (subject to the trust reimbursing them with their costs). However, they were awarded generous remuneration under the court's inherent jurisdiction because they had been honest, had devoted a great deal of time and skill to improving the fortunes of the company, and had brought a benefit to the trust.

In *Boardman v Phipps*, the majority reinforced the principle of strict liability for breaches of fiduciary duty. The defendants were accountable in spite of their honesty and the fact that the trust benefited, and notwithstanding the fact that the possibility of a conflict of interest was very remote. The court favours strict liability as a deterrent. Trustees simply must not put themselves in a position of conflict of interest. If they do, and they make a profit, they will be accountable, regardless of whether they were honest and whether they gained their profit at the expense of the trust. Trustees will not be tempted to try to make a personal profit when they know that they must surrender it regardless of the merits of the case. This means that when they make decisions for the trust, they will not be distracted by thoughts of personal gain. The strict approach also overcomes evidential problems of proving that the trustee was dishonest or profited at the expense of the trust.

Advocates of strict liability also point out that trustees and other fiduciaries are not completely barred from obtaining a personal profit: the courts can order remuneration for exceptional skill and effort which benefits not only the fiduciary but also the beneficiary (*Boardman v Phipps*). Further, the fiduciary can make a profit if it is authorised, eg by the settlor/testator or by the consent of beneficiaries.

However, some would argue that it be better to allow trustees to make a profit, and then decide whether they should be allowed to keep it depending on whether they were honest and whether the trust suffered in any way. Various arguments are made against strict liability – the strict approach not distinguishing between honest and dishonest trustees, and the harsh rules discouraging people from accepting trusteeships.

However, the strict approach of the *Boardman* majority represents the current position in English law in relation to trustees and most fiduciaries. In *Von Westenholz v Gregson* [2022] EWHC 2947 (Ch), two directors of a company were also trustees of a family trust containing shares in the same company. The court found the trustees' actions 'understandable in the circumstances' (they were trying to save the company from liquidation and believed that they were acting in accordance with a loan agreement with the settlor of the trust). However, they had put their duties to the company ahead of their duties as trustees and were, therefore, liable to the trust.

Arguably, the fiduciary duties of company directors in relation to conflict of interest and the use of information have been relaxed slightly by the Companies Act 2006, as it was felt that the equitable rules might stifle entrepreneurial activity. Under s 175(1) of the Companies Act 2006 a director must still avoid a situation in which they have, or may have, a direct or indirect interest that conflicts, or possibly may conflict, with the interests of the company, and this applies in particular to the exploitation of any property, information or opportunity, and it is immaterial whether the company could take advantage of the property, information or opportunity (s 175(2)). However, the fiduciary duty will not be breached if the situation cannot be 'reasonably regarded as likely to give rise to a conflict of interest' (Companies Act, s 175(4)).

## 8.6 Remedies for breach of fiduciary duty

Where there has been a breach of fiduciary duty, the most important question for the successful claimant is likely to centre on the remedy that they will receive.

### 8.6.1 Personal claim

Trustees and other fiduciaries must 'account for' any unauthorised profit which they make. This is a 'personal' remedy, because it requires the fiduciary to pay a sum equal to the amount of the unauthorised profit from their own funds.

With a claim for breach of fiduciary duty, the claimant need not have suffered any loss. For example, if a trustee uses the votes attached to trust shares to become a company director, and receives a salary from the company, the trust has suffered no loss but can still claim the salary as unauthorised profit. The aim is to strip fiduciaries of any gain they make from a conflict situation; it is a 'disgorgement' remedy.

In this way, an action for an account of profits differs from, say, a claim for damages for breach of contract, where the object is to compensate the claimant for loss the claimant has suffered.

### 8.6.2 Proprietary claim

A proprietary claim is an action to recover property which you own (or, by using tracing, property which has replaced it – see **Chapter 9**). There had been some uncertainty about whether a proprietary claim could be made to obtain the actual property now representing the unauthorised fiduciary profit. For example, where the trustee has made an unauthorised profit of £200,000 and has bought company shares with the money, a personal claim would be for an account of £200,000, whereas a proprietary claim would seek to recover the shares.

As a result of the Supreme Court decision in *FHR European Ventures LLP v Cedar Capital Partners LLC* [2014] UKSC 45, any unauthorised profit, regardless of how it is obtained, is held by the fiduciary on constructive trust. The beneficiaries, therefore, have the option of a personal claim or a proprietary claim to the property representing the profit.

A proprietary claim could be advantageous as it enables the principle to recover any increase in value. Additionally, if the defendant fiduciary has been made bankrupt, a proprietary claim has priority over the fiduciary's creditors. In contrast, a claimant bringing a personal claim for an account will rank alongside the ordinary unsecured creditors on the bankruptcy and is unlikely to recover enough to justify the cost of bringing the proceedings.

## 8.7 Express authorisation from the settlor or testator

Duties and powers which impact on the trustees' management and administration of the trust have been identified in **Chapters 7** and **8**. These duties and powers can arise from statute (as in **Chapter 7**) or from the fiduciary nature of the trustees' relationship with the beneficiaries (as here in **Chapter 8**). Regardless of their source, these duties and powers seek to balance the trustees' ability to undertake their role effectively without unnecessary interference in the best interests of the beneficiaries in the circumstances against the obligation to safeguard the needs and interests of those beneficiaries.

In most instances, a settlor or testator will be happy to accept the statutory or fiduciary rules for their trust. However, it is important to remember that the person creating the trust is always able to exclude or amend the statutory provisions or disapply the fiduciary obligations by expressly detailing their own preferences on how their trust should be administered.

Throughout **Chapters 7** and **8,** there have been a number of instances where it is important to check the trust instrument to see whether a settlor or testator has done just that:

- increasing or restricting the trustees' powers of investment under the Trustee Act 2000;
- postponing a right to income under s 31 of the Trustee Act 1925;
- dispensing with the need for the consent of a life tenant to a s 32 Trustee Act 1925 advancement;
- allowing a trustee to purchase trust assets or to retain incidental profits; and
- expanding or limiting the circumstances in which a trustee might receive remuneration for dealing with the trust.

There are other statutory or fiduciary duties which a settlor or testator may seek to adapt to suit their own wishes.

Trustees acting in accordance with the express provisions provided by the settlor or testator will not be in breach of duty (statutory or fiduciary). Of course, a testator or settlor should be aware of and advised carefully when such provisions are to be included in the trust instrument, so they are clear on their effect. However, it is accepted that the inclusion of such express provisions is permissible and in some instances can be beneficial to the administration of the trust for both trustees and beneficiaries alike.

It is also accepted that this freedom extends to a settlor or testator being able to relieve a trustee from liability for any breach even if the particular breach has caused actual loss to the trust.

Such 'exemption clauses', as they are generally called, can relieve trustees from liability for negligent or innocent breaches (they are, however, void insofar as they try to exclude liability for fraudulent breaches - *Armitage v Nurse* [1997] 3 WLR 1046). The clause in *Armitage* protected a trustee from liability for loss or damage to the trust property 'no matter how indolent, imprudent, lacking in diligence, negligent or willful he may have been, so long as he has not acted dishonestly' (Millet LJ). Millet LJ went on to comment that the core trustee duty was merely to perform the trust 'honestly and in good faith'. He did not accept that the core obligations include the 'duties of skill and care, prudence and diligence'.

There is, therefore, concern that exemption clauses can go too far in allowing avoidance of any liability, especially when considering the duties and powers we have considered in this chapter and especially as they can be used to relieve professional as well as lay trustees. The Law Commission acknowledged the issue in its Consultation Paper and 2006 Report on trustee exemption clauses. The Commission report suggested that professional bodies voluntarily adopt practice rules whereby the settlor/testator is made aware that an exemption clause is included in the trust document and its effect. For instance, the Society of Trusts and Estate Practitioners (STEP) does have various rules of practice along these lines, especially if the clause excludes liability for negligence. STEP also provides precedent standard provisions for a trust document which excludes only lay trustees from liability in the event of negligence in certain specific circumstances.

**ACTIVITY Review your understanding – fiduciary duties**

Consider the following questions.

Alice's will appointed Jemima and Ben to be trustees and left her residuary estate on trust for her daughter, Charlotte, for life remainder to Charlotte's children alive at Charlotte's death. Alice died in November 2013. Charlotte is now aged 38 and has a son, David, who is 18.

(1) The trust property includes a house let to tenants. The tenants have been troublesome, and the trustees wish to sell the house. Jemima would like to buy the house herself. Can she do so and, if yes, in what circumstances?

(2) The trust also includes a 40% shareholding in Travco (a private holiday company). Ben asked Travco if he could be appointed director of the company. A resolution appointing him was passed at a shareholders' meeting by a vote of 75% for and 25% against. The 75% in favour included the votes attached to the trust's shares. Since becoming a director, Ben (a qualified accountant) has played an active role in the management of the company and the company has paid him a salary. Must he account to the trust for the salary?

(3) While at a board meeting, Ben was told in confidence of an opportunity to buy some shares in another holiday company, Eastern Tours, which could be a worthwhile investment. He bought shares personally from his savings and sold them last month for twice the amount he paid. He used the proceeds to buy shares in Hopgo plc and they have also appreciated in value. Do the beneficiaries have any claim to the Hopgo shares?

**COMMENT**

(1) This 'self-dealing' purchase would be voidable at the instance of the beneficiaries acting in a reasonable time. The rule has been applied strictly; the courts will not enquire whether the particular trustee was honest or not or consider the circumstances of the sale (*Ex p Lacey*; *Ex p James*). There are ways to avoid the rule: the consent of beneficiaries is not feasible as the class of beneficiaries has not closed yet. Charlotte may have more children before she dies. It would be necessary to check the will for any authorisation from Alice to the purchase of trustee assets by trustees or to apply to the court for consent.

(2) If Ben obtained the directorship by virtue of the trust then he is accountable for the director's salary. According to Re *Gee*, it has to be determined whether he would have

been appointed had all the trust votes been used against him. If this had occurred, the votes would have been 35% in favour and 65% against. Therefore, in law at least, he did obtain the directorship by virtue of the trust (*Re MacAdam*). He is in breach of his fiduciary duty not to profit from the trust. If the will does not authorise retention of directors' fees, the only possibility is to apply to the court, If a court order is not obtained, Ben will have to account for the salary to the beneficiaries.

(3) Ben's purchase of shares in Eastern Tours may fall within the principles of *Boardman v Phipps*. The majority of the House of Lords held that if information or an opportunity comes to the fiduciary only because of their position then the fiduciary (here Ben as trustee) is accountable for any profit they make out of that information or opportunity. Here Ben was appointed director of Travco because of the trust link. It was as a result of the directorship that he gained the information. Arguably, therefore, he did acquire the information only because of the trust. If this is the case, he is accountable for the profit. The other ground for the decision in *Boardman v Phipps* was that the fiduciary must account for any profit if there is the possibility of a conflict of interest. Ben was under a duty to pass on this information to his co-trustee and consider investing trust money in the Eastern Tours shares. He allowed his personal interest to conflict with his duty.

The beneficiaries are entitled to a remedy, either a personal claim for the amount of the profit or a proprietary claim to the Hopgo shares (*FHR European Ventures LLP v Cedar Capital Partners LLC* [2014] UKSC 45) depending on the position.

## SUMMARY

- It is important the identify situations which give rise to a fiduciary relationship, whether linked to the status of a specific type of relationship or whether as a result of specific factual circumstances giving rise to the comparable relationship of trust and confidence.
- In addition to the obligations of acting in good faith and with loyalty, the fundamental duty applicable to all fiduciaries is the duty to avoid conflicts of interest. Knowing when such conflicts arise is key for trustees to prevent them from placing themselves in situations where their duty to the beneficiaries may conflict with their own personal interests. These conflicts can arise from competition with the principal, the receipt of commission, renewal of property subject to a fiduciary relationship, use of information or an opportunity linked to the fiduciary position.
- There are situations particular to the trustee-beneficiary relationship - self-dealing, fair dealing, retention of directors' fees - where specific obligations are placed on the trustees to safeguard against conflicts of interests and rights accrue to the beneficiaries.
- A fiduciary cannot make a profit from their position. Trustees, as fiduciaries, will be strictly called to account for any profit they do gain regardless of whether it has been obtained in good faith or gained without loss to their trust itself.
- Any profit is to be disgorged unless it has been authorised - for trustees, this authorisation can come from the trust instrument, the consent of all the beneficiaries (provided sui juris) or by court order. In the case of remuneration from the trust for time spent and expertise, this authorisation can come from the Trustee Act 2000.
- Where a breach of fiduciary duty has occurred and unauthorised profit gained, the remedy to be pursued will depend on the circumstances. It is possible for the beneficiaries of the trust (and any principal) to seek a personal remedy against the trustee (fiduciary) to account for the amount of the profit gained or to bring a proprietary claim to recover property which now represents the unauthorised profit (allowing increases in value to be recovered and gaining priority in any insolvency situation).

# 9 Remedies Against Trustees and Fiduciaries

**LEARNING OUTCOMES**

By the end of this chapter, you should be able to:

- understand the difference between personal and proprietary remedies and the relevant considerations when deciding which remedy to pursue;
- appreciate how a personal claim can arise against an expressly appointed trustee and how a trustee may defend themselves against such personal actions;
- outline the operation of the various tracing rules in situations where a trustee has misapplied trust money; and
- recognise the use of equitable tracing rules in the context of other fiduciary relationships.

## 9.1 Introduction

A breach of trust occurs if a trustee does any act which they ought not to do and/or fails to do any act which they ought to do. Breaches range from a trustee dishonestly misappropriating trust property to a failure to perform the duties considered in **Chapters 7** and **8**.

Where a trustee has committed a breach of trust resulting in loss to the trust, the beneficiary may seek compensation for the trust from the wrongdoing trustee. This claim is against the trustee personally ('in personam'). They will be required to satisfy a successful claim from their own property. This course of action will be effective provided the trustee has sufficient personal assets to meet the claim.

Alternatively, some breaches involve the trustee taking trust property. Given that the beneficiaries have an equitable interest in the trust property, they can bring a proprietary claim to recover it or any substitute property from the trustees (otherwise called an action 'in rem'). The trust is claiming the return of property owned by the trust, or the property now representing that trust property. In order to identify the property which now represents the trust property, the claimant uses tracing rules, whereby they 'trace' the trust property into the trustee's hands.

There may be circumstances when the trust property no longer exists. In this case, the proprietary remedy is ineffective. Similarly, a proprietary claim is not possible if the defendant does not hold any trust property, for instance, they did misappropriate trust property but have since given it away. The trust property may, of course, now be in the hands of a third party. Such claims are looked at in **Chapter 10**.

A proprietary remedy is preferable where the defendant trustee is bankrupt. A successful personal claim would merely make the beneficiaries ordinary creditors. They would have to share the defendant's assets with the other creditors; it is unlikely that they would recover very much at all. In contrast, a proprietary claim would allow the beneficiaries to recover the trust property ahead of the creditors.

A proprietary action would also be preferable where the property representing the missing trust fund has increased in value. Such a claim would allow the beneficiary to sue for the whole property, including any increases in value. In contrast, a personal claim would be for the loss to the trust fund plus any interest awarded by the court. Conversely, where the misappropriated trust property has gone down in value, recovery of that property through a proprietary claim will yield less than a personal claim for the original loss plus interest.

When the trustee's breach occurred might also determine the appropriate remedy for the beneficiary to seek - personal claims are often statute barred after six years, while proprietary claims against a trustee are not subject to any statutory limitation period.

## 9.2 Personal claims against a trustee

### 9.2.1 Establishing the claim

In order to sue a trustee personally for compensation for breach of trust, a beneficiary must prove that the trustee has breached one of their duties; and that the breach has caused loss to the trust.

#### 9.2.1.1 Identifying the breach

**Chapter 7** (at **7.3 and 7.4**) discussed many of the duties imposed on trustees in the administration of the trust - their duty of care to the beneficiaries (both generally and in relation to investment and delegation), the requirement to be active in the affairs of the trust, to safeguard trust property and to watch over the conduct of fellow trustees, their investment and delegation duties under the Trustee Act 2000, and their obligations to act in the best interests of the beneficiaries at all times.

A trustee might breach these duties in any number of ways - for instance, failing to consider the standard investment criteria (Trustee Act 2000, s 4) when making investment decisions, unauthorised investment of trust funds in a depreciating asset or land outside the UK (Trustee Act 2000, ss 3 and 8), failing to review any delegation agreement (Trustee Act 2000, s 22), non-involvement in the decision-making of the trust (*Bahin v Hughes* [1886] 31 Ch D) or leaving the trust property or the affairs of the trust in the hands of a co-trustee without enquiry or supervision (*Styles v Guy* (1849) 19 LT Ch 185).

Should a trustee misappropriate trust property for their own use, this is an obvious breach of a duty to act honestly and in the best interests of the beneficiaries.

A trustee could also be in breach of trust if they exercise a power in an unauthorised way.

#### 9.2.1.2 Liability of trustees

When considering possible actions against trustees, it is important to remember that trustees are not vicariously liable for the acts of their co-trustees. So one trustee will not automatically be liable to the beneficiaries because a co-trustee has stolen trust property or made poor investment decisions. However, the 'innocent' trustee will be liable if they have committed their own breach which facilitated the original theft or contributed to the poor decision making. For instance, could the trustee have played a more active role in the decision making to prevent the poor investment choices; could they have better secured the trust property and watched over the actions of their co-trustee to safeguard against the theft?

Where a number of trustees are liable for a particular breach (whether as active participants or as passive by-standers) liability among these trustees is joint and several. This means that the beneficiaries can decide whether they wish to bring a claim against one, all or a selection of the liable trustees.

It is possible for a trustee to commit a number of breaches, some of which made a profit and others sustained a loss. As a general rule, the courts do not allow a trustee to set off the profit made on one breach of trust against the loss incurred on another breach. The beneficiaries may keep the profit and at the same time sue for the loss. However, in *Bartlett v Barclays Bank Trust Co Ltd* (No 2) [1980] Ch 515, it was held that set-off is permitted where the profit and loss arise from the same breach or 'transaction'. In *Bartlett*, the profit and loss both arose from speculative property investments, and the trustees were allowed to offset the profit to reduce the compensation which they had to pay the beneficiaries in respect of the unsuccessful investment.

A trustee cannot avoid liability by retiring from the trust. However, they will not be liable for breaches committed after any retirement, unless they retired to facilitate the breach. For example, if they were suspicious about co-trustee's activities and decided to retire in order to avoid dealing with the issue.

9.2.1.3 Causing the loss

Unlike a claim seeking an account of unauthorised profit (discussed in **Chapter 8**), a trustee will only be liable to pay compensation to the beneficiaries if their breach(es) caused the loss to the trust fund - was the trust worth less as a direct consequence of the particular breach? In *Nestle v National Westminster Bank* [1993] 1 WLR 1260 (considered in **7.3.1**), the bank trustee had breached its duty of care when investing the trust fund. However, the claimant beneficiary was unsuccessful because she could not show that the breach had caused loss to the trust fund.

***Target Holdings v Redferns*** **[1996] 1 AC 421**

Target Holdings transferred approximately £1.5 million to Redferns, a firm of solicitors. The money was to be loaned to Crowngate to buy property. Target was to get a mortgage over the property that was to be purchased. Crowngate, however, had orchestrated a scheme to make a fraudulent profit on the property which was actually bought for an amount significantly lower than the reported valuation.

Redferns were under instructions not to release the money until the purchase was completed, and the mortgage was executed. Until then, the solicitors were to hold the money on trust for Target. Breaching these instructions, Redferns in fact released almost all the money to another company before the purchase was completed. The sale subsequently went through, and the mortgage was executed.

Crowngate failed to repay the loan and went into liquidation, and Target was only able to recover £500,000 from the sale of the property. Target sued Redferns solicitors, arguing that it had a duty to account for the money it had wrongly released. Redferns argued that, even though it had breached the trust, this had nothing to do with the loss that Target had incurred.

The House of Lords agreed with Redferns - only losses that were caused by Redferns' breach of the trust terms could be recovered. Target's losses had been caused by the fraudulent mortgage valuation (provided by valuers also in liquidation) and a recession causing a dramatic fall in property prices at the time of the sale. The loss would have been the same regardless of Redfern's breach in releasing the trust property early.

For beneficiaries considering bringing a personal claim for compensation to recover a loss caused to the trust, it is important to identify:

- which trustees are in breach of trust (a trustee is not liable if not guilty of any breach);
- what the breach comprises; and
- that the breach caused loss to the trust fund, as if there is no loss, there is no claim.

Additionally, the beneficiaries have to consider whether a trustee could rely on a defence which would absolve them of personal liability.

### 9.2.2 Defences

#### 9.2.2.1 Knowledge and consent of beneficiary

A trustee has a defence to a claim for breach of trust if a claimant beneficiary consented to or concurred with the breach. However, there are a number of conditions attached to this consent - the beneficiary must have been of full age and capacity; the consent must have been freely given, without undue influence and must be fully informed, the beneficiary having knowledge of all the relevant facts.

In *Re Pauling's Settlement Trust* [1964] Ch 303, the remainder beneficiaries (the children of the life tenant, their mother) sought and received advances which were really to fund their parent's profligate lifestyle. The trustees were found to have made improper advancements (discussed at **7.5.2.1**), but they were able to successfully defend the claim brought by the children for breach of trust for those advances made after the children had reached the age of majority as the presumption of parental undue influence no longer applied, and the children were fully aware of the intended use of the advances. According to Wilberforce J, the beneficiary 'need not know that what [they are] concurring in is a breach of trust, provided that [they] fully understand what [they are] concurring in'.

#### 9.2.2.2 Impounding the beneficial interest

Where a beneficiary has consented to or instigated a trustee's breach, the court can be asked by the trustees to impound the beneficial interest of that beneficiary to meet a successful claim from other beneficiaries.

The court has inherent jurisdiction to make this order, but usually only exercises this jurisdiction if the beneficiary instigated the breach or if they consented to the breach in writing and gained a personal benefit from it.

Alternatively, the court has a statutory jurisdiction under s 62 of the Trustee Act 1925 'to make such order as to the court seems just for impounding all or part of the interest of the beneficiary in the trust estate by way of indemnity to the trustee' if the trustee has committed the breach at the instigation or request or with the consent in writing of a beneficiary.

#### 9.2.2.3 Section 61 of the Trustee Act 1925

Section 61 of the Trustee Act 1925 provides that the court can relieve trustees of liability (wholly or in part) if they acted honestly and reasonably and ought fairly to be excused in respect of the breach.

It is for the trustees to evidence to the court that they acted in good faith *and* reasonably in the circumstances. What is reasonable in the circumstances will likely depend on the status of the trustee as either a lay appointee (as in *Re Evans* [1999] 2 All ER 777) or a professional.

If the court is satisfied on these two issues, it then considers whether the trustees ought fairly to be excused (*Santander UK PLC v RA Legal Solicitors* [2014] EWCA Civ 183).

The courts are reluctant to grant relief to professional trustees (*Bartlett v Barclays Bank Trust Co Ltd* (No 2) [1980] Ch 515), even if they have taken advice (*National Trustee Co of Australia Ltd v General Finance Co* [1905] AC 373). As a matter of policy, the court is also unlikely to provide s 61 relief to breaches committed by a passive trustee because this would encourage trustees not to be active in trust business.

#### 9.2.2.4 Express exemption clause

As seen at **8.7**, the person creating the trust is free to include an exemption clause in the trust instrument relieving trustees of liability. The extent of the relief such a clause provides depends on its drafting. Such a clause may exclude or limit the trustees' statutory or common law duties of care. According to *Armitage v Nurse* [1997] 3 WLR 1026, such clauses can also exclude liability for negligence, including gross negligence, but cannot exclude the trustee's core duty, which is to perform the trust honestly and in good faith for the benefit of the beneficiaries. Such a clause can also not exclude liability for fraud (ie dishonesty).

9.2.2.5 Limitation and laches

Under s 21(1) of the Limitation Act 1980, there is no period of limitation to bringing an action in respect of any fraud or fraudulent breach of trust to which the trustee was a party or privy; or to recovering trust property or the proceeds of trust property in the possession of the trustee.

However, under s 21(3) of the Limitation Act 1980, personal actions in respect of any breach of trust cannot be brought after the expiration of six years from the date on which the cause of action accrued. However, for remainder beneficiaries, time does not start to run until their interest falls into possession (when the life tenant dies).

The equitable doctrine of laches should also be considered in cases where there is no statutory limitation period (Limitation Act 1980, s 36(2)), for instance when considering proprietary actions. The courts will not allow a claimant to succeed where it would be unconscionable to do so.

Laches is applied at the discretion of the court. A successful use of a laches defence requires:

(a) a delay in bringing the action and for the delay to be unreasonable. How long a delay and what makes it unreasonable will depend on the circumstances; and

(b) the defendant to have been prejudiced by the delay. In *Fisher v Brooker* [2009] 1 WLR 1764 (a case involving a claim to royalties from the composition of and involvement in the recording of the Procul Harum song 'Whiter Shade of Pale') the delay was 30 years, but the claim was not defeated by laches as the defendants had not been prejudiced. They had in fact received the royalties in the intervening period which should have been paid to the claimant.

**Figure 9.1** Summary - establishing a trustee's personal liability

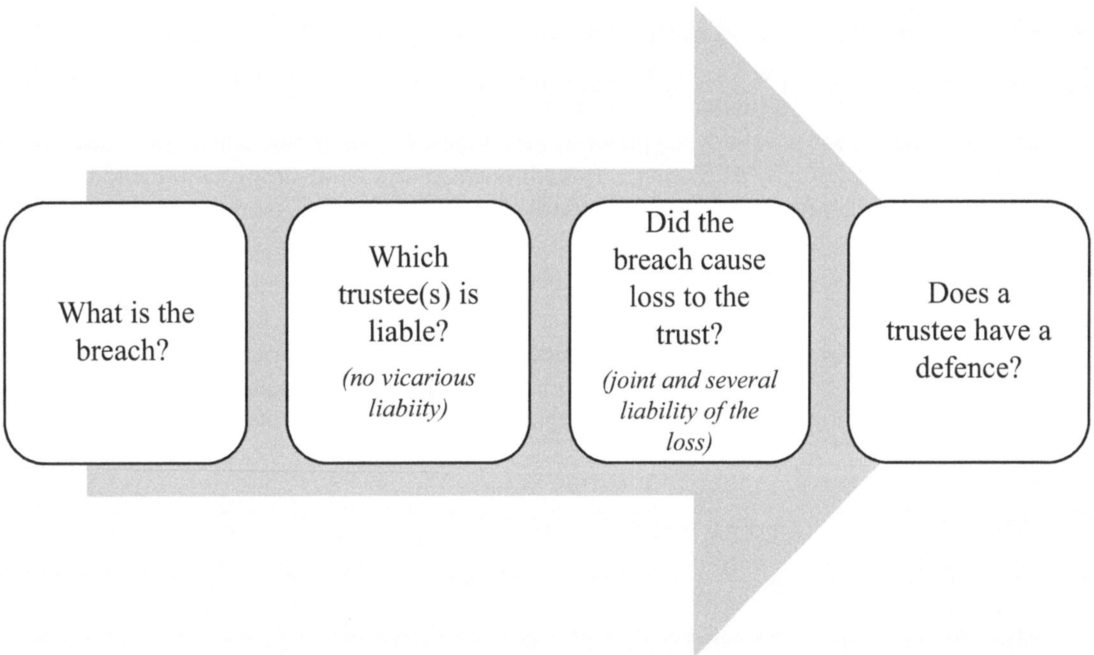

### 9.2.3 Indemnity and contribution

As mentioned in **9.2.1.2**, where more than one trustee is liable for a breach of trust contributing to a loss to the trust, the trustees are joint and severally liable to the beneficiaries. The beneficiaries could, therefore, choose to sue all or only one for the entire loss.

A trustee who is sued for the entire loss has two options against their fellow co-liable trustees.

#### 9.2.3.1 Indemnity

In certain circumstances, they could seek an indemnity (for 100% of the loss) under equitable rules from qualifying co-trustees who are also in breach of trust.

A qualifying co-trustee against whom a full indemnity could be claimed is one who:

- fraudulently obtained a benefit from the breach; or
- received trust property and used it for their own benefit (*Bahin v Hughes* (1886) 31 Ch D 390); or
- is a solicitor exerting a controlling influence over their fellow trustees (*Re Partington* (1887) 57 LT 654) and the other trustees were, as a result of this control, unable to exercise their own judgement, relying totally on the solicitor's advice (*Head v Gould* [1898] 2 Ch 250).

#### 9.2.3.2 Contribution

Where the circumstances for a full indemnity do not exist, a defendant trustee could claim a contribution from co-trustees under s 2 of the Civil Liability (Contribution) Act 1978. The court may order such a contribution as is just and equitable having regard to the extent of each trustee's responsibility for the loss.

## 9.3 Proprietary claims against a trustee

Beneficiaries can bring proprietary claims to recover trust property which a trustee has misappropriated, or to acquire an unauthorised profit which a trustee holds on constructive trust (**8.6.2**). A proprietary claim (or a claim 'in rem') is possible because the beneficiaries have an equitable interest in the property or the unauthorised profit.

A proprietary claim is possible only if the trustee still holds the trust property or replacement property. Such a claim will fail if the trustee has 'dissipated' the trust property, ie spent it in such a way that it is no longer represented by any asset. Examples of dissipation include using the money for a holiday, to pay bills for electricity, telephone and credit card balances, or losing the trust money at a casino. In such cases, there is no property left and the beneficiaries will have to rely on a personal claim.

In some cases, the trustee has stolen trust property and has changed its form; for example, a trustee sold shares belonging to the trust and paid the proceeds into their bank account. Even though the original trust property comprised company shares, the beneficiaries would seek to claim the money in the trustee's bank account in a proprietary action. In order to pursue such a claim, the beneficiaries will be reliant on the equitable tracing rules, a process which enables them to identify trust property through various changes in form.

### 9.3.1 Clean substitution

Where the trustee has simply exchanged the trust property for another asset in a clean substitution, there is no problem tracing the trust property into the replacement asset.

In *Re Hallett's Estate* (1880) 13 Ch D 696, it was said that a beneficiary can elect to take the property purchased or to have a charge over the property to secure the amount due to the trust. This is often referred to as an equitable lien.

In *Foskett v McKeown* [2001] 1 AC 102, Lord Millet considered clean substitution as the simplest case when it came to tracing:

> a trustee wrongfully misappropriates trust property and uses it exclusively to acquire other property for his own benefit. In such a case, the beneficiary is entitled at his option either to assert his beneficial ownership of the proceeds or to bring a personal claim against the trustee for breach of trust and enforce an equitable lien or charge on the proceeds to secure restoration of the trust fund. He will normally exercise the option in the way most advantageous to himself. If the traceable proceeds have increased in value and are worth more than the original asset, he will assert his beneficial ownership and obtain the profit for himself. There is nothing unfair in this.

### 9.3.2 Mixed substitution

Here a trustee buys an asset using partly their own money and partly funds wrongly drawn from the trust. In *Foskett v McKeown*, Lord Millett called this a 'mixed substitution', occurring where trust money represents only part of the cost of acquiring a new asset.

***Foskett v McKeown* [2001] 1 AC 102**

Two property developers, M and D, held sums totalling £2.7 million as trustees on behalf of various investors in an Algarve property development scheme, which was never completed. M took out a life policy. Some of the premiums were paid with his own money, and some with stolen trust money. M died, and the policy paid out £1 million. The investors claimed a pro rata share of the proceeds of the policy. The House of Lords, by a majority, found in the investors' favour.

In *Foskett v McKeown*, Lord Millett held that beneficiary could elect to either:

(a) claim a proportionate share of the asset (corresponding to the proportion the misapplied trust fund bore to the purchase price of the asset); or

(b) enforce a lien (or charge) upon the asset to secure their personal claim against the trustee for the misapplied money.

Where the mixed asset has increased in value, it is more advantageous for the beneficiary to claim a proportionate share of the asset so that the trust will obtain a share of the profit (irrespective of how the increase in value came about). However, where the mixed asset has decreased in value, it would be more beneficial for the beneficiary to claim a lien, forcing the trustee to suffer as much of the decrease in value as possible.

A beneficiary's proprietary claim to the trust property or the traceable property representing it can be maintained against not only the misappropriating trustee but 'anyone who derives title from them except a bona fide purchaser for value without notice of the breach' (Lord Millett in *Foskett*), which means that a beneficiary does have the same remedies against those claiming through the wrongdoer (ie personal representatives and beneficiaries of a deceased trustee's estate).

### 9.3.3 Allocating withdrawals through a bank account

When a trustee mixes trust money with their own personal funds in a bank account and makes withdrawals, it is necessary to allocate the withdrawals either to the trustee's personal funds or the trust fund in order to decide who paid for and, therefore, owns what. The starting tracing rule for this allocation of withdrawals comes from the Court of Appeal decision in *Re Hallett's Estate* (1880) 13 Ch D 696.

***Re Hallett's Estate* (1880) 13 Ch D 696**

A solicitor (Hallett) was a trustee of a family trust and paid trust money into his own bank account, which already contained some of his own money. Later, he paid in money belonging to a client. The fact that solicitors owe their clients fiduciary duties meant that Hallett was also a quasi-trustee of his client's money. Hallett then dissipated some of the money in the account; there was no replacement property to show for his expenditure. Hallett died insolvent, and the issue was who owned the money left in the account. This, in turn, depended on whether Hallett had spent his own money or trust money (consisting of the money derived from the express trust and the client).

It was held that a trustee is deemed to spend their own money first. Thus, the balance remaining in the account belonged to the trust and the client. Given that Hallett died insolvent, the proprietary claim enabled the trust and the client to take their money out of the account ahead of Hallett's creditors.

The presumption from *Re Hallett* (the guilty trustee spends their own money first) worked in the claimants' favour in the case because Hallett's first withdrawal dissipated money from the account. However, where a trustee has mixed trust funds with their own in a bank account and the first withdrawal involves the purchase of a traceable asset, for instance, company shares, with subsequent dissipation, this presumption would render an entirely inappropriate result. Following *Re Hallett*, the shares (ie the traceable asset) would be allocated to the guilty trustee, whereas the trust money would have been dissipated, leaving the beneficiaries without a proprietary claim.

***Re Oatway* [1903] 2 Ch 356**

The trustee withdrew money from a mixed bank account and used it to buy company shares. At the time of the purchase, sufficient funds remained in the account representing amounts misappropriated from the trust. However, later, the trustee withdrew the balance of the bank account and dissipated it. It was held that the beneficiaries were entitled to the company shares purchased with the first withdrawal; the justification was that the beneficiaries' claim had to be satisfied from any identifiable part of the mixed fund before the trustee could set up their own claim. The rule in *Re Hallett's Estate* was subject to the principle that until all the trust monies are restored, the beneficiary has a first charge over all the assets purchased with money from the bank account.

A critical issue is whether beneficiaries would be entitled to recover a share of any increase in value of the purchased property or merely the value of the trust's loss. There is no clear answer.

In *Re Oatway*, the court held that the beneficiary had a lien or charge over the shares equal to the trust money spent on them. However, in *Re Oatway* the shares had not increased in value, so the question was not addressed. However, as already discussed, the House of Lords in *Foskett v McKeown* suggested that the beneficiary should be entitled to a proportionate share of a mixed asset, including any increase in value. However, *Foskett* did not deal directly with money passing through a mixed bank account. Given that both *Re Hallett* and *Re Oatway* operate on the basis that a wrongdoer taking from the trust cannot profit from their wrong and the beneficiaries must be given the opportunity to recover their property, the argument to claim any increase in value could be made.

Where an asset has been purchased but there is also enough money left in the bank account to cover the trust fund, it is unclear which should be used to satisfy the beneficiary's claim. This issue becomes especially relevant if the asset has increased in value. The beneficiary would, no doubt, prefer to claim ownership of the asset. It is unclear whether the beneficiary will be forced to accept the balance in the bank account.

What is clear, however, is that the beneficiaries are only able to trace into a mixed bank account if it can be shown that the misappropriated money is still there. According to *Roscoe v Winder* [1915] 1 Ch 62, if, having dissipated the trust money, the trustee later pays in their own money, this is not regarded as replacing the trust money. The beneficiaries cannot claim the subsequent deposit unless the trustee showed an intention to restore the trust funds. The rule in *Roscoe v Winder* is sometimes called the 'lowest intermediate balance' rule. In other words, the beneficiaries cannot claim anything above the lowest balance to which the account sank after the trust money was paid in. This is consistent with the principle that tracing only allows a claimant to track down their property and is neutral as to the merits of the case.

Another area of controversary is the ability to trace into assets purchased before a misappropriation takes place but where the purchase is with the aid of a mortgage which the misappropriated money is used to repay. This is the concept of 'backward tracing'. Strictly speaking, the beneficiary's property has been dissipated: it has been used to extinguish a liability. However, backward tracing allows the beneficiary to claim the asset acquired with the loan money. The availability of backwards tracing was previously rejected (*Bishopgate Investment Management Ltd v Homan and others* [1995] Ch 211), but more recently has been confirmed, albeit by the Privy Council, as possible where a specific scheme to use the misappropriated funds to release the liability is clearly evidenced (*Brazil v Durant International* [2015] UKPC 35). The justification for allowing such tracing was as a safeguard against 'the development of increasingly sophisticated and elaborate methods of money laundering' (Lord Toulson).

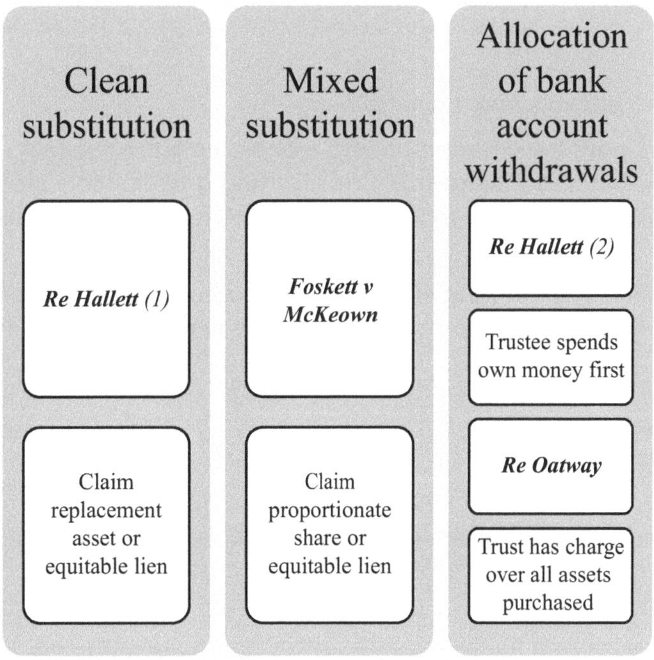


**Figure 9.2** Summary - proprietary claims against a trustee (fiduciary)

### 9.3.4 Allocation of withdrawals between two innocent trust funds

Up to this point, the consideration has been where a trustee dishonestly takes trust money and mixes it with their own. Innocent beneficiaries of the trust are claiming against a guilty trustee. Thus, the tracing rules favour the innocent beneficiaries.

However, some individuals (such as solicitors) may be trustees of several trusts. There is a possibility that such a person could dishonestly take money from a number of trusts and blend it in a bank account or use the mixed fund to purchase an asset. Tracing rules have to be used to unravel what each trust owns.

Where a trustee mixes money from two different trusts, the beneficiaries of both trusts will bring claims against the mixed fund. Both sets of beneficiaries are equally innocent. Thus, the tracing rules for this situation should not favour the beneficiaries of one trust over the beneficiaries of the other.

9.3.4.1 Purchase of asset with the combined fund

Where a trustee has used a combined fund (containing funds from two different trusts) to purchase a traceable asset, beneficiaries of each trust share ownership of the asset pari passu, ie in the same proportions as they contributed to the purchase. Neither trust is allowed to claim a charge over the mixed asset for the amount of their trust fund which has been misappropriated. By insisting on proportionate shares, the courts ensure that the trust funds bear losses and enjoy profits proportionately.

***Example***

*A trustee takes £30,000 from the Henderson family trust and £20,000 from the Robinson family trust. The trustee uses the combined fund of £50,000 to buy shares in Acorn Ltd. The Acorn shares are now worth £30,000. Thus, the Henderson trust contributed three-fifths of the purchase money and therefore owns three-fifths of the shares (worth £18,000). The Robinson trust contributed two-fifths of the purchase price and can, therefore, claim two-fifths of the shares (worth £12,000). Neither trust can claim a charge over the shares for the amount appropriated from their fund as this would be disadvantageous to the other and both trusts are innocent victims of the trustee's fraud.*

9.3.4.2 Allocation of withdrawals from bank account

Here the trustee pays the misappropriated moneys from the two trusts into a current bank account and then makes withdrawals, one involving a dissipation, the second to buy a traceable asset. It is necessary to identify which withdrawal can be allocated to which trust.

The traditional approach is to apply the rule in *Clayton's case* (1816) 1 Mer 572, which sought to ascertain competing claims to funds in a bank account between two innocent parties. The rule is that the first money to be paid in is also the first to be paid out – the FIFO ('first in, first out') principle.

***Example***

*A trustee pays £30,000 from the Henderson family trust into a current bank account and, later, adds £20,000 from the Robinson family trust. The trustee then makes two withdrawals; the first withdrawal of £10,000 is dissipated; the second (£40,000) is used to buy valuable shares.*

*The first money paid into the account (£30,000) belonged to the Henderson family trust, and so the first withdrawal is attributed to Henderson – £10,000 dissipated. The second withdrawal (£40,000) comprises the remaining £20,000 of Henderson money and £20,000 of Robinson money. Thus, the Robinson trust can claim half the shares (thereby recovering its full £20,000). The Henderson trust can also claim half the shares but will recover only £20,000 of the £30,000 originally paid into the account.*

The rule in *Clayton's case* produces a solution which depends on the order of payments into the bank account. The outcome of the case is governed by chance.

A more equitable solution (given that the claimants are equally innocent) would be to divide the balance in the bank account, and any assets purchased out of it, in proportion to the initial contributions to the account. In the Henderson and Robinson example above, the Henderson and Robinson trusts would respectively acquire three-fifths and two-fifths of the value of the shares.

***Barlow Clowes International Ltd (In Liquidation) v Vaughan* [1992] 4 All ER 22**

Here, investors contributed to a common investment scheme. The trustees of the scheme held the monies on separate trusts for each investor. They misapplied the money, and, when the scheme folded, there were insufficient funds to satisfy the claims of all investors. Counsel invited the Court of Appeal to apply the rule in *Clayton's case* so that the misapplied withdrawals would be attributed to the earlier investors; the later investors would then recover the remaining balance in the scheme. The Court of Appeal refused to apply *Clayton* because this was contrary to the intention of the investors. They intended to create a collective scheme in which all would share profits (and losses). It was held that the remaining funds would be shared rateably between the investors in proportion to their contributions.

Woolf LJ said that the rule in *Clayton's case* would not apply in the following circumstances:

(a) where it would be impractical, eg because of the difficulty or expense involved in ascertaining the order of payments in; or

(b) where it would result in an injustice; or

(c) where it would be contrary to the parties' intentions.

Where the trustee mixes money from two or more trusts with their own money, it is necessary to first apply the rules in *Re Hallett* and *Re Oatway* to allocate withdrawals from the account; and then to apply *Clayton* to the balance. As explained above, the court may decide not to apply *Clayton* if it would result in an injustice.

## 9.4 Proprietary claims against those who owe fiduciary duties

Equitable tracing rules are not the exclusive domain of express trusts. They can be used by a claimant who brings a proprietary claim for property in respect of which they were owed fiduciary duties. As seen in **Chapter 8**, there are many different types of fiduciaries, and all are subject to equity's jurisdiction.

For example, if a director steals money from the company's bank account, as with beneficiaries against a fraudulent trustee, so the company will seek to recover its loss. Comparably, if the director has subsequently been made bankrupt, the company will look to bring a proprietary, rather than a personal claim. If the company property has changed in form, the company will have to use tracing to identify its property.

### 9.4.1 Common law tracing

Unlike beneficiaries, the company is the legal owner of the money and so can bring a common law action. However, if the company brings a common law action, it can only use common law tracing rules. There has been no fusion of law and equity in this respect;

a claimant who brings an equitable claim must use equitable tracing, and a claimant at common law must use common law tracing.

There are defects in the common law tracing rules. Common law tracing rules are able to identify an asset through changes in form, for instance if the director bought a painting with the company's money (*Taylor v Plumer* (1815) 3 M & S 562). However, per Lord Ellenborough in *Taylor*, the 'right ceases when the means of ascertainment fail which is the case when the subject is turned into money and compounded in a general mass of the same description'. In other words, common law tracing cannot identify the claimant's property once it has been mixed with other property. Thus, if the director paid the company money into their bank account which already contained their own funds, common law tracing would break down. In contrast, equitable tracing can identify the claimant's property into that mixed fund.

There is a further possible defect of common law tracing rules. In *Agip (Africa) Ltd v Jackson* [1990] Ch 265, Millett J stated that common law tracing also breaks down where funds are transferred between banks electronically. He maintained that common law tracing can only follow a physical asset (such as a cheque) and there is no such asset in an electronic transfer (merely 'a stream of electrons'). Equitable tracing, on the other hand, is not defeated by electronic transfers of funds.

### 9.4.2 Compared to equitable tracing

Common law tracing may not produce the desired result for the company. However, its director owed the company fiduciary duties. Accordingly, the company can bring an equitable proprietary claim and use the equitable tracing rules, which can identify the company's property even after mixing or an electronic transfer.

Equitable tracing rules have clear advantages over their common law counterpart. Litigants have had to argue that they are owed fiduciary duties in novel circumstances in order to be able to use the equitable rules.

While common law tracing was not available to the claimant in *Agip (Africa) Ltd v Jackson* [1991] Ch 547), a fiduciary relationship was found between the company and a senior employee because he had control over the company's funds. This enabled the claimant to trace funds misappropriated by that senior employee into offshore accounts in his name, notwithstanding the movement of the funds via a series of international banks.

***Chase Manhattan Bank v Israel-British Bank* [1979] 3 All ER 1025**

Under the terms of a commercial arrangement, the claimant paid $1 million to the defendant bank. Unfortunately, due to a clerical error the payment was made twice. Due to its own financial issues, the defendant bank became insolvent soon after. The claimant sought to recover the second payment which they could only do using equitable tracing. There was a contractual relationship between the two parties but not a fiduciary relationship; on this basis equitable tracing was not available. However, the court found that a mistaken payment gives rise to a fiduciary relationship – the payer retains an equitable interest in the mistaken payment which the payee has a fiduciary duty to respect.

In *Westdeutsche Landesbank Girozentrale v Islington Borough Council* [1996] AC 669, the House of Lords said that the fiduciary relationship in relation to a mistaken payment only arises if the recipient's conscience is affected – they must know of the mistake to become a trustee. In *Westdeutsche*, it was also said (*obiter*) that a theft gives rise to a constructive trust for the victim. This would suggest that a thief owes their victim fiduciary duties allowing for the use of equitable tracing to recover stolen items (or property representing them).

**ACTIVITY Review your understanding – remedies against trustees**

Please read these facts.

Savita died five years ago. In her will, she left her estate to Zainab and Veena to hold on trust for Nelson for life, remainder to Amrit. There were no express administrative provisions in the will.

Veena is concerned that she might be liable for a breach of trust. She has not been much involved in the administration of the trust and has been content to leave matters in Zainab's hands, as Zainab is a solicitor. Veena says that, at Zainab's request, she has signed some cheques over the years, but is unable to say in whose favour.

The following has occurred:

(a) Six months ago, Nelson was paid £25,000 out of the capital of the trust to purchase a new car. Amrit has recently discovered this and has complained to Veena.

(b) Zainab appears to have paid herself £100,000 from trust funds, transferring it directly into her bank account. At the time of the transfer, Zainab's bank account had a negligible balance. Shortly afterwards, she won £350,000 on the National Lottery and paid this into the same account. She withdrew £50,000 to pay off various creditors. She then spent the remaining £400,000 on a house. The house is now worth £500,000.

Consider what rights and remedies are available against Zainab, and whether Veena might be liable for Zainab's actions.

**COMMENT**

What breaches of trust have been committed?

- The payment of £25,000 to Nelson to purchase a car – s 32 of the Trustee Act 1925 only authorises capital to be advanced to beneficiaries with an interest in capital. As the life tenant, Nelson is entitled to income only.
- Zainab stealing £100,000 of trust money.
- Veena as passive trustee; not being actively involved in the administration of the trust and allowing Zainab to act unsupervised (ie signing cheques simply at Zainab's request without active enquiry as to the payee).

What rights and remedies are available against Zainab?

- As the payment of £25,000 to Nelson was a breach of trust, Zainab would be liable for the loss to the trust. This would be a personal action, dependent on Zainab having the necessary personal wealth to be able to satisfy any judgment. (There would also be rights against Nelson; rights against third parties will be considered in **Chapter 10**.)
- The theft of £100,000 would give rise to a personal action against Zainab for the amount stolen. Alternatively, there would be a proprietary action, if she still has trust property, or property now representing it.

Money has been mixed in an active bank account. As Zainab is a guilty trustee, the rule in *Re Hallett* applies. Zainab is deemed to spend her own money first. Thus, she dissipated her own £50,000 when paying her creditors. The remaining £400,000 used to buy the house comprised £100,000 (trust property) and £300,000 (Zainab's). According to *Re Hallett*, the beneficiaries have a lien over the house for £100,000 and could insist on a sale to realise their charge. It is uncertain whether the beneficiaries would have a share of the increase in the value of the house. Following *Foskett v McKeown*, it is arguable that the beneficiaries should have a one-quarter share of the increased value of the house.

There would be no defences available to Zainab.

Could Veena be liable for Zainab's actions?

- If the actions against Zainab satisfy the loss to the trust, there is no further loss to claim from Veena.
- However, while not vicariously liable for Zainab's actions, on the basis of her own breach (detailed above) and on the basis of joint and several liability, the beneficiaries could elect to sue her personally for the losses.
- If Veena were to be sued, the equitable indemnity rules apply where the trustee has blindly followed the decisions of a solicitor co-trustee (*Re Partington*). Zainab is a solicitor, but Veena would also have to establish that Zainab exercised such a controlling influence that Veena did not exercise her own judgement (*Head v Gould*).
- Alternatively, she would be able to claim contribution from Zainab under the Civil Liability (Contribution) Act 1978. The court can order such contribution as would be just and equitable having regard to the extent of each trustee's liability for the loss. It is likely that Veena would be able to claim more than 50% from Zainab.

## SUMMARY

- When considering remedies available against trustees who breach their duties, beneficiaries are able to bring both personal and proprietary remedies. It is essential to recognise the aims of and differences between the two.
- The financial status of the defendant is a crucial factor in determining how best to proceed against the wrongdoer. What has happened to the misapplied trust property is also relevant. A claimant is unable to use a proprietary remedy if the target property no longer exists, ie because it has been dissipated in some way.
- Beneficiaries seeking to bring a personal action against a trustee need to be able to identify the breaches that have been committed and by which trustee(s), that the breaches have brought about the loss to the trust and whether a trustee might benefit from a defence which relieves them of liability.
- Tracing is available at common law and in equity. Tracing is not a remedy, nor it is a cause of action; tracing is a process which allows beneficiaries (and fiduciary principals) to exert their proprietary rights to claim in priority over creditors on an insolvency or to benefit from an asset's increase in value.
- Common law tracing is available to those claimants having legal title to misappropriated funds, but there are limitations to its use, primarily its requirement for the property to be clearly identifiable. Tracing at common law fails where property has been mixed.
- Equitable tracing is more flexible as it allows tracing into mixed funds. However, the ability to use equitable tracing rules depends on the existence of a fiduciary relationship between the claimant and the defendant. Equitable tracing can, therefore, be deployed by beneficiaries against trustees as well as by other claimants who are owed fiduciary duties (ie a company against a director).

- Where trust property has been misappropriated by a trustee, different equitable tracing rules will apply to enable the beneficiaries to recover that property depending on how the stolen property has been deployed. It is important to be able to understand why and how the rules arose, their effect and their relevance to a given circumstance – for instance where a trustee purchases property with a mixture of personal funds and trust money, or where the stolen money has passed through the trustee's bank account.
- It is important to recognise that these same tracing rules can be applied in the context of proprietary claims arising from breaches by other fiduciaries.

# 10 Remedies Against Third Parties

**LEARNING OUTCOMES**

By the end of this chapter, you should be able to:

- understand the requirements for the various equitable personal claims against third parties following a breach of trust or fiduciary duty;
- appreciate when equitable proprietary actions are or are not available against third parties who have received property derived from a breach of trust or fiduciary duty;
- identify the different approaches to be taken to those proprietary actions depending on a third party's status as a wrongdoer or innocent volunteer; and
- outline legal remedies which may be appropriate to consider against third parties and when they are available.

## 10.1 Introduction

Trustees or fiduciaries who breach their duties may be assisted by third parties in that breach or may transfer property taken in breach of trust or fiduciary duty to third parties. These 'third parties' are often called 'strangers', as they are not the actual trustees or fiduciaries but have become implicated in the breach, and consequently equity, in certain circumstances, allows for claims to be brought against them.

There are numerous reasons why the beneficiaries of a trust (or a fiduciary principal) might decide to bring claims against these third party 'strangers' instead of the trustee who has stolen from the trust or the fiduciary who has breached their fiduciary duty. The trustee (or other fiduciary) may be bankrupt and/or own no assets, while the third party is wealthy or is a professional likely to have insurance to cover such claims. The whereabouts of the trustee or fiduciary may be unknown, making proceedings against them difficult to bring, while the location of the third party is established. The beneficiaries may wish to reclaim trust property which has sentimental value, but which is now in the hands of a third party; the third party has substituted trust property for an asset which has subsequently increased in value. In some situations, it may be worthwhile claiming against the trustee and third party in the alternative, so that if the claim against one fails, the claimant can fall back on the other action.

## 10.2 Equitable personal claims against third parties

The beneficiaries of a trust or fiduciary relationship may sue a third-party stranger personally if they can establish the stranger's liability as an accessory, or as a recipient, or as a person who has 'meddled' in trust or fiduciary affairs.

There has been some confusion in the terminology used to describe the liability of the stranger in these three instances. It had been suggested that a successful claim against the stranger made them a constructive trustee. However, in *Williams v Central Bank of Nigeria* [2014] UKSC 10, the majority of the Supreme Court held that only intermeddlers were constructive trustees. Strangers who were found to be accessories or recipients were liable to account *as though they were trustees*, but they were *not* actual or constructive trustees. They were not subject to the duties of ordinary trustees (such as investment and safeguarding the trust property). Their only duty was to account for and restore the trust property.

### 10.2.1 Accessory liability

Accessory liability can also be called 'dishonest assistance'. A third-party stranger is liable under this head if they dishonestly assist a breach of trust or fiduciary duty.

#### 10.2.1.1 Assistance

Assistance is an action which actively assists in the breach. In *Brinks Ltd v Abu-Saleh (No 3)* (1995) The Times, 23 October), a wife who occasionally accompanied her husband on car trips to Switzerland was held not to have dishonestly assisted in a breach of trust. While she thought that he might have been involved in tax evasion, she had no awareness of the true purpose of the journeys (he was laundering the proceeds of a bullion theft occasioned by an employee's fiduciary breach). Her presence was not 'assistance of a nature sufficient to make her an accessory to the breach of trust' (Rimer J). She was there merely to make the trip more enjoyable for her husband rather than providing cover for the money laundering.

Disapproving of the decision in *Abu-Saleh (No 3)*, the Privy Council in *Barlow Clowes International Ltd (In Liquidation) v Eurotrust International Ltd* [2006] 1 WLR 1376 held that it was not necessary for a defendant to appreciate that they were assisting a breach of trust or fiduciary duty. The defendant was liable if they knew they were assisting some illegal scheme; they need not know the details. This point was later confirmed in *Group Seven Ltd v Notable Services* LLP [2019] EWCA Civ 614.

#### 10.2.1.2 Dishonesty

The meaning of 'dishonesty' in this context has been an area of some controversy.

***Royal Brunei Airlines v Tan* [1995] 3 All ER 97**

Borneo Leisure Travel (BLT) sold flight tickets for Royal Brunei Airlines and agreed to hold the money on trust for the airline until it was paid over. BLT breached the trust by using the flight ticket money in its own business rather than keeping it in a separate trust bank account as agreed. By the time the airline found out what was happening, BLT had become insolvent and was not worth suing. Tan was the main shareholder and director of BLT and had instigated the breach of trust. The airline decided to sue Tan for compensation on the ground that he had dishonestly assisted BLT to breach its trust. Tan argued that for the liability to arise, both the breach and the assistance provided by the stranger have to be dishonest. As BLT's actions had not been fraudulent, Tan could not be liable.

Lord Nicholls confirmed that a stranger can be liable if they participate in or instigate a breach of trust (irrespective of whether this breach was committed in good faith or fraudulently). It is only the stranger who must be dishonest for the liability to arise.

Lord Nicholls went on to say that dishonesty means 'conscious impropriety'; it involves advertent conduct. Neither carelessness nor negligence equate to dishonesty. Dishonesty is 'not acting as an honest person would in the circumstances'. On this basis, Tan was liable.

According to *Royal Brunei*, the standard of honesty is objective. A defendant who does not act in accordance with the objective standard of honesty is liable; it is no defence for the defendant to plead that, by their personal moral code, they saw nothing wrong with their behaviour. However, the assessment of honesty also involves subjective factors. The court will assess how a hypothetical honest person would have acted knowing the facts the defendant actually knew. The court will also take account of the defendant's experience and intelligence, and the circumstances in which the activities occur (such as the usual action taken in that line of business or commerce).

This approach was temporarily thrown into disarray by the House of Lords in *Twinsectra v Yardley* [2002] 2 WLR 882. The majority held that a defendant is dishonest if, in addition to their conduct being dishonest by the ordinary standards of reasonable and honest people, the defendant realised that, by those standards, their conduct is dishonest. This seemed to be at odds with the purely objective approach in *Royal Brunei* and was rather worrying because Privy Council decisions (*Royal Brunei*) are not binding on British courts, unlike House of Lords' decisions (*Twinsectra*).

Two of the judges who were in the majority in *Twinsectra* (Lords Hoffman and Steyn) had the opportunity to clarify their views in the Privy Council case of *Barlow Clowes International Ltd (In Liquidation) v Eurotrust International Ltd* [2006] 1 WLR 1376. They said that their views expressed in *Twinsectra* had been misunderstood; dishonesty required 'consciousness of those elements of the transaction which make participation transgress ordinary standards of honest behaviour. It did not also require ... thought about what those standards were' (Lord Hoffman). The test remained as stated in *Royal Brunei*: did the defendant act as an honest person would have acted in the circumstances?

*Barlow Clowes* was subsequently followed by the Court of Appeal in *Abou-Rahmah v Abacha* [2006] EWCA Civ 1492 and *Starglade Properties Ltd v Nash* [2010] EWCA Civ 1314. In *Ivey v Genting Casinos (UK) Ltd* [2017] 3 WLR 1212, the Supreme Court considered the issue of dishonesty in criminal proceedings. However, Lord Hughes JSC also addressed dishonesty in civil proceedings such as those involving accessory liability. He confirmed that the 'standard by which the law determines what is dishonest is objective'. In light of *Ivey*, in *Group Seven Ltd v Notable Services* LLP [2019] EWCA Civ 614, a case involving the alleged dishonest assistance of an accountant in a £100 million fraud, the Court of Appeal was happy to treat as 'settled law' that the touchstone of accessory liability was dishonesty, and that the standard of appraisal was objective as applied to the facts (which would include the defendant's knowledge, skills and expertise).

### 10.2.2 Recipient liability

This cause of action is also called 'knowing receipt' and it arises where the following elements are present:

(a) the trustee transfers trust property to a stranger in breach of trust (or a fiduciary transfers property in breach of fiduciary duty); and

(b) the stranger receives the property for their own benefit; and

(c) the stranger receives the property with the requisite degree of knowledge that the transfer of the property was in breach of trust or fiduciary duty, or they later acquire that knowledge and then deal with the property in a manner inconsistent with the trust or fiduciary duty.

10.2.2.1 Knowledge

The element of recipient liability which has caused the most controversy is the defendant's state of mind – the requisite degree of knowledge required for the liability to arise.

***Bank of Credit and Commerce International (Overseas) Ltd and Anor v Akindele*** **[2000] 4 All ER 221**

In 1985, Akindele entered into an artificial loan agreement under which he provided BCCI with $10 million. The agreement was a breach of the fiduciary duties of the directors of BCCI. In 1988, the directors of BCCI paid Akindele $16.79 million out of the company's funds under the terms of the agreement. When BCCI became insolvent, the liquidators claimed that Akindele was accountable for $6.79 million on the grounds of recipient liability.

Akindele had undoubtedly received BCCI's money for his own benefit in breach of the directors' fiduciary duties. The issue was whether he had the requisite state of mind for recipient liability.

The Court of Appeal acknowledged that dishonesty was the test for knowing assistance (accessory liability), but the judges did not adopt the same test for recipient liability. For recipient liability it was necessary to show that the defendant's knowledge made it unconscionable for them to retain the property.

It was held that Akindele's knowledge was not such that it would be unconscionable for him to retain the money. He had no reason to suspect the dealings of BCCI's directors, and the artificial nature of the agreement and high rate of interest were not sufficient to render him liable. Earlier general rumours of irregularities concerning BCCI and its directors were not enough to suggest anything improper at the time of the agreement. Unconscionability did not arise.

10.2.2.2 How much knowledge is unconscionable?

In *BCCI v Akindele*, it was unclear what is meant by 'unconscionable' and Nourse LJ did not elaborate, save for saying that it was wider than dishonesty.

Consequently, there have been discussions as to the level of knowledge required to render the receipt unconscionable and so wrongful. Historically, case law provided for a spectrum of levels of knowledge (see *Baden, Delvaux & Lecuit v Societe Generale* [1992] 4 All ER 161). More recently, however, the courts have moved away from this spectrum.

The court acknowledges that actual knowledge about the provenance of the receipt would give rise to liability. It is also accepted that deliberately shutting one's eyes to the obvious or deliberately failing to make enquiries would constitute such unconscionable knowledge.

However, the issue of whether unconscionability includes 'constructive knowledge' (knowledge of circumstances which would have caused a reasonable person to deduce that there might have been some wrongdoing) and/or 'constructive notice' (knowledge which would have been acquired had the defendant made the enquiries a reasonable person would have made) has given rise to judicial speculation.

It has been suggested that constructive knowledge may be sufficient on the basis that the defendant does have some knowledge which would put a reasonable person on notice (*Armstrong v Winnington* [2013] Ch 156).

As far as constructive notice is concerned. in *Akindele*, Nourse LJ cited, with approval, statements made by Megarry VC in *Re Montagu's Settlement Trusts* [1987] Ch 264 that recipient liability required 'conscious impropriety' on the part of the defendant and that constructive notice was, therefore, not sufficient. Megarry VC's comments were also approved, *obiter*, by the House of Lords in *Westdeutsche Landesbank Girozentrale v Islington London Borough Council* [1996] AC 669. It is, therefore, unlikely that unconscionability encompasses constructive notice.

### 10.2.3 Intermeddling

Where someone, not a trustee, does acts characteristic of a trustee, they will be liable for any misapplication of trust property or other loss caused to the trust just as if they had been appointed an express trustee (*Mara v Browne* (1896) 1 Ch 199). Such a person who assumes the role of trustee is called a 'trustee de son tort' (a trustee of his own wrong). A typical example arises where an agent, such as a solicitor or an accountant, exercises trustee functions over trust property beyond the scope of their agency. In *Lyell v Kennedy* (1889) 14 App Cas 437, an agent of the trustee continued to collect rent from the tenants of trust properties after his instructions ceased on the death of the trustee. It was held that the agent was liable to the beneficiaries as a trustee de son tort.

***Example***

*Carl, who holds property on trust for Fatima for life remainder to Sunil, instructs Abdul, an investment adviser, to sell some of the trust 's shareholdings. Abdul sells the shares, but Carl goes on an Arctic expedition before Abdul accounts to him for the proceeds. Not knowing what to do with the money, Abdul invests it in shares in Totaltech Ltd. Totaltech has subsequently become insolvent and the shares are worthless.*

*There is no liability in selling the shares; Abdul was merely acting within his instructions as agent. However, Abdul could be personally liable as a 'trustee de son tort' because he acted as a trustee by investing the proceeds of sale (trust funds). Carl left no instructions regarding investment of the proceeds of sale, and, therefore, Abdul acted outside his authority as agent.*

**Table 10.1** Summary – equitable personal claims against third parties

| **Circumstance** | **Claim** | **Requirements for claim** |
|---|---|---|
| Third party has received property subject to trust/ fiduciary relationship | Recipient liability (knowing receipt) | • Breach of duty<br>• Receipt of property for own benefit<br>• Knowledge which makes it unconscionable to retain property (*BCCI v Akindele*) |
| Third party has received property subject to trust/ fiduciary relationship and dealt with it without authority | Intermeddling ('trustee de son tort') | • Receipt on behalf of others<br>• Acting as if trustee (without instructions) (*Mara v Browne*) |
| Third party has assisted breach of duty | Accessory liability (dishonest assistance) | • Breach of duty<br>• Active assistance<br>• Objective dishonesty (in light of third party's circumstances) (*Royal Brunei v Tan*) |

## 10.3 Equitable proprietary claims against third parties

Where the trustee (or fiduciary) has transferred the property to a third-party stranger in breach of trust or fiduciary duty, a proprietary action could be brought against that stranger (providing the stranger has not dissipated their receipt). The aim would be to recover the property or its replacement, and the latter will involve tracing. How tracing will operate in these claims will depend on the status of the stranger.

### 10.3.1 Bona fide purchaser

The third-party recipient may be a 'bona fide purchaser of the legal interest for value without notice' that it was property transferred to them in breach of duty. As discussed in **1.4.3**, this third-party recipient will have paid consideration for the trust property at market value, will have acted in good faith when the purchase occurred and will not have been aware of the existence of the trust's or the fiduciary principal's rights over the property. Such bona fide purchasers take the property free from any equitable interests. No proprietary claim can be brought against this third party.

In this scenario, the recipient retains the asset they have purchased; the beneficiaries' equitable rights transfer to the proceeds of sale which the trustee or fiduciary received.

### 10.3.2 Proprietary claims against wrongdoers

Here, the stranger is an intermeddler or is guilty of recipient liability (they received property arising from a breach of duty and had sufficient knowledge which means that their conscience is affected - *BCCI v Akindele* as discussed in **10.2.2.1**). In this circumstance, beneficiaries or fiduciary principals can bring a proprietary claim against the recipient to recover property received or its replacement, and as the third-party stranger is a wrongdoer, they are liable *as if they were trustees*. It follows that the tracing rules relevant to proprietary claims against guilty trustees or fiduciaries discussed in **Chapter 9** (**9.3** and **9.4**) will apply here also.

#### 10.3.2.1 Clear substitution

Where the wrongdoer has simply exchanged the property they received for another asset in a clean substitution, *Re Hallett's Estate* (1880) 13 Ch D 696 says that a claimant can elect to take the substitute property or to have a charge over the property to secure the amount due to the trust (the equitable lien).

#### 10.3.2.2 Mixed substitution

Where the wrongdoer has purchased an asset with their own funds and the money received in breach of duty (or money representing the asset they received), the rule from *Foskett v McKeown* [2001] 1 AC 102 will allow the claimant a lien over the purchased asset for the amount of the fiduciary receipt contributing to the purchase, or, alternatively, they can claim ownership of a proportion of the asset (corresponding to the proportion of the purchase price contributed).

#### 10.3.2.3 Allocating withdrawals through a bank account

Where the wrongdoer has mixed a monetary receipt in their bank account, the equitable tracing rules on withdrawals from a mixed bank account apply. Under the rule in *Re Hallett* the wrongdoer is deemed to spend their own money first. If this results in the allocation of dissipated withdrawals to the innocent trust or fiduciary principal and traceable assets to the wrongdoer then *Re Oatway* says that the claimant's charge (or lien) will exist over the mixed fund and any assets purchased with it.

### 10.3.3 Proprietary claims against innocent volunteers

Where the third party had no knowledge or notice of the breach of trust or fiduciary duty and provided no consideration for the transfer and has not intermeddled, a proprietary claim can still be brought against them, but as an 'innocent volunteer'. Here the tracing rules are kinder than those applicable to trustees or fiduciaries.

#### 10.3.3.1 Clean substitution

In a case of clear substitution – the straight exchange of money or property received by the innocent volunteer for another asset with no mixing – there is no difficulty in bringing a proprietary claim against that innocent volunteer to recover substituted property, despite the recipient's lack of awareness as to the provenance of the original property. The trust (fiduciary principal) retains their beneficial interest against 'everyone who takes the property or its traceable proceeds' (Lord Millett, in *Foskett v McKeown* [2001] 1 AC 102).

#### 10.3.3.2 Mixed substitution

A trustee gives trust property or money to an innocent volunteer, who adds it to their own funds and uses the mixture to buy an asset. Here, equity has the dilemma of choosing between two innocent parties: the beneficiaries on the one hand, and the innocent volunteer on the other. The solution which equity adopts is that the trust and the innocent volunteer share the asset pro rata in proportion to their contributions to the purchase price. Thus, if the trust contributed two-thirds of the purchase price, it could claim two-thirds of the asset regardless of whether the asset had increased or decreased in value.

As the recipient is an innocent volunteer there is no question of the trust/fiduciary principal electing for a lien. The trust/fiduciary principal and the volunteer are both innocent parties and must be treated equally (Lord Millett, *Foskett v McKeown* [2001] 1 AC 102).

#### 10.3.3.3 Withdrawals from a mixed bank account

Where the innocent volunteer places the receipt into their own bank account which already holds (or comes to hold) their own money, and later makes withdrawals from that account, it is necessary to determine which money is used for which withdrawal.

Discussed in **9.3.4.2**, the rule in *Clayton's case* (1816) 1 Mer 572 also applies here, namely on a 'first in, first out' basis. Accordingly, if there was already money in the account before the deposit of misappropriated money, the first withdrawals, whether for a traceable or a dissipated asset, will be attributed to the recipient.

The rule in *Clayton's case* is a rule of convenience which was developed in the context of banking law; it may not produce an equitable result in every instance. There is modern support for the view that it will not be used if its application would be impractical, or if it would lead to an unjust result (*Barlow Clowes v Vaughan* [1992] 4 All ER 22 discussed in **9.3.4.2**). In *Russell-Cooke Trust Co v Prentis* [2002] All ER (D) 22, Lindsay J went as far as to say that the so-called 'rule' in *Clayton's case* ought to be known as the 'exception' in *Clayton's case*. However, *Clayton* will continue to apply if there are not factors to displace it.

#### 10.3.3.4 Defence – inequitable result

Innocent volunteers will have a defence if they can show that tracing and the resulting proprietary claim would produce an inequitable result. This defence is never available to trustees and fiduciaries who have misappropriated property subject to trust or fiduciary duties or to wrongdoers like recipients or intermeddlers.

***Re Diplock*** **[1948] Ch 465**

By his will Caleb Diplock directed his executors to apply his residue 'for such charitable institutions or other charitable or benevolent object or objects in England' as they should in their absolute discretion select. The executors assumed that the will created a valid charitable trust and distributed the residue among hospitals and other charities.

The next of kin successfully challenged the validity of the trust on the grounds it was not exclusively charitable and failed as a non-charitable trust for uncertainty of object. The next of kin had exhausted their remedy against the executors and claimed the rest of the money from the charities.

The charities had used the Diplock money to pay off debts and, in combination with money of their own, to alter and improve buildings which they already owned.

It was accepted that the money used to pay debts had been dissipated and was thus untraceable.

The court confirmed that tracing was not restricted to actions against a trustee or fiduciary but also applied where an innocent volunteer had mixed trust money with their own. The court went on to say that if the fund had been used in acquisition of new property, tracing would have presented no particular difficulty.

However, the court held that the money used for the alterations and improvements could not be traced (denying the beneficiaries of their claim) for two reasons:

(a) The improvements may not have added to the value of the buildings. In this case, the trust money no longer existed, and so was dissipated.

(b) Where the competition is between two innocent parties, the equitable owners of the trust property 'must submit to equality of treatment with the innocent volunteer'. Where the innocent volunteer has contributed the land and the trust has contributed to improvements, tracing does not produce this equality of treatment. The sale of the land to satisfy any equitable charge would deprive the volunteer of the land. Giving the volunteer some of the sale proceeds instead of the land which they had previously owned does not produce an equal result. It was, therefore, inequitable to allow tracing.

**Figure 10.1** Summary - proprietary claims against third parties

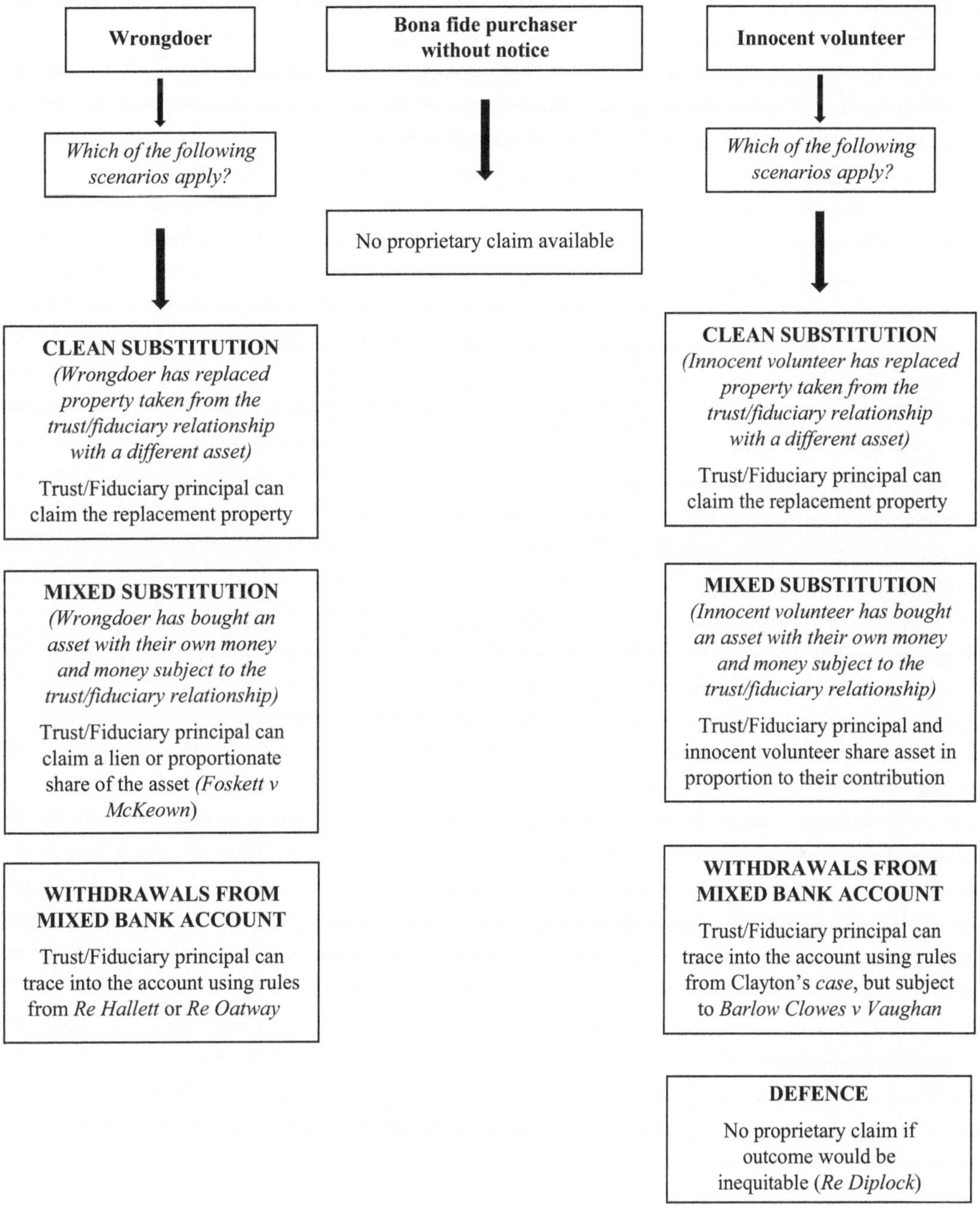


## 10.4 Common law claim for restitution

Where a legal owner has been deprived of their property without their consent as a result of fraud, theft or mistake, they could bring a legal claim against the person now holding the property on the grounds of unjust enrichment. The claimant will seek the remedy of restitution. If successful, the defendant will have to return the unjust enrichment received. Restitution is a personal claim, not proprietary, and thus will not have priority on the bankruptcy of the defendant.

### 10.4.1 Claimant must be a legal owner

Restitution claims are available only where the claimant holds *legal* title to the property which has been misappropriated.

So, a company as the legal owner of misappropriated company money would be able to claim restitution against a third-party recipient of that money. Similarly, a trustee could bring a restitution claim to recover trust property misappropriated by a co-trustee as they would hold legal title to the trust property.

However, beneficiaries are unable to bring a claim in restitution as they do not hold the legal title to the trust property. They have the equitable interest in the property and so must rely solely on equitable remedies against the recipient.

### 10.4.2 Strict liability

Restitution does not depend on any wrongdoing on the part of the defendant. The defendant need not be the person who deprived the claimant of their property. They may be someone who later receives the property innocently. Strict liability applies to restitution claims; there is no need to prove that the defendant acted dishonestly, nor indeed any reason to inquire into the defendant's state of mind or their knowledge of the provenance of the stolen money.

In this respect, a common law action for unjust enrichment and restitution is easier to establish than the equitable claim for recipient liability.

### 10.4.3 Proof of receipt of the claimant's property

A claimant for restitution has to prove that the defendant received the claimant's property. Where the property changed in form before it reached the defendant, it will be necessary to use common law tracing to establish that the property received by the defendant is indeed the claimant's. Common law tracing has to be employed (not equitable) because restitution is a common law claim. If common law tracing fails to identify the property at the time of receipt by the defendant, the action for restitution will fail.

***Example 1***

*A director withdraws money from a company's funds. They use the money to buy a car which they give to their son.*

*Restitution would be feasible in this case because the money was not mixed before it reached the son; it merely changed form. Thus, common law tracing can establish that the car received by the son was the company's property.*

***Example 2***

*A director sold a company asset and gave the proceeds of sale to their son. The son paid the proceeds into a building society account containing his own money*

*Restitution would also be feasible in this case because the proceeds of sale were not mixed before they reached the son. Common law tracing can establish that the proceeds received by the son were the company's property. It does not matter that the son mixed the money after the crucial moment of receipt.*

***Example 3***

*A director withdrew money from the company's funds, paid it into their own bank account containing their own money and then drew a cheque in favour of their son.*

*In this case, restitution would be unsuccessful because the company's money was mixed with other funds before it reached the son. Common law tracing will be unable to identify the money paid to son as being the claimant's money.*

### 10.4.4 Defences

There are two possible defences to a claim of common law restitution.

#### 10.4.4.1 Bona fide purchaser

It is not possible to claim restitution against a bona fide purchaser for value without notice because they have not been unjustly enriched.

#### 10.4.4.2 Change of position

An innocent defendant who has so changed their position that it would be unjust to compel them to make restitution can claim this defence. An example is where the defendant spent the money in an exceptional and irretrievable manner before finding out they were not entitled to it. The defendant has nothing left to meet the claim and the court might consider it unjust to require the defendant to restore the money out of their own resources (*Lipkin Gorman v Karpnale Ltd* [1992] 4 All ER 512).

The defence does not arise in all cases where the defendant has spent the money. In *Lipkin Gorman*, Lord Templeman suggested that the defence can only be claimed where the defendant has spent the money in a way they would not otherwise have done (ie in an 'exceptional' way). For instance, if the receipt has been used to discharge an existing liability (ie payment of a credit card bill), there will have been no change of position as the liability will have had to have been paid anyway.

The defence is also available only if the defendant changed their position in good faith. Thus, a defendant will still be liable if they spent the money knowing that it belonged to someone else. The Court of Appeal considered the meaning of 'good faith' in *Abou-Rahmah v Abacha* [2006] EWCA Civ 1492. In *Abou-Rahmah*, a restitution claim was made against the Bank, but it successfully defended the claim on the grounds of change of position because it had transferred the money to its customer. Two of the judges in the Court of Appeal held that the Bank had not denied itself the defence on the grounds of bad faith. Following an earlier case, they said that bad faith embraced 'a failure to act in a commercially acceptable way and sharp practice of a kind that falls short of outright dishonesty'.

**Figure 10.2** Summary – considerations for a common law restitution claim

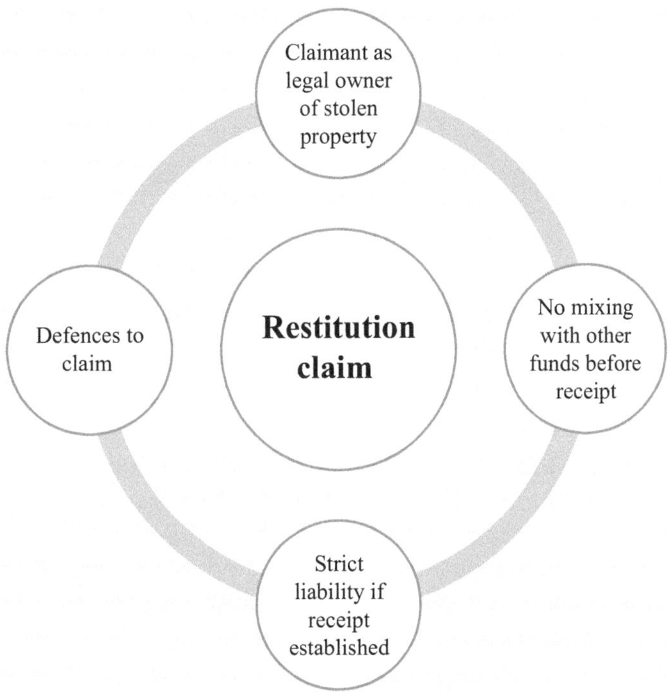

***Lipkin Gorman v Karpnale Ltd* [1992] 4 All ER 512**

In compliance with Law Society rules, the partners in a firm of solicitors, Lipkin Gorman, held clients' money in a separate bank account. They were trustees of the account for their clients. One partner, Cass, stole over £200,000 from the client account and gambled the money at the Playboy Club casino. He lost over £150,000. The money was mostly withdrawn by cheques made out to 'cash' which Cass then used to obtain cash to pay for the gambling chips. The Playboy Club did not know where the money came from.

The Club paid the money into its general funds and used it to pay the few winnings which Cass secured and towards general overheads of the business.

As the Club had no knowledge of the source of the money (rendering an equitable claim for recipient liability unavailable) the other partners in Lipkin Gorman (as legal owners of the bank account from which the money was originally stolen) sued the owners of the Playboy Club for unjust enrichment.

The money had undergone changes in form before reaching the defendant; it had changed from money in a bank account (a debt owed to the bank's customer) to a cheque to cash. However, there had been no mixing before the Club received the money. Therefore, common law tracing could identify that the cash received by the Club was in fact the claimant's money. The fact that the Club mixed the money with other funds after receipt was immaterial.

The House of Lords held that the Club did not have the defence of bona fide purchaser. As gaming contracts were void under the Gaming Act 1845, the Club could not be regarded as having provided consideration for Cass's payments and was not, therefore, a 'purchaser'.

The Club argued that it had the defence of change of position; it would be inequitable to require it to make restitution because it had spent the money in good faith in an exceptional and irretrievable manner. The defendant was partially successful. There was no doubt that it spent the money in good faith. However, the defence was not available to the extent that the money had been spent on general business running costs because that expenditure was not 'exceptional'; the Club would have spent its own money on these outgoings in the normal course of its business. The defence was allowed to the extent that the money had been spent on Cass's winnings (around £50,000) because, in this respect, the Club did change its position as a result of receiving the claimant's money.

**ACTIVITY Review your understanding – claims against third parties**

Consider the following facts.

Hallmark Bank is the trustee of a trust created by Camilla's father. The terms of the trust directed the bank to hold on trust for Camilla for life remainder to her legitimate children but if there were none for Oxfam.

Camilla has two children, Harry and Lucinda, and cannot have any more. Camilla has always pretended that she was married to Harry and Lucinda's father, Pedro. Pedro recently died. On Lucinda's 21st birthday (when Harry was 18), Camilla decided to surrender her life interest. The bank agreed to pay the trust capital to Harry and Lucinda in equal shares. The bank asked to see Camilla's marriage certificate, and she produced a certificate that had been forged with the help of her art teacher, Kyle. Kyle believed that Camilla wanted to use the certificate to get a Spanish passport by representing that she was married to Pedro, a Spanish citizen.

was aware of an illegal activity

The bank duly paid the trust capital to Harry and Lucinda. Harry spent the money in paying off debts and travelling; Lucinda used her share as a deposit on a new house. Neither had any idea that the trust was confined to Camilla's legitimate children.

Oxfam could consider a claim against Hallmark Bank. However, as an alternative, think about what claims, if any, it might bring against:

(1) Harry and/or Lucinda;

(2) Camilla; and

(3) Kyle.

**Comment**

(1) Harry and/or Lucinda

- Personal claim
    - o Received property in breach of trust because the bank breached its duty to distribute to the correct beneficiaries. It does not matter that the breach was innocent.
    - o Received the property for their own benefit.
    - o Neither aware that they were not entitled to the money (they would not be expected to investigate their entitlement by reading the trust instrument). Unlikely that it would be unconscionable for them to retain the property (*BCCI v Akindele*).
    - o No liability to pay compensation on the grounds of recipient liability.
- Proprietary claim
    - o Harry – a proprietary claim against him is useless as he has dissipated the money.
    - o Lucinda – a proprietary claim is possible against her, even though she is an innocent volunteer. She has contributed the trust's money to the purchase of a new house. In a mixed substitution such as this, Oxfam, as the actual beneficiary of the trust (there being no legitimate children), will be able to claim a share of the house proportionate to its monetary contribution. It will not be able to claim a lien. Nor will Lucinda be able to claim the *Re Diplock* defence as she used her receipt to acquire a new asset, rather than to improve a property she already owned.

(2) Camilla and Kyle

Both are likely to be liable as dishonest accessories. There was a breach of trust by the bank (see above). Camilla assisted (or even instigated) that breach by representing that she was married and presenting a false marriage certificate. Kyle assisted the breach by forging the marriage certificate. The question is whether they acted as an honest person would have acted in the circumstances (*Royal Brunei Airlines v Tan*).

Given her awareness of the situation, Camille clearly acted dishonestly. As far as Kyle is concerned, it is not necessary for him to know that he was assisting in a breach of trust. In *Barlow Clowes v Eurotrust*, it was held that it was sufficient to establish dishonest assistance, if the defendant knows they are participating in some fraud. Here an honest person would not have produced a false marriage certificate knowing that it was to be used for some fraudulent activity (obtaining the passport) which satisfies the *Tan* dishonesty test.

**SUMMARY**

- Being able to pursue equitable personal and proprietary claims against third parties can provide a useful alternative to suing trustees or fiduciaries.
- The relevant equitable principles which cover such claims operate in the same way whether one is concerned with a family-type trust or a commercial fiduciary relationship.
- Third parties can be implicated in a breach of trust or fiduciary duty either by assisting in a breach of duty by a trustee or a fiduciary or by receiving property subject to the trust or the fiduciary relationship for their own benefit or meddling in trust affairs.
- When considering the claim against the third-party accessory, it is the third party's dishonesty which will determine liability – if they did not act as an honest person would have done in comparable circumstances they can be called to compensate the trust or the fiduciary principal for the loss occasioned by the breach in full.
- A person who has received property subject to the trust or the fiduciary relationship for their own benefit can be subject to personal and/or proprietary claims. The personal claim for compensation will depend on the recipient's knowledge making it unconscionable for them to retain their receipt. Knowledge in this circumstance is more than dishonesty and is likely to range from actual knowledge to deliberately shutting one's eyes to the obvious or deliberately failing to make enquiries to knowledge of circumstances which would have caused a reasonable person to deduce that there might have been some wrongdoing ('constructive knowledge').
- No proprietary claim is available against a third party who is a bona fide purchaser of the property without notice of its provenance. No proprietary claim is available where the receipt has been dissipated by the third party.
- Tracing will, however, be available to a claimant bringing proprietary claims against other third-party recipients. The relevant rules to deploy depend on the status of the recipient. A recipient liable as a wrongdoer (personally guilty under recipient liability or as a 'trustee de son tort') will be treated as a trustee and so be subject to harsher tracing rules. Where there is no recipient liability, the tracing rules against the innocent volunteer are kinder and are subject to a defence where the proprietary claim gives rise to an unjust result.
- Where the claimant is a legal owner of property which has been misappropriated, it is possible to consider a legal action for restitution as well as the equitable claims.

# Appendix

## An Example of a Discretionary Trust

What follows is an example of a discretionary trust, highlighting the structure and containing some of the provisions which might be contained in a professionally drafted trust document. Please note this example is illustrative only and should not be used as a precedent. The precise wording would be amended in light of a settlor's specific instructions and circumstances. However, there is a commentary on some of the clauses at the end.

## DISCRETIONARY SETTLEMENT

### Settlement

DATE: []

### Parties:

(1) Name and address (the 'Settlor'); and

(2) Names and addresses (the 'Trustees').

### Recitals

(A) The Settlor wishes to make this Settlement and has transferred or delivered to the Trustees or otherwise placed under their control the property specified in the Schedule. Further money, investments or other property may be paid or transferred to the Trustees by way of addition.

(B) It is intended that this Settlement shall be irrevocable.

### Part 1 – Operative Provisions

1 **Definitions and construction**

In this Deed, where the context admits, the following definitions and rules of construction shall apply.

1.1 The '**Trust Fund**' shall mean:

(a) the property specified in the Schedule;

(b) all money, investments or other property paid or transferred by any person to, or so as to be under the control of, and, in either case, accepted by the Trustees as additions;

(c) all accumulations (if any) of income added to the Trust Fund; and

(d) the money, investments and property from time to time representing the above.

1.2 The '**Trust Period**' shall mean the period ending on the earlier of:

(a) the last day of the period of 125 years from the date of this Deed, which period, and no other, shall be the applicable perpetuity period; and

(b) such date as the Trustees shall at any time specify by deed.

1.3 The '**Beneficiaries**' shall mean:

(a) the Settlor's children and remoter issue;

(b) the spouses, widows and widowers (whether or not such widows or widowers have remarried) of the Settlor's children and remoter issue;

(c) [another beneficiary];

(d) [Charities]; and

(e) [such other objects or persons as are added under clause 2].

1.4 '**Charity**' shall mean any trust, foundation, company or other organisation established only for purposes regarded as charitable under the law of England and Wales.

1.5 The expression '**the Trustees**' shall, where the context admits, include the trustees for the time being of this Settlement.

1.6 References to the children, grandchildren and issue of any person shall include his children, grandchildren and remoter issue, whether legitimate, legitimated, illegitimate or adopted.

**2 Power to add beneficiaries**

The Settlor, or such person as the Settlor shall have nominated in writing, may, at any time during the Trust Period, add to the Beneficiaries such objects or persons or classes of objects or persons as the Settlor or such other person shall determine.

**3 Discretionary trust of capital and income**

The Trustees shall hold the capital and income of the Trust Fund upon trust for or for the benefit of such of the Beneficiaries, at such ages or times, in such shares, upon such trusts and in such manner generally as the Trustees shall in their discretion appoint. Any such appointment may include such powers and provisions for the maintenance, education or other benefit of the Beneficiaries or for the accumulation of income and such administrative powers and provisions as the Trustees think fit.

**4 Income trusts in default of appointment**

The provisions of this clause shall apply during the Trust Period until, subject to and in default of any appointment under clause 3.

4.1 The Trustees shall pay or apply the income of the Trust Fund to or for the benefit of such of the Beneficiaries as shall for the time being be in existence, in such shares and in such manner generally as the Trustees shall in their discretion from time to time think fit.

4.2 Notwithstanding the provisions of sub-clause 4.1, the Trustees may at any time in their discretion accumulate the income by investing it in any investments authorised by this Deed or by law.

5 **Ultimate default trusts**

Subject as above and if and so far as not wholly disposed of for any reason whatever by the above provisions, the capital and income of the Trust Fund shall be held upon trust for [X] absolutely.

---

## Part 2 – Administrative Provisions

The standard provisions [and all /the following of the special provisions] of the Society of Trust and Estate Practitioners (2nd Edition) shall apply to this settlement.

**Schedule**

[details of the original trust property would be detailed here]

**Execution**

**Comment**

*Title – Discretionary Settlement*

The term 'Settlement' in this context is generally used to include any arrangement whereby an individual 'settles' property on trust for a group of beneficiaries or objects. 'Settlement' refers to the whole arrangement; the 'trusts' are the terms upon which the property is held. The use of terminology in this area is not always consistent. This discretionary settlement might also commonly be referred to as a 'discretionary trust'.

*Definitions*

The '*Trust Period*' is the maximum 'life' of the settlement. The maximum length of time the law allows the trust to continue is governed by the perpetuity period, which was mentioned **Chapter 2**. One hundred and twenty-five years is the perpetuity period prescribed by the Perpetuities and Accumulations Act 2009.

The '*Beneficiaries*' are widely defined to include the settlor's children, grandchildren, etc ('remoter issue') and their spouses. These settlements often include the settlor's brothers and sisters and their families. If wished, other named individuals or charities can be included. Together all those included form the 'class of objects'. As discussed in **Chapter 2**, they must satisfy the requirements of certainty of objects. These 'beneficiaries' are only possible beneficiaries until they are chosen, if at all, by the trustees to benefit under the discretionary trusts.

*Power to add beneficiaries*

Not only can the class of beneficiaries, or objects, be widely drawn as above, but it is also possible for other objects to be added later. In this settlement, the settlor retains this power, or can give it to someone they nominate. It could, for instance, be granted to the trustees. Some settlements grant the power to the trustees from the outset.

*Primary provisions regarding capital and income*

Clause 3 is the main provision bestowing on the trustees the discretion how the trust fund and the income it earns is to be distributed between the 'beneficiaries', as defined in clause 1. You will see that the discretion permits the choice of some beneficiaries rather than all.

The chosen beneficiary may benefit by a new trust, rather than by an outright gift. The distribution to a chosen beneficiary, whether directly to the beneficiary or by way of trust, is known as an 'appointment'.

*Default provisions regarding income*

The trustees will invest the trust fund. Clause 4 states how the trustees are to deal with the income the investments generate prior to the trust property and its income being appointed to the chosen beneficiaries under Clause 3.

Clause 4.1 imposes a duty to distribute the income but gives a discretion as to the recipient. Clause 4.2 gives the trustees the power to accumulate (ie keep back and not distribute) income. This is known as 'accumulation' of income. In the absence of this power to retain the income, they would be under an obligation to distribute it.

*Ultimate default trusts*

This is a 'long stop' provision. The clause provides that if for any reason at the end of the trust period there is any trust property which has not been distributed to the chosen beneficiaries, it is to go to a named person. This will often be a charity.

*Administrative provisions*

A properly drafted settlement is likely to contain a large number of clauses dealing with routine administration matters. These administrative provisions provide the necessary guidance and powers to enable trustees to undertake their role effectively. As discussed in **Chapters 7** and **8**, the settlor is free to include whatever administrative provisions they consider appropriate, although they often rely on guidance received from their advisors in this regard. Historically, it had been necessary to set the relevant provisions out in full in each settlement (there are numerous books and precedents available which detail possible wording for these provisions). However, in 1992, STEP (the Society of Estate and Trust Practitioners) condensed all this material into a series of 'standard provisions' seeking to avoid technical words which might be unfamiliar to the lay reader. The provisions were amended in 2012 and 2023 to take account of changes in the law and practice developments. There is a series of core 'standard provisions' as well as a number of 'special provisions' which can be incorporated (in full or in part) at the discretion of the settlor and their practitioner. A 2023 Practice Direction from the Principal Registry of the Family Division permits the incorporation of these provisions by reference, without having to provide the full text of the provisions themselves. The full provisions and guidance material can be accessed on the STEP website (https://www.step.org/public-policy/step-standard-provisions).

*Schedule*

The original trust property (the subject-matter of the trust) is always detailed. However, during the lifetime of the trust, the nature of this property can change as trustees make investment decisions or make appointments of capital to beneficiaries.

*Execution*

All parties to the settlement (settlor and all trustees) will need to sign the document. As it is a deed, these signatures will need to be witnessed.

# Index

## K



## L



## M



## N



## O



## P